NINETEEN EIGHTY-FOUR
TO
1984

NINETEEN EIGHTY-FOUR
TO
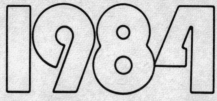

A Companion to the Classic Novel of Our Time

Edited by C. J. Kuppig

Carroll & Graf Publishers inc.   New York

Note to Readers: For convenience, page references to *Nineteen Eighty-Four* in this volume have been standardized to the pagination of the Signet Classic Paperback edition.

Copyright © 1984 by Carroll & Graf Publishers, Inc.

All rights reserved.

Carroll & Graf Publishers, Inc.
260 Fifth Avenue
New York, N.Y. 10001

Library of Congress Cataloging in Publication Data

Main entry under title
  Nineteen Eighty-four to 1984.
    1. Orwell, George, 1903–1950. Nineteen Eighty-four — —
Addresses, essays, lectures.   I. Kuppig, Christopher J.
II. Orwell, George, 1903–1950. Nineteen Eighty-four.
PR6029.R8N5325   1984   823'.912   84-9574

ISBN: 0-88184-085-8

Manufactured in the United States of America

CONTENTS

I
The Origins of Nineteen Eight-Four

II
The Response to Nineteen Eighty-Four

III
The Legacy of Nineteen Eighty-Four

THE ORIGINS OF
NINETEEN EIGHTY-FOUR

Such, Such Were the Joys
George Orwell

This autobiographical sketch, first published in *Partisan Review* in 1952—after Orwell's death—is the focus of one of the most intriguing debates surrounding the origins of *Nineteen Eighty-Four*.

Ostensibly, the piece recounts Orwell's traumatic, brutalizing childhood experience at a Sussex prep school called St. Cyprian's. His recollections of tawdry surroundings, physical deprivation, and mental torture in the guise of pedagogy would be interesting enough in themselves, as they appear in numerous of Orwell's mature writings—and especially in the character of Winston Smith and the world of 1984. But there is strong evidence that this is the last essay Orwell completed before his death, undertaken—whether initially or in revision of an earlier version—during the same period in 1947 that he was completing the first draft of *Nineteen Eighty-Four*.

Bernard Crick, in an appendix to his 1981 study of Orwell, provides the most definitive statement on the dating of the essay, and elsewhere in his book he wisely discards both sides of the argument over which gave rise to the other: Orwell's sadomasochistic remembrances of his childhood taking new form in the horrors visited upon Winston and Julia in *Nineteen Eighty-Four*, or vice versa.

Indeed, another point in the debate arises over the factual accuracy of Orwell's account. The boyhood portrait he paints of himself as unattractive, unpopular, somewhat prone to sloth, and the hapless victim of an especially cruel headmaster and headmistress has received ample comment. Neither his friend Cyril

Connolly, who attended St. Cyprian's with him and later wrote *Enemies of Promise* (1938) about his experience there, nor Orwell's own sister, Avril, recall Orwell as being particularly unhappy at that time. Both agree that Orwell's memories were likely embroidered to serve dramatic purpose.

Regardless, Orwell has left behind a small mystery that can only be solved to the individual satisfaction of readers of both *Nineteen Eighty-Four* and "Such, Such Were the Joys." For it is undeniable that on some level childhood experiences imprint themselves indelibly on the personalities of us all. Our elemental understandings about the power and authority of others radiate outward, first from our feelings about our parents, then to teachers and peers, and eventually to our beliefs about leaders and governments.

Taken this way, the essay cannot be anything but revelatory. For in *Nineteen Eighty-Four* Orwell has clearly taken the insights about child psychology that he reveals in "Such, Such Were the Joys" to their extreme limit. No more perfect an example exists in reality or fiction of the emotional complex revolving around dependency and subjection, power and impotence, love and hate, than that of the relationship between Big Brother and the Party members of Oceania.

I

Soon after I arrived at St. Cyprian's (not immediately, but after a week or two, just when I seemed to be settling into the routine of school life) I began wetting my bed. I was now aged eight, so that this was a reversion to a habit which I must have grown out of at least four years earlier.

Nowadays, I believe, bed-wetting in such circumstances is taken for granted. It is a normal reaction in children who have been removed from their homes to a strange place. In those days, however, it was looked on as a disgusting crime which the child committed on purpose and for which the proper cure was a beating. For my part I did not need to be told it was a crime. Night after night I prayed, with a fervour never previously attained in my prayers, "Please God, do not let me wet my bed! Oh, please God, do not let me wet my bed!", but it made remarkably little difference. Some nights the thing happened, others not. There was no volition about it, no consciousness. You did not properly speaking *do* the deed: you merely woke up in the morning and found that the sheets were wringing wet.

After the second or third offence I was warned that I should be beaten next time, but I received the warning in a curiously round-about way. One afternoon, as we were filing out from tea, Mrs W——, the Headmaster's wife, was sitting at the head of one of the tables, chatting with a lady of whom I knew nothing, except that she was on an afternoon's visit to the school. She was an intimidating, masculine-looking person wearing a riding-habit, or something that I took to be a riding-habit. I was just leaving the room when Mrs W—— called me back, as though to introduce me to the visitor.

Mrs W—— was nicknamed Flip, and I shall call her by that name, for I seldom think of her by any other. (Officially, however, she was addressed as Mum, probably a corruption of the "Ma'am" used by public schoolboys to their housemasters' wives.) She was a stocky square-built woman with hard red cheeks, a flat top to her head, prominent brows and deep-set, suspicious eyes. Although a great deal of the time she was full of false heartiness, jollying one along with mannish slang ("*Buck* up, old chap!" and so forth), and even using one's Christian name, her eyes never lost their anxious, accusing look. It was very difficult to look her in the face without feeling guilty, even at moments when one was not guilty of anything in particular.

"Here is a little boy," said Flip, indicating me to the strange lady, "who wets his bed every night. Do you know what I am going to do if you wet your bed again?" she added, turning to me. "I am going to get the Sixth Form to beat you."

The strange lady put on an air of being inexpressibly shocked, and exclaimed "I-should-*think*-so!" And here there occurred one of those wild, almost lunatic misunderstandings which are part of the daily experience of childhood. The Sixth Form was a group of older boys who were selected as having "character" and were empowered to beat smaller boys. I had not yet learned of their existence, and I mis-heard the phrase "the Sixth Form" as "Mrs. Form". I took it as referring to the strange lady—I thought, that is, that her name was Mrs. Form. It was an improbable name, but a child has no judgement in such matters. I imagined, therefore, that it was *she* who was to be deputed to beat me. It did not strike me as strange that this job should be turned over to a casual visitor in no way connected with the school. I merely assumed that "Mrs. Form" was a stern disciplinarian who enjoyed beating people (somehow her appearance seemed to bear this out) and I had an immediate terrifying vision of her arriving for the occasion in full riding kit and armed with a hunting-whip. To this day I can feel myself almost swooning with shame as I stood, a very small, round-faced boy in short corduroy knickers, before the two women. I could not speak. I felt that I should die if "Mrs Form" were to beat me. But my dominant feeling was not fear or even resentment: it was simply shame because one more person, and that a woman, had been told of my disgusting offence.

A little later, I forget how, I learned that it was not after all "Mrs. Form" who would do the beating. I cannot remember whether it was that very night that I wetted my bed again, but at any rate I did wet it again quite soon. Oh, the despair, the feeling of cruel injustice, after all my prayers and resolutions, at once again waking between the clammy sheets! There was no chance of hiding what I had done. The grim statuesque matron, Margaret by name, arrived in the dormitory to inspect my bed. She pulled back the clothes, then drew herself up, and the dreaded words seemed to come rolling out of her like a peal of thunder:

"REPORT YOURSELF to the Headmaster after breakfast!"

I put REPORT YOURSELF in capitals because that was how it appeared in my mind. I do not know how many times I heard that phrase during my early years at St. Cyprian's. It was only very rarely that it did not mean a beating. The words always had a portentous sound in my ears, like muffled drums or the words of the death sentence.

When I arrived to report myself, Flip was doing something or other at the long shiny table in the ante-room to the study. Her uneasy eyes searched me as I went past. In the study the Headmaster, nicknamed Sambo, was waiting. Sambo was a round-shouldered, curiously oafish-looking man, not large but shambling in gait, with a chubby face which was like that of an overgrown baby, and which was capable of good humour. He knew, of course, why I had been sent to him, and had al-

ready taken a bone-handled riding-crop out of the
cupboard, but it was part of the punishment of
reporting yourself that you had to proclaim your
offence with your own lips. When I had said my
say, he read me a short but pompous lecture, then
seized me by the scruff of the neck, twisted me
over and began beating me with the riding-crop.
He had a habit of continuing his lecture while he
flogged you, and I remember the words "you dir-ty
lit-tle boy" keeping time with the blows. The beating did not hurt (perhaps, as it was the first time,
he was not hitting me very hard), and I walked out
feeling very much better. The fact that the beating
had not hurt was a sort of victory and partially
wiped out the shame of the bed-wetting. I was
even incautious enough to wear a grin on my face.
Some small boys were hanging about in the passage outside the door of the ante-room.

"D'you get the cane?"

"It didn't hurt," I said proudly.

Flip had heard everything. Instantly her voice
came screaming after me:

"Come here! Come here this instant! What was
that you said?"

"I said it didn't hurt," I faltered out.

"How dare you say a thing like that? Do you
think that is a proper thing to say? Go in and
REPORT YOURSELF AGAIN!"

This time Sambo laid on in real earnest. He
continued for a length of time that frightened and
astonished me—about five minutes, it seemed—
ending up by breaking the riding-crop. The bone
handle went flying across the room.

"Look what you've made me do!" he said furi-
ously, holding up the broken crop.

I had fallen into a chair, weakly snivelling. I
remember that this was the only time throughout
my boyhood when a beating actually reduced me

to tears, and curiously enough I was not even now crying because of the pain. The second beating had not hurt very much either. Fright and shame seemed to have anaesthetised me. I was crying partly because I felt that this was expected of me, partly from genuine repentance, but partly also because of a deeper grief which is peculiar to childhood and not easy to convey: a sense of desolate loneliness and helplessness, of being locked up not only in a hostile world but in a world of good and evil where the rules were such that it was actually not possible for me to keep them.

I knew that the bed-wetting was (a) wicked and (b) outside my control. The second fact I was personally aware of, and the first I did not question. It was possible, therefore, to commit a sin without knowing that you committed it, without wanting to commit it, and without being able to avoid it. Sin was not necessarily something that you did: it might be something that happened to you. I do not want to claim that this idea flashed into my mind as a complete novelty at this very moment, under the blows of Sambo's cane: I must have had glimpses of it even before I left home, for my early childhood had not been altogether happy. But at any rate this was the great, abiding lesson of my boyhood: that I was in a world where it was *not possible* for me to be good. And the double beating was a turning-point, for it brought home to me for the first time the harshness of the environment into which I had been flung. Life was more terrible, and I was more wicked, than I had imagined. At any rate, as I sat snivelling on the edge of a chair in Sambo's study, with not even the self-possession to stand up while he stormed at me, I had a conviction of sin and folly and weakness, such as I do not remember to have felt before.

In general, one's memories of any period must

necessarily weaken as one moves away from it. One is constantly learning new facts, and old ones have to drop out to make way for them. At twenty I could have written the history of my schooldays with an accuracy which would be quite impossible now. But it can also happen that one's memories grow sharper after a long lapse of time, because one is looking at the past with fresh eyes and can isolate and, as it were, notice facts which previously existed undifferentiated among a mass of others. Here are two things which in a sense I remembered, but which did not strike me as strange or interesting until quite recently. One is that the second beating seemed to me a just and reasonable punishment. To get one beating, and then to get another and far fiercer one on top of it, for being so unwise as to show that the first had not hurt—that was quite natural. The gods are jealous, and when you have good fortune you should conceal it. The other is that I accepted the broken riding-crop as my own crime. I can still recall my feeling as I saw the handle lying on the carpet— the feeling of having done an ill-bred clumsy thing, and ruined an expensive object. *I* had broken it: so Sambo told me, and so I believed. This acceptance of guilt lay unnoticed in my memory for twenty or thirty years.

So much for the episode of the bed-wetting. But there is one more thing to be remarked. This is that I did not wet my bed again—at least, I did wet it once again, and received another beating, after which the trouble stopped. So perhaps this barbarous remedy does work, though at a heavy price, I have no doubt.

II

St. Cyprian's was an expensive and snobbish school which was in process of becoming more snobbish, and, I imagine, more expensive. The public school with which it had special connections was Harrow, but during my time an increasing proportion of the boys went on to Eton. Most of them were the children of rich parents, but on the whole they were un-aristocratic rich, the sort of people who live in huge shrubberied houses in Bournemouth or Richmond, and who have cars and butlers but not country estates. There were a few exotics among them—some South American boys, sons of Argentine beef barons, one or two Russians, and even a Siamese prince, or someone who was described as a prince.

Sambo had two great ambitions. One was to attract titled boys to the school, and the other was to train up pupils to win scholarships at public schools, above all at Eton. He did, towards the end of my time, succeed in getting hold of two boys with real English titles. One of them, I remember, was a wretched drivelling little creature, almost an albino, peering upwards out of weak eyes, with a long nose at the end of which a dewdrop always seemed to be trembling. Sambo always gave these boys their titles when mentioning them to a third person, and for their first few days he actually addressed them to their faces as "Lord So-and-so."

Needless to say he found ways of drawing attention to them when any visitor was being shown round the school. Once, I remember the little fair-haired boy had a choking fit at dinner, and a stream of snot ran out of his nose onto his plate in a way horrible to see. Any lesser person would been called a dirty little beast and ordered out of the room instantly, but Sambo and Flip laughed it off in a "boys will be boys" spirit.

All the very rich boys were more or less undisguisedly favoured. The school still had a faint suggestion of the Victorian "private academy" with its "parlour boarders", and when I later read about that kind of school in Thackeray I immediately saw the resemblance. The rich boys had milk and biscuits in the middle of the morning, they were given riding lessons once or twice a week, Flip mothered them and called by their Christian names, and above all they were never caned. Apart from the South Americans, whose parents were safely distant, I doubt whether Sambo ever caned any boy whose father's income was much above £2,000 a year. But he was sometimes willing to sacrifice financial profit to scholastic prestige. Occasionally, by special arrangment, he would take at greatly reduced fees some boy who seemed likely to win scholarships and thus bring credit on the school. It was on these terms that I was at St. Cyprian's myself: otherwise my parents could not have afforded to send me to so expensive a school.

I did not at first understand that I was being taken at reduced fees; it was only when I was about eleven that Flip and Sambo began throwing the fact in my teeth. For my first two or three years I went through the ordinary educational mill: then, soon after I had started Greek (one started Latin at eight, Greek at ten), I moved into the scholarship class, which was taught, so far as classics went, largely by Sambo himself. Over a period of two or three years the scholarship boys were crammed with learning as cynically as a goose is crammed for Christmas. And with what learning! This business of making a gifted boy's career depend on a competitive examination, taken when he is only twelve or thirteen, is an evil thing at best, but there do appear to be preparatory schools which send scholars to Eton, Winchester, etc. without teaching them to see everything in terms of marks. At St Cyprian's the whole process was frankly a preparation for a sort of confidence trick. Your job was to learn exactly those things that would give an examiner the impression that you knew more than you did know, and as far as possible to avoid burdening your brain with anything else. Subjects which lacked examination-value, such as geography, were almost completely neglected, mathematics was also neglected if you were a "classical", science was not taught in any form—indeed it was so despised that even an interest in natural history was discouraged—and even the books you were encouraged to read in your spare time were chosen with one eye on the "English paper." Latin and Greek, the main scholarship subjects, were what counted, but even these were deliberately taught in a flashy, unsound way. We never, for example, read right throgh even a single book of a Greek or Latin author: we merely read short passages which were picked out because they were the kind of thing likely to be set as an "unseen translation." During the last year or so before we went up for our scholarships, most of our time was spent in simply working our way through the scholarship papers of previous years. Sambo had sheaves of these in his possesion, from every one of the major public schools. But the greatest outrage of all was the teaching of history.

There was in those days a piece of nonsense called the Harrow History Prize, an annual competition for which many preparatory schools entered. It was a tradition for St. Cyprian's to win it every year, as well we might, for we had mugged up every paper that had been set since the competition started, and the supply of possible questions was not inexhaustible. They were the kind of stupid question that is answered by rapping out a name or a quotation. Who plundered the Begams? Who was beheaded in an open boat? Who caught the Whigs bathing and ran away with their clothes? Almost all our historical teaching was on this level. History was a series of unrelated, unintelligible but—in some way that was never explained to us—important facts with resounding phrases tied to them. Disraeli brought peace with honour. Clive was astonished at his moderation. Pitt called in the New World to redress the balance of the Old. And the dates, and the mnemonic devices! (Did you know, for example, that the initial letters of "A black Negress was my aunt: there's her house behind the barn" are also the initial letters of the battles in the Wars of the Roses?) Flip, who "took" the higher forms in history, revelled in this kind of thing. I recall positive orgies of dates, with the keener boys leaping up and down in their places in their eagerness to shout out the right answers, and at the same time not feeling the faintest interest in the meaning of the mysterious events they were naming.

"1587?"

"Massacre of St Bartholomew!"

"1707?"

"Death of Aurangzeeb!"

"1713?"

"Treaty of Utrecht!"

"1773?"

"Boston Tea Party!"

"1520?"

"Oo, Mum, please, Mum—"

"Please, Mum, please, Mum! Let me tell him, Mum!"

"Well! 1520?"

"Field of the Cloth of Gold!"

And so on.

But history and such secondary subjects were not bad fun. It was in "classics" that the real strain came. Looking back, I realise that I then worked harder than I have ever done since, and yet at the time it never seemed possible to make quite the effort that was demanded of one. We would sit round the long shiny table, made of some very pale-coloured hard wood, with Sambo goading, threatening, exhorting, sometimes joking, very occasionally praising, but always prodding, prodding away at one's mind to keep it up to the right pitch of concentration, as one might keep a sleepy person awake by sticking pins into him.

"Go on, you little slacker! Go on, you idle, worthless little boy! The whole trouble with you is that you're bone and horn idle. You eat too much, that's why. You wolf down enormous meals, and then when you come here you're half asleep. Go on, now, put your back into it. You're not *thinking*. Your brain doesn't sweat."

He would tap away at one's skull with his silver pencil, which, in my memory, seems to have been about the size of a banana, and which certainly was heavy enough to raise a bump: or he would pull the short hairs round one's ears, or, occasionally, reach out under the table and kick one's shin. On some days nothing seemed to go right, and then it would be: "All right, then, I know what you want. You've been asking for it the whole morning. Come along, you useless little slacker. Come into the study." And then whack, whack, whack, whack, and back one would come, red-wealed and smarting —in later years Sambo had abandoned his riding-crop in favour of a thin rattan cane which hurt very much more—to settle down to work again. This did not happen very often, but I do remember, more than once, being led out of the room in the middle of a Latin sentence, receiving a beating and then going straight ahead with the same sentence, just like that. It is a mistake to think such methods do not work. They work very well for their special purpose. Indeed, I doubt whether classical education ever has been or can be success-fully carried on without corporal punishment. The boys themselves believed in its efficacy. There was a boy named Beacham, with no brains to speak of, but evidently in acute need of a scholarship. Sambo was flogging him towards the goal as one might do with a foundered horse. He went up for a schol-arship at Uppingham, came back with a conscious-ness of having done badly, and a day or two later received a severe beating for idleness. "I wish I'd had that caning before I went up for the exam," he said sadly—a remark which I felt to be contemp-tible, but which I perfectly well understood.

The boys of the scholarship class were not all treated alike. If a boy were the son of rich parents to whom the saving of fees was not all-important, Sambo would goad him along in a comparatively fatherly way, with jokes and digs in the ribs and perhaps an occasional tap with the pencil, but no hair-pulling and no caning. It was the poor but "clever" boys who suffered. Our brains were a gold-mine in which he had sunk money, and the dividends must be squeezed out of us. Long before I had grasped the nature of my financial relation-ship with Sambo, I had been made to understand that I was not on the same footing as most of the other boys. In effect there were three castes in the school. There was the minority with an aristocratic or millionaire background, there were the children of the ordinary suburban rich, who made up the bulk of the school, and there were a few underlings like myself, the sons of clergymen, Indian civil servants, struggling widows and the like. These poorer ones were discouraged from going in for "extras" such as shooting and carpentry, and were humiliated over clothes and petty possessions. I never, for instance, succeeded in getting a cricket bat of my own, because "Your parents wouldn't be able to afford it". This phrase pursued me throughout my schooldays. At St. Cyprian's we were not allowed to keep the money we brought back with us, but had to "give it in" on the first day of term, and then from time to time were allowed to spend it under supervision. I and similarly placed boys were always choked off from buying expensive toys like model aeroplanes, even if the necessary money stood to our credit. Flip, in particular, seemed to aim consciously at inculcating a humble outlook in the poorer boys. "Do you think that's the sort of thing a boy like you should buy?" I remember her saying to somebody— and she said this in front of the whole school: "You know you're not going to grow up with money, don't you? Your people aren't rich. You must learn to be sensible. Don't get above yourself!" There was also the weekly pocket-money, which we took out in sweets, dispensed by Flip from a large table. The millionaires had sixpence a week, but the normal sum was threepence. I and one or two others were only allowed twopence. My parents had not given instructions to this effect, and the saving of a penny a week could not conceivably have made any difference to them: it was a mark of status. Worse yet was the detail of the birthday cakes. It was usual for each boy, on his birthday, to have a large iced cake with candles, which was shared out at tea between the whole school. It was provided as a matter of routine and went on his parents' bill. I never had such a cake, though my parents would have paid for it readily enough. Year after year, never daring to ask, I would miserably hope that this year a cake would appear. Once or twice I even rashly pretended to my companions that this time I *was* going to have a cake. Then came tea-time, and no cake, which did not make me more popular.

Very early it was impressed upon me that I had no chance of a decent future unless I won a scholarship at a public school. Either I won my scholarship, or I must leave school at fourteen and become, in Sambo's favourite phrase "a little office boy at forty pounds a year." In my circumstances it was natural that I should believe this. Indeed, it was universally taken for granted at St. Cyprian's that unless you went to a "good" public school (and only about fifteen schools came under this heading) you were ruined for life. It is not easy to convey to a grown-up person the sense of strain, of nerving oneself for some terrible, all-deciding combat, as the date of the examination crept nearer—eleven years old, twelve years old, then thirteen, the fatal year itself! Over a period of about two years, I do not think there was ever a day when "the exam," as I called it, was quite out of my waking thoughts. In my prayers it figured invariably: and whenever I got the bigger portion of a wishbone, or picked up a horseshoe, or bowed seven times to the new moon, or succeeded in passing through a wishing-gate without touching the sides, then the wish I earned by doing so went on "the exam" as a matter of course. And yet curiously enough I was also tormented by an almost irresistible impulse *not* to work. There were days when my heart sickened at the labours ahead of me, and I stood stupid as an animal before the most elementary difficulties. In the holidays, also, I could not work. Some of the scholarship boys received extra tuition from a certain Mr. Batchelor, a likeable, very hairy man who wore shaggy suits and lived in a typical bachelor's "den"—booklined walls, overwhelming stench of tobacco—somewhere in the town. During the holidays Mr. Batchelor used to send us extracts from Latin authors to translate, and we were supposed to send back a wad of work once a week. Somehow I could not do it. The empty paper and the black Latin dictionary lying on the table, the consciousness of a plain duty shirked, poisoned my leisure, but somehow I could not start, and by the end of the holidays I would only have sent Mr. Batchelor fifty or a hundred lines. Undoubtedly part of the reason was that Sambo and his cane were far away. But in term-time, also, I would go through periods of idleness and stupidity when I would sink deeper and deeper into disgrace and even achieve a sort of feeble, snivelling defiance, fully conscious of my guilt and yet unable or unwilling—I could not be sure which—to do any better. Then Sambo or Flip would send for me, and this time it would not even be a caning.

Flip would search me with her baleful eyes. (What colour were those eyes, I wonder? I remember them as green, but actually no human being has green eyes. Perhaps they were hazel.) She would start off in her peculiar, wheedling, bullying style, which never failed to get right through one's guard and score a hit on one's better nature.

"I don't think it's awfully decent of you to behave like this, is it? Do you think it's quite playing the game by your mother and father to go on idling your time away, week after week, month after month? Do you *want* to throw all your chances away? You know your people aren't rich, don't you? You know they can't afford the same things as other boys' parents. How are they to send you to a public school if you don't win a scholarship? I know how proud your mother is of you. Do you *want* to let her down?"

"I don't think he wants to go to a public school any longer," Sambo would say, addressing himself to Flip with a pretence that I was not there. "I think he's given up that idea. He wants to be a little office boy at forty pounds a year."

The horrible sensation of tears—a swelling in the breast, a tickling behind the nose—would already have assailed me. Flip would bring out her ace of trumps:

"And do you think it's quite fair to *us*, the way you're behaving? After all we've done for you? You *do* know what we've done for you, don't you?" Her eyes would pierce deep into me, and though she never said it straight out, I did know. "We've had you here all these years—we even had you here for a week in the holidays so that Mr. Batchelor could coach you. We don't *want* to have to send you away, you know, but we can't keep a boy here just to eat up our food, term after term. *I* don't think it's very straight, the way you're behaving. Do you?"

I never had any answer except a miserable "No, Mum," or "Yes, Mum," as the case might be. Evidently it was *not* straight, the way I was behaving. And at some point or other the unwanted tear would always force its way out of the corner of my eye, roll down my nose, and splash.

Flip never said in plain words that I was a non-paying pupil, no doubt because vague phrases like "all we've done for you" had a deeper emotional appeal. Sambo, who did not aspire to be loved by his pupils, put it more brutally, though, as was usual with him, in pompous language. "You are living on my bounty" was his favourite phrase in this context. At least once I listened to these words between blows of the cane. I must say that these scenes were not frequent, and except on one occasion they did not take place in the presence of other boys. In public I was reminded that I was poor and that my parents "wouldn't be able to afford" this or that, but I was not actually reminded of my dependent position. It was a final unanswerable argument, to be brought forth like an instrument of torture when my work became exceptionally bad.

To grasp the effect of this kind of thing on a child of ten or twelve, one has to remember that the child has little sense of proportion or probability. A child may be a mass of egoism and rebelliousness, but it has no accumulated experience to give it confidence in its own judgements. On the whole it will accept what it is told, and it will believe in the most fantastic way in the knowledge and powers of the adults surrounding it. Here is an example.

I have said that at St. Cyprian's we were not allowed to keep our own money. However, it was possible to hold back a shilling or two, and sometimes I used furtively to buy sweets which I kept hidden in the loose ivy on the playing-field wall. One day when I had been sent on an errand I went into a sweet-shop a mile or more from the school and bought some chocolates. As I came out of the shop I saw on the opposite pavement a small sharp-faced man who seemed to be staring very hard at my school cap. Instantly a horrible fear went through me. There could be no doubt as to who the man was. He was a spy placed there by Sambo! I turned away unconcernedly, and then, as though my legs were doing it of their own accord, broke into a clumsy run. But when I got round the next corner I forced myself to walk again, for to run was a sign of guilt, and obviously there would be other spies posted here and there about the town. All that day and the next I waited for the summons to the study, and was surprised when it did not come. It did not seem to me strange that the headmaster of a private school should dispose of an army of informers, and I did not even imagine that he would have to pay them. I assumed that any adult, inside the school or outside, would collaborate voluntarily in preventing us from breaking the rules. Sambo was all-powerful; it was natural that his agents should be everywhere. When this episode happened I do not think I can have been less than twelve years old.

I hated Sambo and Flip, with a sort of shamefaced, remorseful hatred, but it did not occur to me to doubt their judgement. When they told me that I must either win a public-school scholarship or become an office boy at fourteen, I believed that those were the unavoidable alternatives before me. And above all, I believed Sambo and Flip when they told me they were my benefactors. I see now, of course, that from Sambo's point of view I was a good speculation. He sank money in me, and he looked to get it back in the form of prestige. If I had "gone off," as promising boys sometimes do, I imagine that he would have got rid of me swiftly. As it was I won him two scholarships when the time came, and no doubt he made full use of them in his prospectuses. But it is difficult for a child to realise that a school is primarily a commercial venture. A child believes that the school exists to educate and that the schoolmaster disciplines him either for his own good, or from a love of bullying. Flip and Sambo had chosen to befriend me, and their friendship included canings, reproaches and humiliations, which were good for me and saved me from an office stool. That was their version, and I believed in it. It was therefore clear that I owed them a vast debt of gratitude. But I was *not* grateful, as I very well knew. On the contrary, I hated both of them. I could not control my subjective feelings, and I could not conceal them from myself. But it is wicked, is it not, to hate your benefactors? So I was taught, and so I believed. A child accepts the codes of behaviour that are presented to it, even when it breaks them. From the age of eight, or even earlier, the consciousness of sin was never far away from me. If I contrived to seem callous and defiant, it was only a thin cover over a mass of shame and dismay. All through my boyhood I had a profound conviction that I was no good, that I was wasting my time, wrecking my talents, behaving with monstrous folly and wickedness and ingratitude—and all this, it seemed, was inescapable, because I lived among laws which were absolute, like the law of gravity, but which it was not possible for me to keep.

III

No one can look back on his schooldays and say with truth that they were altogether unhappy.

I have good memories of St. Cyprian's, among a horde of bad ones. Sometimes on summer afternoons there were wonderful expeditions across the Downs to a village called Birling Gap, or to Beachy

Head, where one bathed dangerously among the chalk boulders and came home covered with cuts. And there were still more wonderful midsummer evenings when, as a special treat, we were not driven off to bed as usual but allowed to wander about the grounds in the long twilight, ending up with a plunge into the swimming bath at about nine o'clock. There was the joy of waking early on summer mornings and getting in an hour's undisturbed reading (Ian Hay, Thackeray, Kipling and H.G. Wells were the favourite authors of my boyhood) in the sunlit, sleeping dormitory. There was also cricket, which I was no good at but with which I conducted a sort of hopeless love affair up to the age of about eighteen. And there was the pleasure of keeping caterpillars—the silky green and purple puss-moth, the ghostly green poplar-hawk, the privet-hawk, large as one's third finger, specimens of which could be illicitly purchased for sixpence at a shop in the town—and, when one could escape long enough from the master who was "taking the walk", there was the excitement of dredging the dew-ponds on the Down for enormous newts with orange-coloured bellies. This business of being out for a walk, coming across something of fascinating interest and then being dragged away from it by a yell from the master, like a dog jerked onwards by the leash, is an important feature of school life, and helps to build up the conviction, so strong in many children, that the things you most want to do are always unattainable.

Very occasionally, perhaps once during each summer, it was possible to escape altogether from the barrack-like atmosphere of school, when Brown, the second master, was permitted to take one or two boys for an afternoon of butterfly hunting on a common a few miles away. Brown was a man with white hair and a red face like a strawberry, who was good at natural history, making models and plaster casts, operating magic lanterns, and things of that kind. He and Mr. Batchelor were the only adults in any way connected with the school whom I did not either dislike or fear. Once he took me into his room and showed me in confidence a plated, pearl-handled revolver—his "six-shooter," he called it—which he kept in a box under his bed. And oh, the joy of those occasional expeditions! The ride of two or three miles on a lonely little branch line, the afternoon of charging to and fro with large green nets, the beauty of the enormous dragonflies which hovered over the tops of the grasses, the sinister killing-bottle with its sickly smell, and then tea in the parlour of a pub with large slices of pale-caloured cake! The essence of it was in the railway journey, which seemed to put magic distances between yourself and school.

Flip, characteristically, disapproved of these expeditions, though not actually forbidding them. "And have you been catching *little butterflies*?" she would say with a vicious sneer when one got back, making her voice as babyish as possible. From her point of view, natural history ("bug-hunting" she would probably have called it) was a babyish pursuit which a boy should be laughed out of as early as possible. Moreover it was somehow faintly plebeian, it was traditionally associated with boys who wore spectacles and were no good at games, it did not help you to pass exams, and above all it smelt of science and therefore seemed to menace classical education. It needed a considerable moral effort to accept Brown's invitation. How I dreaded that sneer of *little butterflies*! Brown, however, who had been at school since its early days, had built up a certain independence for himself: he seemed able to handle Sambo, and ignored Flip a good deal. If it ever happened that both of them were away, Brown acted as deputy headmaster, and on those occasions instead of reading the appointed lesson for the day at morning chapel, he would read us stories from the Apocrypha.

Most of the good memories of my childhood, and up to the age of about twenty, are in some way connected with animals. So far as St. Cyprian's goes, it also seems, when I look back, that all my good memories are of summer. In winter your nose ran continually, your fingers were too numb to button your shirt (this was an especial misery on Sundays, when we wore Eton collars), and there was the daily nightmare of football—the cold, the mud, the hideous greasy ball that came whizzing at one's face, the gouging knees and trampling boots of the bigger boys. Part of the trouble was that in winter, after the age of about ten, I was seldom in good health, at any rate during term-time. I had defective bronchial tubes and a lesion in one lung which was not discovered till many years later. Hence I not only had a chronic cough, but running was a torment to me. In those days however, "wheeziness," or "chestiness," as it was called, was either diagnosed as imagination or was looked on as essentially a moral disorder, caused by overeating. "You wheeze like a concertina," Sambo would say disapprovingly as he stood behind my chair; "You're prepetually stuffing yourself with food, that's why." My cough was referred to as a "stomach cough," which made it sound both disgusting and reprehensible. The cure for it was hard running, which, if you kept it up long enough, ultimately "cleared your chest."

It is curious, the degree—I will not say of actual hardship, but of squalor and neglect—that was taken for granted in upper-class schools of that period. Almost as in the days of Thackeray, it seemed natural that a little boy of eight or ten should be a miserable, snotty-nosed creature, his face almost permanently dirty, his hands chapped, his nails bitten, his handkerchief a sodden horror, his bottom frequently blue with bruises. It was partly the prospect of actual physical discomfort that made the thought of going back to school lie in one's breast like a lump of lead during the last few days of the holidays. A characteristic memory of St. Cyprian's is the astonishing hardness of one's bed on the first night of term. Since this was an expensive school, I took a social step upwards by attending it, and yet the standard of comfort was in every way far lower than in my own home, or, indeed, than it would have been in a prosperous working-class home. One only had a hot bath once a week, for instance. The food was not only bad, it was also insufficient. Never before or since have I seen butter or jam scraped on bread so thinly. I do not think I can be imagining the fact that we were underfed, when I remember the lengths we would go in order to steal food. On a number of occasions I remember creeping down at two or three o'clock in the morning through what seemed like miles of pitch-dark stairways and passages—barefooted, stopping to listen after each step, paralysed with about equal fear of Sambo, ghosts and burglars—to steal stale bread from the pantry. The assistant masters had their meals with us, but they had somewhat better food, and if one got half a chance it was usual to steal left-over scraps of bacon rind or fried potato when their plates were removed.

As usual, I did not see the sound commercial reason for this underfeeding. On the whole I accepted Sambo's view that a boy's appetite is a sort of morbid growth which should be kept in check as much as possible. A maxim often repeated to us at St. Cyprian's was that it is healthy to get up from a meal feeling as hungry as when you sat down. Only a generation earlier than this it had been common for school dinners to start off with a slab of unsweetened suet pudding, which, it was frankly said, "broke the boys' appetites." But the underfeeding was probably less flagrant at preparatory schools, where a boy was wholly dependent on the official diet, than at public schools, where he was allowed—indeed, expected—to buy extra food for himself. At some schools, he would literally not have had enough to eat unless he had bought regular supplies of eggs, sausages, sardines, etc.; and his parents had to allow him money for this purpose. At Eton, for instance, at any rate in College, a boy was given no solid meal after midday dinner. For his afternoon tea he was given only tea and bread and butter, and at eight o'clock he was given a miserable supper of soup or fried fish, or more often bread and cheese, with water to drink. Sambo went down to see his eldest son at Eton and came back in snobbish ecstasies over the luxury in which the boys lived. "They give them fried fish for supper!" he exclaimed, beaming all over his chubby face. "There's no school like it in the world." Fried fish! The habitual supper of the poorest of the working class! At very cheap boarding schools it was no doubt worse. A very early memory of mine is of seeing the boarders at a grammar school—the sons, probably, of farmers and shopkeepers—being fed on boiled lights.

Whoever writes about his childhood must beware of exaggeration and self-pity. I do not want to claim that I was a martyr or that St Cyprian's was a sort of Dotheboys Hall. But I should be falsifying my own memories if I did not record that they are largely memories of disgust. The overcrowded, underfed, underwashed life that we led *was* disgusting, as I recall it. If I shut my eyes and say "school," it is of course the physical sur-roundings that first come back to me: the flat playing-field with its cricket pavilion and the little shed by the rifle range, the draughty dormitories, the dusty splintery passages, the square of asphalt in front of the gymnasium, the raw-looking pine-wood chapel at the back. And at almost every point some filthy detail obtrudes itself. For example, there were the pewter bowls out of which we had our porridge. They had overhanging rims, and un-der the rims there were accumulations of sour porridge, which could be flaked off in long strips. The porridge itself, too, contained more lumps, hairs and unexplained black things than one would have thought possible, unless someone were put-ting them there on purpose. It was never safe to start on that porridge without investigating it first. and there was the slimy water of the plunge bath—it was twelve or fifteen feet long, the whole school was supposed to go into it every morning, and I doubt whether the water was changed at all frequently—and the always-damp towels with their cheesy smell: and, on occasional visits in the winter, the murky sea-water of the local Baths, which came straight in from the beach and on which I once saw floating a human turd. And the sweaty smell of the changing-room with its greasy basins, and, giving on this, the row of filthy, dilapidated lavatories, which had no fastenings of any kind on the doors, so that whenever you were sitting there someone was sure to come crashing in. It is not easy for me to think of my schooldays without seeming to breathe in a whiff of something cold and evil-smelling—a sort of compound of sweaty stockings, dirty towels, faecal smells blowing along corridors, forks with old food between the prongs, neck-of-mutton stew, and the banging doors of the lavatories and the echoing chamber-pots in the dormitories.

It is true that I am by nature not gregarious, and the WC and dirty-handkerchief side of life is necessarily more obtrusive when great numbers of human beings are crushed together in a small space. It is just as bad in an army, and worse, no doubt, in a prison. Besides, boyhood is the age of disgust. After one has learned to differentiate, and before one has become hardened—between seven and eighteen, say—one seems always to be walking the tight-rope over a cesspool. Yet I do not think I exaggerate the squalor of school life, when I remember how health and cleanliness were neglected, in spite of the hoo-ha about fresh air and cold water and keeping in hard training. It was common to remain constipated for days together. Indeed, one was hardly encouraged to keep one's bowels open, since the only aperients tolerated were castor oil or another almost equally horrible drink called liquorice powder. One was supposed to go into the plunge bath every morning, but some boys shirked it for days on end, simply making themselves scarce when the bell sounded, or else slipping along the edge of the bath among the crowd, and then wetting their hair with a little dirty water off the floor. A little boy of eight or nine will not necessarily keep himself clean unless there is someone to see that he does it. There was a new boy named Hazel, a pretty, mother's darling of a boy, who came a little while before I left. the first thing I noticed about him was the beautiful pearly whiteness of his teeth. By the end of that term his teeth were an extraordinary shade of green. During all that time, apparently, no one had taken sufficient interest in him to see that he brushed them.

But of course the differences between home and

school were more than physical. That bump on the hard mattress, on the first night of term, used to give me a feeling of abrupt awakening, a feeling of: "This is reality, this is what you are up against." Your home might be far from perfect, but at least it was a place ruled by love rather than by fear, where you did not have to be perpetually on your guard against the people surrounding you. At eight years old you were suddenly taken out of this warm nest and flung into a world of force and fraud and secrecy, like a gold-fish into a tank full of pike. Against no matter what degree of bullying you had no redress. You could only have defended yourself by sneaking, which, except in a few rigidly defined circumstances, was the unforgivable sin. To write home and ask your parents to take you away would have been even less thinkable, since to do so would have been to admit yourself unhappy and unpopular, which a boy will never do. Boys are Erewhonians: they think that misfortune is disgraceful and must be concealed at all costs. It might perhaps have been considered permissible to complain to your parents about bad food, or an unjustified caning, or some other ill-treatment inflicted by masters and not by boys. The fact that Sambo never beat the richer boys suggests that such complaints were made occasionally. But in my own peculiar circumstances I could never have asked my parents to intervene on my behalf. Even before I understood about the reduced fees, I grasped that they were in some way under an obligation to Sambo, and therefore could not protect me against him. I have mentioned already that throughout my time at St. Cyprian's I never had a cricket bat of my own. I had been told this was because "your parents couldn't afford it." One day in the holidays, by some casual remark, it came out that they had provided ten shillings to buy me one: yet no cricket bat appeared. I did not protest to my parents, let alone raise the subject with Sambo. How could I? I was dependent on him, and the ten shillings was merely a fragment of what I owed him. I realise now, of course, that it is immensely unlikely that Sambo had simply stuck to the money. No doubt the matter had slipped his memory. But the point is that I assumed that he had stuck to it, and that he had a right to do so if he chose.

How difficult it is for a child to have any real independence of attitude could be seen in our behaviour towards Flip. I think it would be true to say that every boy in the school hated and feared her. Yet we all fawned on her in the most abject way, and the top layer of our feelings towards her was a sort of guilt-stricken loyalty. Flip, although the discipline of the school depended more on her than on Sambo, hardly pretended to dispense strict justice. She was frankly capricious. An act which might get you a caning one day might next day be laughed off as a boyish prank, or even commended because it "showed you had guts." There were days when everyone cowered before those deep-set, accusing eyes, and there were days when she was like a flirtatious queen surrounded by courtier-lovers, laughing and joking, scattering largesse, or the promise of largesse ("And if you win the Harrow History Prize I'll give you a new case for your camera!"), and occasionally even packing three or four favoured boys into her Ford car and carrying them off to a teashop in town, where they were allowed to buy coffee and cakes. Flip was inextricably mixed up in my mind with Queen Elizabeth, whose relations with Leicester and Essex and Raleigh were intelligible to me from a very early age. A word we all constantly used in speaking of Flip was "favour." "I'm in good favour," we would say, or "I'm in bad favour." Except for the handful of wealthy or titled boys, no one was permanently in good favour, but on the other hand even the outcasts had patches of it from time to time. Thus, although my memories of Flip are mostly hostile, I also remember considerable periods when I basked under her smiles, when she called me "old chap" and used my Christian name, and allowed me to frequent her private library, where I first made acquaintance with *Vanity Fair*. The high-water mark of good favour was to be invited to serve at table on Sunday nights when Flip and Sambo had guests to dinner. In clearing away, of course, one had a chance to finish off the scraps, but one also got a servile pleasure from standing behind the seated guests, and darting deferentially forward when something was wanted. Whenever one had the chance to suck up, one did suck up, and at the first smile one's hatred turned into a sort of cringing love. I was always tremendously proud when I succeeded in making Flip laugh. I have even, at her command, written *vers d'occasion*, comic verses to celebrate memorable events in the life of the school.

I am anxious to make it clear that I was not a rebel, except by force of circumstances. I accepted the codes that I found in being. Once, towards the end of my time, I even sneaked to Brown about a suspected case of homosexuality. I did not know very well what homosexuality was, but I knew that it happened and was bad, and that this was one of the contexts in which it was proper to sneak. Brown told me I was "a good fellow," which made me feel horribly ashamed. Before Flip one seemed as helpless as a snake before the snake-charmer. She had a hardly varying vocabulary of praise and abuse, a whole series of set phrases, each of which promptly called forth the appropriate response.

There was "*Buck* up, old chap!", which inspired one to paroxysms of energy; there was "Don't *be* such a fool!" (or, "It's path*et*ic, isn't it?"), which made one feel a born idiot; and there was "It isn't very straight of you, is it?", which always brought one to the brink of tears. And yet all the while, at the middle of one's heart, there seemed to stand an incorruptible inner self who knew that whatever one did—whether one laughed or snivelled or went into frenzies of gratitude for small favours—one's only true feeling was hatred.

IV

I had learned early in my career that one can do wrong against one's will, and before long I also learned that one can do wrong without ever discovering what one has done or why it was wrong. There were sins that were too subtle to be explained, and there were others that were too terrible to be clearly mentioned. For example, there was sex, which was always smouldering just under the surface and which suddenly blew up into a tremendous row when I was about twelve.

At some preparatory schools homosexuality is not a problem, but I think that St. Cyprian's may have acquired a "bad tone" thanks to the presence of the South American boys, who would perhaps mature a year or two earlier than an English boy. At that age I was not interested, so I do not actually know what went on, but I imagine it was group masturbation. At any rate, one day the storm suddenly burst over our heads. There were summonses, interrogations, confessions, floggings, repentances, solemn lectures of which one understood nothing except that some irredeemable sin known as "swinishness" or "beastliness" had been committed. One of the ringleaders, a boy named Horne, was flogged, according to eye-witnesses, for a quarter of an hour continuously before being expelled. His yells rang through the house. But we were all implicated, more or less, or felt ourselves to be implicated. Guilt seemed to hang in the air like a pall of smoke. A solemn, black-haired imbecile of an assistant master, who was later to be a Member of Parliament, took the older boys to a secluded room and delivered a talk on the Temple of the Body.

"Don't you realise what a wonderful thing your body is?" he said gravely. "You talk of your motor-car engines, your Rolls-Royces and Daimlers and so on. Don't you understand that no engine ever made is fit to be compared with your body? And then you go and wreck it, ruin it—for life!"

He turned his cavernous black eyes on me and added sadly:

"And you, whom I'd always believed to be quite a decent person after your fashion—you, I hear, are one of the very worst."

A feeling of doom descended upon me. So I was guilty too. I too had done the dreadful thing, whatever it was, that wrecked you for life, body and soul, and ended in suicide or the lunatic asylum. Till then I had hoped that I was innocent, and the conviction of sin which now took possession of me was perhaps all the stronger because I did not know what I had done. I was not among those who were interrogated and flogged, and it was not until the row was well over that I even learned about the trivial accident that had connected my name with it. Even then I understood nothing. It was not till about two years later that I fully grasped what that lecture on the Temple of the Body had referred to.

At this time I was in an almost sexless state, which is normal, or at any rate common, in boys of that age; I was therefore in the position of simultaneously knowing and not knowing what used to be called the Facts of Life. At five or six, like many children, I had passed through a phase of sexuality. My friends were the plumber's children up the road, and we used sometimes to play games of a vaguely erotic kind. One was called "playing at doctors," and I remember getting a faint but definitely pleasant thrill from holding a toy trumpet, which was supposed to be a stethoscope, against a little girl's belly. About the same time I fell deeply in love, a far more worshipping kind of love than I have ever felt for anyone since, with a girl named Elsie at the convent school which I attended. She seemed to me grown up, so I suppose she must have been fifteen. After that, as so often happens, all sexual feelings seemed to go out of me for many years. At twelve I knew more than I had known as a young child, but I understood less, because I no longer knew the essential fact that there is something pleasant in sexual activity. Between roughly seven and fourteen, the whole subject seemed to me uninteresting and, when for some reason I was forced to think of it, disgusting. My knowledge of the so-called Facts of Life was derived from animals, and was therefore distorted, and in any case was only intermittent. I knew that animals copulated and that human beings had bodies resembling those of animals: but that human beings also copulated I only knew, as it were, reluctantly, when something, a phrase in the Bible, perhaps, compelled me to remember it. Not having desire, I had no curiosity, and was willing to leave many questions unanswered. Thus, I knew in principle how the baby gets into the woman, but I did not know how it gets out again, because I had never followed the subject up. I knew all the dirty words, and in my bad moments I would repeat them to myself, but I did not know what the worst of them meant, nor wanted to know. They were abstractly wicked, a sort of verbal charm. While I remained in this state, it was easy for me to remain ignorant of any sexual misdeeds that went on about me, and to be hardly wiser even when the row broke. At most, through the veiled and terrible warnings of Flip, Sambo and all the rest of them, I grasped that the crime of which we were all guilty was somehow connected with the sexual organs. I had noticed, without feeling much interest, that one's penis sometimes stands up of its own accord (this starts happening to a boy long before he has any conscious sexual desires), and I was inclined to believe, or half-believe, that *that* must be the crime. At any rate, it was something to do with the penis—so much I understood. Many other boys, I have no doubt, were equally in the dark.

After the talk on the Temple of the Body (days later, it seems in retrospect: the row seemed to continue for days), a dozen of us were seated at the long shiny table which Sambo used for the scholarship class, under Flip's lowering eye. A long, desolate wail rang out from a room somewhere above. A very small boy named Ronalds, aged no more than about ten, who was implicated in some way, was being flogged, or was recovering from a flogging. At the sound, Flip's eyes searched our faces, and settled upon me.

"You see," she said.

I will not swear that she said "You see what you have done," but that was the sense of it. We were all bowed down with shame. It was *our* fault. Somehow or other we had led poor Ronalds astray: *we* were responsible for his agony and his ruin. Then Flip turned upon another boy named Heath. It was thirty years ago, and I cannot remember for certain whether she merely quoted a verse from the Bible, or whether she actually brought out a Bible and made Heath read it; but at any rate the text indicated was: "Whoso shall offend one of these little ones that believe in me, it were better for him that a millstone were hanged about his neck, and that he were drowned in the depth of the sea."

That, too, was terrible. Ronalds was one of these little ones, we had offended him; it were better that a millstone were hanged about our necks and that we were drowned in the depth of the sea.

"Have you thought about that, Heath—have you thought what it means?" Flip said. And Heath broke down into snivelling tears.

Another boy, Beacham, whom I have mentioned already, was similarly overwhelmed with shame by the accusation that he "had black rings round his eyes."

"Have you looked in the glass lately, Beacham?" said Flip. "Aren't you ashamed to go about with a face like that? Do you think everyone doesn't know what it means when a boy has black rings round his eyes?"

Once again the load of guilt and fear seemed to settle down upon me. Had *I* got black rings round my eyes? A couple of years later I realised that these were supposed to be a symptom by which masturbators could be detected. But already, without knowing this, I accepted the black rings as a sure sign of depravity, *some* kind of depravity. And many times, even before I grasped the supposed meaning, I have gazed anxiously into the glass, looking for the first hint of that dreaded stigma, the confession which the secret sinner writes upon his own face.

These terrors wore off, or became merely intermittent, without affecting what one might call my official beliefs. It was still true about the madhouse and the suicide's grave, but it was no longer acutely frightening. Some months later it happened that I once again saw Horne, the ringleader who had been flogged and expelled. Horne was one of the outcasts, the son of poor middle-class parents, which was no doubt part of the reason why Sambo had handled him so roughly. The term after his expulsion he went on to Eastbourne College, the small local public school, which was hideously despised at St. Cyprian's and looked on as "not really" a public school at all. Only a very few boys from St. Cyprian's went there, and Sambo always spoke of them with a sort of contemptuous pity. You had no chance if you went to a school like that: at the best your destiny would be a clerkship. I thought of Horne as a person who at thirteen had already forfeited all hope of any decent future. Physically, morally and socially he was finished. Moreover I assumed that his parents had only sent him to Eastbourne College because after his disgrace no "good" school would have him.

During the following term, when we were out for a walk, we passed Horne in the street. He looked completely normal. He was a strongly built, rather good-looking boy with black hair. I immediately noticed that he looked better than when I had last seen him—his complexion, previously rather pale, was pinker and that he did not seem embarrassed at meeting us. Apparently he was not ashamed either of having been expelled, or of being

at Eastbourne College. If one could gather anything from the way he looked at us as we filed
past, it was that he was glad to have escaped from
St. Cyprian's. But the encounter made very little
impression on me. I drew no inference from the
fact that Horne, ruined in body and soul, appeared
to be happy and in good health. I still believed in
the sexual mythology that had been taught me by
Sambo and Flip. The mysterious, terrible dangers
were still there. Any morning the black rings might
appear round your eyes and you would know that
you too were among the lost ones. Only it no longer
seemed to matter very much. These contradictions
can exist easily in the mind of a child, because of
its own vitality. It accepts—how can it do otherwise?—the nonsense that its elders tell it, but its
youthful body, and the sweetness of the physical
world, tell it another story. It was the same with
Hell, which up to the age of about fourteen I officially believed in. Almost certainly Hell existed,
and there were occasions when a vivid sermon
could scare you into fits. But somehow it never
lasted. The fire that waited for you was real fire, it
would hurt in the same way as when you burnt
your finger, and *forever*, but most of the time you
could contemplate it without bothering.

V

The various codes which were presented to you at
St. Cyprian's—religious, moral, social and intellectual—contradicted one another if you worked

out their implications. The essential conflict was between the tradition of nineteenth-century asceticism and the actually existing luxury and snobbery of the pre-1914 age. On the one side were low-church Bible Christianity, sex puritanism, insistence on hard work, respect for academic distinction, disapproval of self-indulgence: on the other, contempt for "braininess," and worship of games, contempt for foreigners and the working class, an almost neurotic dread of poverty, and, above all, the assumption not only that money and privilege are the things that matter, but that it is better to inherit them than to have to work for them. Broadly, you were bidden to be at once a Christian and a social success, which is impossible. At the time I did not perceive that the various ideals which were set before us cancelled out. I merely saw that they were all, or nearly all, unattainable, so far as I was concerned, since they all depended not only on what you did but on what you *were*.

Very early, at the age of only ten or eleven, I reached the conclusion—no one told me this, but on the other hand I did not simply make it up out of my own head: somehow it was in the air I breathed—that you were no good unless you had £100,000. I had perhaps fixed on this particular sum as a result of reading Thackeray. The interest on £100,000 would be £4,000 a year (I was in favour of a safe 4 per cent), and this seemed to me the minimum income that you must possess if you were to belong to the real top crust, the people in the country houses. But it was clear that I could never find my way into that paradise, to which you did not really belong unless you were born into it. You could only *make* money, if at all, by a mysterious operation called "going into the City," and when you came out of the City, having won your £100,000, you were fat and old. But the truly enviable thing about the top-notchers was that they were rich while young. For people like me, the ambitious middle class, the examination-passers, only a bleak, laborious kind of success was possible. You clambered upwards on a ladder of scholarships into the Civil Service or the Indian Civil Service, or possibly you became a barrister. And if at any point you "slacked" or "went off" and missed one of the rungs in the ladder, you became "a little office boy at forty pounds a year." But even if you climbed to the highest niche that was open to you, you could still only be an underling, a hanger-on of the people who really counted.

Even if I had not learned this from Sambo and Flip, I would have learned it from the other boys. Looking back, it is astonishing how intimately, intelligently snobbish we all were, how knowledgeable about names and addresses, how swift to detect small differences in accents and manners and the cut of clothes. There were some boys who seemed to drip money from their pores even in the bleak misery of the middle of a winter term. At the beginning and end of the term, especially, there was naively snobbish chatter about Switzerland, and Scotland with its ghillies and grouse moors, and "my uncle's yacht," and "our place in the country," and "my pony" and "my pater's touring car." There never was, I suppose, in the history of the world a time when the sheer vulgar fatness of wealth, without any kind of aristocratic elegance to redeem it, was so obtrusive as in those years before 1914. It was the age when crazy millionaires in curly top-hats and lavender waistcoats gave champagne parties in rococo house-boats on the Thames, the age of diabolo and hobble skirts, the age of the "knut" in his grey bowler and cut-away coat, the age of *The Merry Widow*, Saki's novels, *Peter Pan* and *Where the Rainbow Ends*, the age when people talked about chocs and cigs and ripping and topping and heavenly, when they went for divvy week-ends at Brighton and had scrumptious teas at the Troc. From the whole decade before 1914 there seems to breathe forth a smell of the more vulgar, un-grown-up kinds of luxury, a smell of brilliantine and *Crème-de-menthe* and soft-centred chocolates—an atmosphere, as it were, of eating everlasting strawberry ices on green lawns to the tune of the Eton Boating Song. The extraordinary thing was the way in which everyone took it for granted that this oozing, bulging wealth of the English upper-middle classes would last for ever, and was part of the order of things. After 1918 it was never quite the same again. Snobbishness and expensive habits came back, certainly, but they were self-conscious and on the defensive. Before the war the worship of money was entirely unreflecting and untroubled by any pang of conscience. The goodness of money was as unmistakable as the goddness of health or beauty, and a glittering car, a title or a horde of servants was mixed up in people's minds with the idea of actual moral virtue.

At St. Cyprian's, in term-time, the general bareness of life enforced a certain democracy, but any mention of the holidays, and the consequent competitive swanking about cars and butlers and country houses, promptly called class distinctions into being. The school was pervaded by a curious cult of Scotland, which brought out the fundamental contradiction in our standard of values. Flip claimed Scottish ancestry, and she favoured the Scottish boys, encouraging them to wear kilts in their ancestral tartan instead of the school uniform, and even christened her youngest child by a Gaelic name. Ostensibly we were supposed to admire the Scots because they were "grim" and "dour" ("stern" was perhaps the key word), and irresistible on the field of battle. In the big schoolroom there was a steel engraving of the charge of the Scots Greys at Waterloo, all looking as though they enjoyed every moment of it. Our picture of Scotland was made up of burns, braes, kilts, sporrans, claymores, bagpipes and the like, all somehow mixed up with the invigorating effects of porridge, Protestantism and a cold climate. But underlying this was something quite different. The real reason for the cult of Scotland was that only very rich people could spend their summers there. And the pretended belief in Scottish superiority was a cover for the bad conscience of the occupying English, who had pushed the Highland peasantry off their farms to make way for the deer forests, and then compensated them by turning them into servants. Flip's face always beamed with innocent snobbishness when she spoke of Scotland. Occasionally she even attempted a trace of Scottish accent. Scotland was a private paradise which a few initiates could talk about and make outsiders feel small.

"You going to Scotland this hols?"

"Rather! We go every year."

"My pater's got three miles of river."

"My pater's giving me a new gun for the twelfth. There's jolly good black game where we go. Get out, Smith! What are you listening for? You've never been in Scotland. I bet you don't know what a blackcock looks like."

Following on this, imitations of the cry of a blackcock, of the roaring of a stag, of the accent of "our ghillies", etc etc.

And the questionings that new boys of doubtful social origin were sometimes put through—questionings quite surprising in their meanminded particularity, when one reflects that the inquisitors were only twelve or thirteen!

"How much a year has your pater got? What part of London do you live in? Is that Knightsbridge or Kensington? How many bathrooms has your house got? How many servants do your people keep? Have you got a butler? Well, then, have you got a cook? Where do you get your clothes made? How many shows did you go to in the hols? How much money did you bring back with you?" etc. etc.

I have seen a little new boy, hardly older than eight, desperately lying his way through such a catechism:

"Have your people got a car?"

"Yes."

"What sort of car?"

"Daimler."

"How many horse-power?"

(Pause, and leap in the dark.) "Fifteen."

"What kind of lights?"

The little boy is bewildered.

"What kind of lights? Electric or acetylene?"

(A longer pause, and another leap in the dark.) "Acetylene."

"Coo! He says his pater's car's got acetylene lamps. They went out years ago. It must be as old as the hills."

"Rot! He's making it up. He hasn't got a car. He's just a navvy. Your pater's a navvy."

And so on.

By the social standards that prevailed about me, I was no good, and could not be any good. But all the different kinds of virtue seemed to be mysteriously interconnected and to belong to much the same people. It was not only money that mattered: there were also strength, beauty, charm, athleticism and something called "guts" or "character," which in reality meant the power to impose your will on others. I did not possess any of these qualities. At games, for instance, I was hopeless. I was a fairly good swimmer and not altogether contemptible at cricket, but these had no prestige value, because boys only attach importance to a game if it requires strength and courage. What counted was football, at which I was a funk. I loathed the game, and since I could see no pleasure or usefulness in it, it was very difficult for me to show courage at it. Football, it seemed to me, is not really played for the pleasure of kicking a ball about, but is a species of fighting. The lovers of football are large, boisterous, nobbly boys who are good at knocking down and trampling on slightly smaller boys. That was the pattern of school life—a continuous triumph of the strong over the weak. Virtue consisted in winning: it consisted in being bigger, stronger, handsomer, richer, more popular, more elegant, more unscrupulous than other people —in dominating them, bullying them, making them suffer pain, making them look foolish, getting the better of them in every way. Life was hierarchical and whatever happened was right. There were the strong, who deserved to win and always did win, and there were the weak, who deserved to lose and always did lose, everlastingly.

I did not question the prevailing standards, because so far as I could see there were no others. How could the rich, the strong, the elegant, the fashionable, the powerful, be in the wrong? It was their world, and the rules they made for it must be the right ones. And yet from a very early age I was aware of the impossibility of any *subjective* conformity. Always at the centre of my heart the inner self seemed to be awake, pointing out the difference between the moral obligation and the psychological *fact*. It was the same in all matters, worldly or other-worldly. Take religion, for instance. You were supposed to love God, and I did not question this. Till the age of about fourteen I believed in God, and believed that the accounts given of him were true. But I was well aware that I did not love him. On the contrary, I hated him, just as I hated Jesus and the Hebrew patriarchs. If I had sympathetic feelings towards any character in the Old Testament, it was towards such people as Cain, Jezebel, Haman, Agag, Sisera: in the New Testament my friends, if any, were Ananias, Caiaphas, Judas and Pontius Pilate. But the whole business of religion seemed to be strewn with psychological impossibilities. The Prayer Book told you, for example, to love God and fear him: but how could you love someone whom you feared? With your private affections it was the same. What you *ought* to feel was usually clear enough, but the appropriate emotion could not be commanded. Obviously it was my duty to feel grateful towards Flip and Sambo; but I was not grateful. It was equally clear that one ought to love one's father, but I knew very well that I merely disliked my own father, whom I had barely seen before I was eight and who appeared to me simply as a gruff-voiced elderly man forever saying "Don't." It was not that one did not want to possess the right qualities or feel the correct emotions, but that one could not. The good and the possible never seemed to coincide.

There was a line of verse that I came across not actually while I was at St. Cyprian's, but a year or two later, and which seemed to strike a sort of leaden echo in my heart. It was: "The armies of unalterable law." I understood to perfection what it meant to be Lucifer, defeated and justly defeated, with no possibility of revenge. The schoolmasters with their canes, the millionaires with their Scottish castles, the athletes with their curly hair—these

were the armies of unalterable law. It was not
easy, at that date, to realise that in fact it *was*
alterable. And according to that law I was damned.
I had no money, I was weak, I was ugly, I was
unpopular, I had a chronic cough, I was cowardly,
I smelt. This picture, I should add, was not altogether fanciful. I was an unattractive boy. St.
Cyprian's soon made me so, even if I had not been
so before. But a child's belief in its own shortcomings
is not much influenced by facts. I believed, for
example, that I "smelt," but this was based simply
on general probability. It was notorious that dis-
agreeable people smelt, and therefore presumably
I did so too. Again, until after I had left school for
good I continued to believe that I was preternatu-
rally ugly. It was what my schoolfellows had told
me, and I had no other authority to refer to. The
conviction that it was *not possible* for me to be a
success went deep enough to influence my actions
till far into adult life. Until I was about thirty I
always planned my life on the assumption not
only that any major undertaking was bound to
fail, but that I could only expect to live a few years
longer.

But this sense of guilt and inevitable failure was
balanced by something else: that is, the instinct to
survive. Even a creature that is weak, ugly, cowardly, smelly and in no way justifiable still wants
to stay alive and be happy after its own fashion. I
could not invert the existing scale of values, or
turn myself into a success, but I could accept my
failure and make the best of it. I could resign
myself to being what I was, and then endeavour to
survive on those terms.

To survive, or at least to preserve any kind of
independence, was essentially criminal, since it
meant breaking rules which you yourself recognised.
There was a boy named Johnny Hale who for some

months oppressed me horribly. He was a big, powerful, coarsely handsome boy with a very red face and curly black hair, who was forever twisting somebody's arm, wringing somebody's ear, flogging somebody with a riding-crop (he was a member of the Sixth Form), or performing prodigies of activity on the football field. Flip loved him (hence the fact that he was habitually called by his Christian name) and Sambo commended him as a boy who "had character" and "could keep order." He was followed about by a group of toadies who nicknamed him Strong Man.

One day, when we were taking off our overcoats in the changing-room, Hale picked on me for some reason. I "answered him back," whereupon he gripped my wrist, twisted it round and bent my forearm back upon itself in a hideously painful way. I remember his handsome, jeering red face bearing down upon mine. He was, I think, older than I, besides being enormously stronger. As he let go of me a terrible, wicked resolve formed itself in my heart. I would get back on him by hitting him when he did not expect it. It was a strategic moment, for the master who had been "taking" the walk would be coming back almost immediately, and then there could be no fight. I let perhaps a minute go by, walked up to Hale with the most harmless air I could assume, and then, getting the weight of my body behind it, smashed my fist into his face. He was flung backwards by the blow, and some blood ran out of his mouth. His always sanguine face turned almost black with rage. Then he turned away to rinse his mouth at the washing-basins.

"*All right!*" he said to me between his teeth as the master led us away.

For days after this he followed me about, challenging me to fight. Although terrified out of my wits, I steadily refused to fight. I said that the blow in the face had served him right, and there was an end of it. Curiously enough he did not simply fall upon me there and then, which public opinion would probably have supported him in doing. So gradually the matter tailed off, and there was no fight.

Now, I had behaved wrongly, by my own code no less than his. To hit him unawares was wrong. But to refuse afterwards to fight knowing that if we fought he would beat me—that was far worse: it was cowardly. If I had refused because I disapproved of fighting, or because I genuinely felt the matter to be closed, it would have been all right; but I had refused merely because I was afraid. Even my revenge was made empty by that fact. I had struck the blow in a moment of mindless violence, deliberately not looking far ahead and merely determined to get my own back for once and damn the consequences. I had had time to realise that what I did was wrong, but it was the kind of crime from which you could get some satisfaction. Not all was nullified. There had been a sort of courage in the first act, but my subsequent cowardice had wiped it out.

The fact I hardly noticed was that though Hale formally challenged me to fight, he did not actually attack me. Indeed, after receiving that one blow he never oppressed me again. It was perhaps twenty years before I saw the significance of this. At the time I could not see beyond the moral dilemma that is presented to the weak in a world governed by the strong: Break the rules, or perish. I did not see that in that case the weak have the right to make a different set of rules for themselves; because, even if such an idea had occurred to me, there was no one in my environment who could have confirmed me in it. I lived in a world of boys, gregarious animals, questioning nothing, accepting the law of the stronger and avenging their own humiliations by passing them down to someone smaller. My situation was that of countless other boys, and if potentially I was more of a rebel than most, it was only because, by boyish standards, I was a poorer specimen. But I never did rebel intellectually, only emotionally. I had nothing to help me except my dumb selfishness, my inability—not, indeed, to despise myself, but to *dislike* myself—my instinct to survive.

It was about a year after I hit Johnny Hale in the face that I left St. Cyprian's forever. It was the end of a winter term. With a sense of coming out from darkness into sunlight I put on my Old Boy's tie as we dressed for the journey. I well remember the feeling of that brand-new silk tie round my neck, a feeling of emancipation, as though the tie had been at once a badge of manhood and an amulet against Flip's voice and Sambo's cane. I was escaping from bondage. It was not that I expected, or even intended, to be any more successful at a public school than I had been at St. Cyprian's. But still, I was escaping. I knew that at a public school there would be more privacy, more neglect, more chance to be idle and self-indulgent and degenerate. For years past I had been resolved—unconsciously at first, but consciously later on—that when once my scholarship was won I would "slack off" and cram no longer. This resolve, by the way, was so fully carried out that between the ages of thirteen and twenty-two or three I hardly ever did a stroke of avoidable work.

Flip shook hands to say good-bye. She even gave me my Christian name for the occasion. But there was a sort of patronage, almost a sneer, in her face and in her voice. The tone in which she said good-bye was nearly the tone in which she had been used to say *little butterflies*. I had won two scholarships, but I was a failure, because success was measured not by what you did but by what you *were*. I was "not a good type of boy" and could bring no credit on the school. I did not possess character or courage or health or strength or money, or even good manners, the power to look like a gentleman.

"Good-bye," Flip's parting smile seemed to say; "it's not worth quarrelling now. You haven't made much of a success of your time at St. Cyprian's, have you? And I don't suppose you'll get on awfully well at a public school either. We made a mistake, really, in wasting our time and money on you. This kind of education hasn't much to offer to a boy with your background and your outlook. Oh, don't think we don't understand you! We know all about those ideas you have at the back of your head, we know you disbelieve in everything we've taught you, and we know you aren't in the least grateful for all we've done for you. But there's no use in bringing it all up now. We aren't responsible for you any longer, and we shan't be seeing you again. Let's just admit that you're one of our failures and part without ill-feeling. And so, good-bye."

That at least was what I read into her face. And yet how happy I was, that winter morning, as the train bore me away with the gleaming new silk tie (dark green, pale blue and black, if I remember rightly) round my neck! The world was opening before me, just a little, like a grey sky which exhibits narrow crack of blue. A public school would be better fun than St. Cyprian's, but at bottom equally alien. In a world where the prime necessities were money, titled relatives, athleticism, tailor-made clothes, neatly-brushed hair, a charming smile, I was no good. All I had gained was a breathing-space. A little quietude, a little self-indulgence, a little respite from cramming—and then, ruin. What kind of ruin I did not know: perhaps the colonies or an office stool, perhaps prison or an early death. But first a year or two in which one could "slack off" and get the benefit of one's sins, like Doctor Faustus. I believed firmly in my evil destiny, and yet I was acutely happy. It is the advantage of being thirteen that you can not only live in the moment, but do so with full consciousness, foreseeing the future and yet not caring about it. Next term I was going to Wellington. I had also won a scholarship at Eton, but it was uncertain whether there would be a vacancy, and I was going to Wellington first. At Eton you had a room to yourself—a room which might even have a fire in it. At Wellington you had your own cubicle, and could make yourself cocoa in the evenings. The privacy of it, the grown-upness! And there would be libraries to hang about in, and summer afternoons when you could shirk games and mooch about the countryside alone, with no master driving you along. Meanwhile there were the holidays. There was the .22 rifle that I had bought the previous holidays (the Crackshot, it was called, costing twenty-two and sixpence), and Christmas was coming next week. There were also the pleasures of overeating. I thought of some particularly voluptuous cream buns which could be bought for twopence each at a shop in our town. (This was 1916, and food-rationing had not yet started.) Even the detail that my journey-money had been slightly miscalculated, leaving about a shilling over—enough for an unforeseen cup of coffee and a cake or two somewhere on the way—was enough to fill me with bliss. There was time for a bit of happiness before the future closed in upon me. But I did know that the future was dark. Failure, failure,

failure—failure behind me, failure ahead of me—
that was by far the deepest conviction that I carried away.

VI

All this was thirty years ago and more. The question is: Does a child at school go through the same
kind of experiences nowadays?

The only honest answer, I believe, is that we do
not with certainty know. Of course it is obvious
that the present-day *attitude* towards education is
enormously more humane and sensible than that
of the past. The snobbishness that was an integral
part of my own education would be almost unthinkable today, because the society that nourished it is dead. I recall a conversation that must
have taken place about a year before I left St.
Cyprian's. A Russian boy, large and fair-haired, a
year older than myself, was questioning me.

"How much a year has your father got?"

I told him what I thought it was, adding a few
hundreds to make it sound better. The Russian
boy, neat in his habits, produced a pencil and a
small note-book and made a calculation.

"My father has over two hundred times as much
money as yours," he announced with a sort of
amused contempt.

That was in 1915. What happened to that money
a couple of years later, I wonder? And still more I

wonder, do conversations of that kind happen at preparatory schools now?

Clearly there has been a vast change of outlook, a general growth of "enlightenment," even among ordinary, unthinking middle-class people. Religious belief, for instance, has largely vanished, dragging other kinds of nonsense after it. I imagine that very few people nowadays would tell a child that if it masturbates it will end in the lunatic asylum. Beating, too, has become discredited, and has even been abandoned at many schools. Nor is the underfeeding of children looked on as a normal, almost meritorious act. No one now would openly set out to give his pupils as little food as they could do with, or tell them that it is healthy to get up from a meal as hungry as you sat down. The whole status of children has improved, partly because they have grown relatively less numerous. And the diffusion of even a little psychological knowledge has made it harder for parents and schoolteachers to indulge their aberrations in the name of discipline. Here is a case, not known to me personally, but known to someone I can vouch for, and happening within my own lifetime. A small girl, daughter of a clergyman, continued wetting her bed at an age when she should have grown out of it. In order to punish her for this dreadful deed, her father took her to a large garden party and there introduced her to the whole company as a little girl who wetted her bed: and to underline her wickedness he had previously painted her face black. I do not suggest that Flip and Sambo would actually have done a thing like this, but I doubt whether it would have much surprised them. After all, things do change. And yet—!

The question is not whether boys are still buckled into Eton collars on Sunday, or told that babies are dug up under gooseberry bushes. That kind of thing is at an end, admittedly. The real question is whether it is still normal for a school-child to live for years amid irrational terrors and lunatic misunderstandings. And here one is up against the very great difficulty of knowing what a child really feels and thinks. A child which appears reasonably happy may actually be suffering horrors which it cannot or will not reveal. It lives in a sort of alien under-water world which we can only penetrate by memory or divination. Our chief clue is the fact that we were once children ourselves, and many people appear to forget the atmosphere of their own childhood almost entirely. Think for instance of the unnecessary torments that people will inflict by sending a child back to school with clothes of the wrong pattern, and refusing to see that this matters! Over things of this kind a child will sometimes utter a protest, but a great deal of the time its attitude is one of simple concealment. Not to expose your true feelings to an adult seems to be instinctive from the age of seven or eight onwards. Even the affection that one feels for a child, the desire to protect and cherish it, is a cause of misunderstanding. One can love a child, perhaps, more deeply than one can love another adult, but it is rash to assume that the child feels any love in return. Looking back on my own childhood, after the infant years were over, I do not believe that I ever felt love for any mature person, except my mother, and even her I did not trust, in the sense that shyness made me conceal most of my real feelings from her. Love, the spontaneous, unqualified emotion of love, was something I could only feel for people who were young. Towards people who were old—and remember that "old" to a child means over thirty, or even over twenty-five—I could feel reverence, respect, admiration or compunction, but I seemed cut off from them by a veil of fear and shyness mixed up with physical distaste. People are too ready to forget the child's *physical* shrinking from the adult. The enormous size of grown-ups, their ungainly, rigid bodies, their coarse, wrinkled skins, their great relaxed eyelids, their yellow teeth, and the whiffs of musty clothes and beer and sweat and tobacco that disengage from them at every movement! Part of the reason for the ugliness of adults, in a child's eyes, is that the child is usually looking upwards, and few faces are at their best when seen from below. Besides, being fresh and unmarked itself, the child has impossibly high standards in the matter of skin and teeth and complexion. But the greatest barrier of all is the child's misconception about age. A child can hardly envisage life beyond thirty, and in judging people's ages it will make fantastic mistakes. It will think that a person of twenty-five is forty, that a person of forty is sixty-five, and so on. Thus, when I fell in love with Elsie I took her to be grown-up. I met her again, when I was thirteen and she, I think, must have been twenty-three; she now seemed to me a middle-aged woman, somewhat past her best. And the child thinks of growing old as an almost obscene calamity, which for some mysterious reason will never happen to itself. All who have passed the age of thirty are joyless grotesques, endlessly fussing about things of no importance and staying alive without, so far as the child can see, having anything to live for. Only child life is real life. The schoolmaster who imagines that he is loved and trusted by his boys is in fact mimicked and laughed at behind his back. An adult who does not seem dangerous nearly always seems ridiculous.

I base these generalisations on what I can recall of my own childhood outlook. Treacherous though memory is, it seems to me the chief means we have of discovering how a child's mind works. Only by resurrecting our own memories can we realise how incredibly distorted is the child's vision of the world. Consider this, for example. How would St. Cyprian's appear to me now, if I could go back, at my present age, and see it as it was in 1915? What should I think of Sambo and Flip, those terrible, all-powerful monsters? I should see them as a couple of silly, shallow, ineffectual people, eagerly clambering up a social ladder which any thinking person could see to be on the point of collapse. I would no more be frightened of them than I would be frightened of a doormouse. Moreover, in those days they seemed to me fantastically old, whereas—though of this I am not certain—I imagine they must have been somewhat younger than I am now. And how would Johnny Hale appear, with his blacksmith's arms and his red, jeering face? Merely a scruffy little boy, barely distinguishable from hundreds of other scruffy little boys. The two sets of facts can lie side by side in my mind, because those happen to be my own memories. But it would be very difficult for me to see with the eyes of any other child, except by an effort of the imagination which might lead me completely astray. The child and the adult live in different worlds. If that is so, we cannot be certain that school, at any rate boarding school, is not still for many children as dreadful an experience as it used to be. Take away God, Latin, the cane, class distinctions and sexual taboos, and the fear, the hatred, the snobbery and the misunderstanding might still all be there. It will have been seen that my own main trouble was an utter lack of any sense of proportion or probability. This led me to accept outrages and believe absurdities, and to suffer torments over things which were in fact of no importance. It is not enough to say that I was "silly" and "ought to have known better." Look back into your own childhood and think of the nonsense you used to believe and the trivialities which could make you suffer. Of course my own case had its individual variations, but essentially it was that of countless other boys. The weakness of the child is that it starts with a blank sheet. It neither understands nor questions the society in which it lives, and because of its credulity other people can work upon it, infecting it with the sense of inferiority and the dread of offending against mysterious, terrible laws. It may be that everything that happened to me at St. Cyprian's could happen in the most "enlightened" school, though perhaps in subtler forms. Of one thing, however, I do feel fairly sure, and that is that boarding schools are worse than day schools. A child has a better chance with the sanctuary of its home near at hand. And I think the characteristic faults of the English upper and middle classes may be partly due to the practice, general until recently, of sending children away from home as young as nine, eight or even seven.

I have never been back to St. Cyprian's. Reunions, old boys' dinners and such-like leave me something more than cold, even when my memories are friendly. I have never even been down to Eton, where I was relatively happy, though I did once pass through it in 1933 and noted with interest that nothing seemed to have changed, except that the shops now sold radios. As for St. Cyprian's, for years I loathed its very name so deeply that I could not view it with enough detachment to see the significance of the things that happened to me there. In a way, it is only within the last decade that I have really thought over my schooldays, vividly though their memory has always haunted me. Nowadays, I believe, it would make very little impression on me to see the place again, if it still exists. (I remember hearing a rumour some years ago that it had been burnt down.) If I had to pass through Eastbourne I would not make a detour to avoid the school: and if I happened to pass the school itself I might even stop for a moment by the low brick wall, with the steep bank running down from it, and look across the flat playing field at the ugly building with the square of asphalt in front of it. And if I went inside and smelt again the inky, dusty smell of the big schoolroom, the rosiny smell of the chapel, the stagnant smell of the swimming bath and the cold reek of the lavatories, I think I should only feel what one invariably feels in revisiting any scene of childhood: How small everything has grown, and how terrible is the deterioration in myself! But it is a fact that for many years I could hardly have borne to look at it again. Except upon dire necessity I would not have set foot in Eastbourne. I even conceived a prejudice against Sussex, as the county that contained St. Cyprian's, and as an adult I have only once been in Sussex, on a short visit. Now, however, the place is out of my system for good. Its magic works no longer, and I have not even enough animosity left to make me hope that Flip and Sambo are dead or that the story of the school being burnt down was true.

Utopias in Negative
George Woodcock

With a series of novels and short fictions published in the wake of World War I, a centuries-old tradition of utopian ideas was turned on its head. Beginning with the novel *We*, written by the Russian émigré Yevgeny Zamyatin, who had been imprisoned by both the czarist and revolutionary regimes, the ideal of a positive end to progress in a perfect society of material plenty and social justice—a utopia—was dashed by a darker vision of an unchanging state that maintained its stasis by control, coercion, and the eradication of all individual freedom. The notion of *dystopia* had been born.

George Woodcock, author of a significant study of Orwell entitled *The Crystal Spirit* (1971), traces the lineage of *Nineteen Eighty-Four* within the utopian and dystopian traditions. Orwell's reading of Zamyatin's *We*, Woodcock explains, provided much of the narrative framework for his own novel. Orwell's self-admitted debt to Zamyatin—as well as Aldous Huxley's for themes in *Brave New World*—has been a subject of ongoing controversy, the harshest critics holding that Orwell essentially plagiarized *We*. But, as Woodcock points out, there are many dissimilarities among the three novels and their authors as well as points of likeness.

Seventy years ago Oscar Wilde, the most demonstrative of individualists, wrote in *The Soul of Man Under Socialism*: "A map of the world that does not include Utopia is not worth even glancing at, for it leaves out the one country at which Humanity is always landing. And when Humanity lands there, it looks out, and seeing a better country, sets sail. Progress is the realisation of Utopias." His remarks were typical of the attitude towards utopianism that existed among the *avant garde* of two generations ago.

Writers of today, even writers adhering politically to the independent left, would be more inclined to echo an almost equally well-quoted statement of Nicholas Berdiaeff,* similar in its premises to Wilde's, but opposite in its conclusion: "Utopias are realisable. Life marches towards utopias. And perhaps a new century is beginning, a century in which the intellectuals and the cultivated class will dream of the means of avoiding utopias and of returning to a non-utopian society, less 'perfect' and more free."

When one considers these differing statements, each more or less appropriate to its era, it becomes evident that Wilde's view was based on a common misunderstanding of the nature of Utopia. Utopia is not progressive. Most of the "ideal" societies of literature are intentionally static; every conflict has been eliminated, every social problem has been solved, and change has come to a stop like a train in a terminus; time has ended and society is frozen into a crystalline permanence. Wilde, a progressivist by nature, saw Utopias as steps by which to scale the heavens of freedom; for him Utopia was a means. But no Utopian thinker has seen his vision as anything but an end, an image of heaven translated into earthly terms.

For four centuries after the publication of Sir Thomas More's romance, Utopia focussed the hopes

*Nikolai Alexanderovich Berdyayav (1874–1948), Russian Christian existentialist philosopher. [ed.]

of men with uneasy social consciences. Now it gives shape to their fears, and, as Berdiaeff suggested, the reason is that the visionary societies of dead thinkers have at last begun to move out of theory and to assume in the modern world a portentous actuality.

Utopia, as it was envisaged by More and Campanella, by Cabet and Fourier and Bellamy, by Plato in his anticipatory Republic and Wells in his quasi-scientific fantasies, can be defined as a society permanently constituted and rigidly regulated according to a plan which its founders believe will serve the best interests of the people as a whole. If one accepts this definition, it is possible to argue that world society has become steadily more Utopian in structure since the First World War. In intention, Russia is more Utopian than it is orthodoxly Marxist, and in other countries the hopes of New Dealers and Welfare Staters, who seek to shape society by intensified control rather than by voluntary initiative, have moved towards the realization of Utopia. Even a cursory reading of the literature of social fantasy shows that many of its features have assumed concrete form in the modern world; more than that, the pattern of static rigidity which characterizes Utopia settles over contemporary societies as the area of collective control is broadened, while the growing complexity of administration breeds élites of specialists who resemble the ruling groups of many ideal communities from *The Republic* onwards.

Yet, though so much of the Utopian dream is being fulfilled, our age has in one respect failed to meet the expectations of More and his successors; planned societies have brought little marked increase in human happiness. And it is avoiding the issue to blame this, as some disgruntled idealists have done, on the personal weaknesses of those who construct such societies. Rather than in human frailty, the error seems to lie in the Utopian outlook itself. Does not happiness, regarded in terms of a free and full life, depend on social fluidity? Does not any pre-determined way of living result in a constriction of initiative that is not only intolerable to human beings, but also harmful to the very efficiency it aims to achieve? These are questions which writers have asked with growing anxiety for the past three decades, and which have led to the emergence of a criticism of Utopian conceptions more rigorous than anything since Proudhon exposed the fallacious visions of Cabet and Fourier a century ago.

One result of this increasingly critical attitude has been the virtual disappearance of the orthodox Utopia as a literary form. Wells was the last important Utopian; his *Men Like Gods* appeared in 1922, and only two years later there was published in New York the first of the significant contemporary anti-Utopian novels. It was entitled *We*, and was written by the Russian novelist, Evgeny Zamiatin. Even in the 1920's, Zamiatin was unable to publish his novel in Russia. It first appeared in an English translation, and only in 1953 was a Russian version published, by an émigré group in New York; Zamiatin himself died obscurely in exile in 1937.

II

We was not merely the predecessor of such recent anti-Utopias as Huxley's *Brave New World* and Orwell's *1984*; it also set the pattern which they have followed. But before discussing these books in any detail, it is desirable to consider how they differ from the various negative quasi-Utopias which appeared before 1924. These can be divided into two categories: the romances in which an imaginary country is used to satirise existing society, and those in which conservative thinkers attack Utopian radicalism. The first class is the more numerous; it begins with Restoration key romances of political intent like Mary Manley's *New Atlantis*, which lampooned Sara Churchill, and includes such literary masterpieces as *Gulliver's Travels* and *Erewhon*. But the writers who create this kind of fiction do not attack the problem of Utopia directly; Swift, no less than Mrs. Manley, was much too busy satirizing the errors of his own time to be concerned with the world of the future.

The more direct anti-Utopias of the period before the First World War differ from those of Zamiatin and Huxley and Orwell in that they attack the collectivist idea rather than its concrete manifestations, which were not nearly so evident in 1900 as they are today. The Utopians had put forward hypothetical visions, and the anti-Utopians countered with other hypothetical visions. Thus, books like Eugene Richter's *Pictures of the Socialist Future*, and the various blasts against Bellamy, are inconsiderable largely because their authors lacked any knowledge of how Utopia might work out in reality.

One early anti-Utopia is more interesting than the rest; it is E. M. Forster's story, *The Machine Stops*, which was written in 1912. In a limited way, it anticipates *We* and *Brave New World* since, like them, it has a strong element of neo-Luddism. Forster imagines a world which has finally become dominated by machinery. Men have abandoned the surface of the earth and gone underground, where each person lives alone in a room exactly like those of all his fellows, with whom he is in contact through television. The inhabitants of this underground world do not work, for everything is provided by a vast machine, the prototype of the modern mechanical brain; the press of a button satisfies in a completely synthetic manner every cultural and physical need.

Thus, eleven years before Capek wrote *RUR*, Forster envisaged a situation in which the Machine had virtually ceased to be man's servant and had become his master. "The Machine," say the people for whom it cares, "feeds us and clothes us and houses us; through it we speak to one another, through it we see one another, in it we have our being. The Machine is the friend of ideas and the enemy of superstition; the Machine is omnipotent, eternal; blessed is the Machine." But one day the Machine grinds to a stop, and with it all men die, starved and asphyxiated in the underground rooms which have now become their prisons. "Man, the flower of all flesh, the noblest of all creatures visible, man who had once made God in his image, and had mirrored his strength on the constellations, beautiful naked man was dying, strangled in the garments he had woven. Century after century he had toiled, and here was his reward."

But, though *The Machine Stops* is nearer in insight to the anti-Utopias of our time than any other story written before the First World War, it still seems to lack immediacy, partly because it criticises what is still outside practical probability, and partly because it concentrates on the technological aspect of Utopianism and pays scanty attention to its social and political implications.

More than any other historical development, the 1914 war precipitated the changes that began to give substance both to Utopia and to the criticisms of the anti-Utopians. The development in warfare of the aeroplane and the submarine, the invention of radio and the promise of television, the appearance of the assembly line system in industry, all these seemed to bring within reach the changes dreamed of by the Utopians, while there began a mounting trend towards political collectivism.

Thus the anti-Utopian novels of the present generation have been written by men who have looked closely at the reality which congeals out of the fantasies of the past, and who have rejected what they see. They do not reject it out of ignorance, or a lack of idealism, for none of the authors of the anti-Utopian romances I am about to discuss has been without liberal ideals or political experience. Zamiatin underwent political exile under the Tsar, and lived through the October Revolution and its aftermath. Huxley became a pacifist propagandist with marked leanings towards Kropotkinist anarchism. Orwell remained a libertarian socialist to the end of his life. Thus, the main criticism of Utopia in our day has come, not from the conservatives, but from the disillusioned Left, from the maverick radicals who are the spiritual descendants of Proudhon and Tolstoy.

III

In *We*, Zamiatin envisages an age, almost a millenium ahead, in which the majority of men are subjects of a United State which consists of a number of cities scattered over the earth and isolated by Green Walls and barriers of electrical charges from the rural spaces around and between them. This isolation from nature is deliberate, since the rulers of the United State aim to turn man into a machine, to replace the organic by the inorganic, to provide a synthetic happiness by eliminating everything that can arouse natural passions or personal inclinations. Theoretically, men and women have ceased to be persons, and, losing their names, they have become "numbers" or "unifs."

All the "numbers" wear similar garments, and each carries on the metal plate that identifies him a watch to symbolize the rigid time schedule to which daily life is subordinated; significantly, the most distinguished literary work that has been preserved from the past is the Railway Time Table. In the United State all the apartments are built with walls of glass, so that the actions of the "numbers" are public, and really solitary activity is almost impossible. Only at times of sexual intercourse can the curtains be lowered for brief periods; such intercourse is strictly regulated by a Sexual Bureau, which issues tickets entitling the holders to the use of whatever persons they may choose, since, as a further denial of individuality, all "numbers" are held to be available to each other. Physical norms are established for childbearing, and a woman who does not qualify and becomes pregnant is executed; children are cared for by the state, and the family is remembered only as an incomprehensible folly of the distant past. Mechanization enters into every aspect of life; the "numbers" are nourished by synthetic petroleum foods, and even culture is de-humanized, music being composed by machines and university classes taught by robot professors.

This soulless society is ruled by a dictator called

the Benefactor, and his government is periodically endorsed by elections held on what is significantly called "The Day of Uniformity." He is supported by a political police, the Guardians, who hover above the city in planes equipped with observation tubes and whose task is facilitated by sensitive membranes which stretch across the streets and pick up conversations. Scientific tortures are used to extract confessions, and criminals are liquidated literally, by means of an electrical machine which reduces them to puddles of colorless water. Informing, considered a sacred duty, is illustrated in this bitter scene: "Above was the shining, golden, sun-like sign: 'Bureau of the Guardians.' Inside, a long queue of bluish-grey unifs awaiting their turns, faces shining like the oil lamps of an ancient temple. They came to accomplish a great thing: they come to put on the altar of the United State their beloved ones, their friends, and their own selves."

All these means are used to support "the instinct of non-freedom," for the prevailing philosophy of the United State regards freedom as inseparable from crime. "The only means to deliver man from crime is to deliver him from freedom." Furthermore, the loss of freedom is the only way to happiness. "The Benefactor, the Machine, the Guardians—all these are good. All these are magnificent, beautiful, noble, lofty, crystalline, pure. For all these preserve our non-freedom, that is to say, our happiness."

It is logical that in such a society the past should be despised and, as far as possible, eliminated. Making explicit what is implied in almost all Utopian visions, the rulers of the United State try to erect a perfectly "crystalline" and immutable order. As D. 503, the narrator, remarks: "The ideal is to be found where nothing *happens*," where no element of the spontaneous or unpredictable impinges on the ordered pattern of existence.

Yet the impulses of rebellion remain; even though every manifestation of nature has been eliminated within the Green Walls, the winds still blow clouds overhead, still bring pollen and gossamer to stir the atavistic feelings of the "numbers," to remind them of the life from which their society departed centuries ago. "Even in our day," says D.503, "one hears from time to time, coming from the bottom, the primitive depths, the echo of the apes."

D.503, who tells his story in a diary kept at great risk of discovery by the Guardians, is one of those who listen to these uncomfortable echoes; he is perpetually reminded of them by the physical peculiarity of his hairy hands. "It is very strange," he interjects in a piece of orthodox preaching for the United State, "while I was writing today of loftiest summit of human history, all the while I breathed the purest mountain air of thought, but within me it was and remains cloudy, cobwebby, and there is a kind of cross-like, four-pawed X. Or perhaps it is my paws, my hairy paws. I don't like to talk about them. I dislike them. They are a trace of a primitive epoch."

It is this lingering resistance to regimentation, shown also in his tendency towards passionate love, that leads D.503 into the sin of overt rebellion. Through a woman who insists on re-living the evil past in secret, who commits such cardinal sins as smoking, wearing skirts and drinking alcohol, he meets a group of conspirators who have established contact with the naked and hairy survivors of free humanity lurking in the forests beyond the Green Wall. The conspirators meet in an old house, from the centuries before the United State, which has been preserved as a museum; this is appropriate, since in Utopia revolution reverses its process, and turns into a movement towards the freedom of the past.

The Green Wall is blown up, and for a time it appears as though the unregenerate instincts of the "numbers" will re-assert themselves. But as *We* comes to an end the Guardians are winning, the leading rebels are tortured and killed, and those who escape death, including D.503, are subjected to a new operation which removes from them the unpredictable faculty of fancy and turns them into automata in human form, devoid of the last vestiges of individuality.

The basic elements of the society Zamiatin imagines can be traced to a variety of possible sources. The theme of radical ideas ending paradoxically in a slave society was developed by Dostoevsky in *The Possessed*, and the implications of scientific Utopianism were discussed negatively as well as positively by H. G. Wells, who envisaged, in such stories as *The Time Machine*, the chance that science misused might atrophy mankind, in the direction of either physical ineptitude or mental brutalization. The reformed prison system introduced in Europe during the nineteenth century gave currency to the classification of people as numbers instead of as individuals, while a society of rightless "unifs," ruled by a class of ruthless and self-righteous Guardians, has distant roots in Plato. Uniform dress was a feature of More's *Utopia*, while strict time schedules made their appearance in Cabet's *Voyage en Icarie*. A system of regulating sexual intercourse was stressed in Campanella's *The City of the Sun*, Plutarch described eugenic experiments which were said to have formed part of that most ancient attempt to build Utopia in real life, the Sparta of Lycurgus, and mutual bodily availability was a leading idea in de Sade's *La Philosophie dans le Boudoir*. Doubtless a closer search would reveal other details in which Zamiation may have been influenced be earlier writers.* Yet *We* gains originality from the fact that Zamiatin was the first novelist to place all these fragmentary anticipations into the coherent context of actuality, the context of those tendencies towards industrial regimentation, towards the closer regulation of daily living, which he saw emerging in the world of the 1920's. Thus *We* appears as the first major anti-Utopia, the first novel of literary importance that presented a relatively complete vision of the negative results involved in the realization of Utopia.

IV

Between *We* and the anti-Utopian novels that followed it—Huxley's *Brave New World* and Orwell's *1984*, the resemblances are so close in both details and structure as to leave little doubt of Zamiatin's direct influence on his successors. Indeed, in the case of Orwell the influence was admitted frankly; he first read *We* several years before starting work on *1984*, and my own introduction to Zamiatin's book came in 1943 when Orwell lent me a French translation, which he later made the subject of one of his weekly literary pieces in the London *Tribune*.

---

*He was in England between 1914 and 1917 and may well have read Forster's *The Machine Stops*, as well as Butler's ambiguous discussion in *Erewhon* of the possibilities inherent in over-mechanization.

So far as the societies described in these three novels are concerned, the similarities are numerous and clear. All three authors saw Utopia as a possible—even a probable—outcome of twentieth century technological and political developments. They all suggested that, if this Utopian future came about, it would involve the total elimination of even the idea of freedom, the falsification or destruction of history and the sense of the past, and the reduction of culture to a rudimentary and mechanical function. They all envisaged the economic structure of Utopia as collectivist and its political structure as a pyramid controlled by an exclusive élite with the help of efficient police systems. They all foresaw a radical interference in sexual life, and some form of mental or physical conditioning to make the individual docile and obedient; always, such conditioning involved the rejection of nature and privacy, the systematic destruction of passionate personal relationships and of any association that might exist outside the state. Finally, the resemblances between the three Utopias embrace such practical details as the imposition of uniforms upon the inhabitants and the production of literature and music by entirely mechanical means.

Perhaps even more striking than the resemblances between the societies described by these three writers are the close structural similarities between their novels. In each case the hero is an inhabitant of Utopia who, because of some peculiarity of physique or experience, has become conscious of his difference from the general depersonalised herd. D.503 has his hairy hands as mementoes of the animal past, Bernard Marx in *Brave New World* is made self-conscious by a stunted physique due to some accident in pre-natal conditioning, and Winston Smith in *1984* stumbles accidentally on a piece of evidence which makes him aware of the deliberate and systematized falsification of truth in the state of Oceania. For each of these heroes, rebellion is accompanied by a desire for possessive and passionate sexual relations and by a longing to reconstruct the past, symbolised in *We* by the old house where the conspirators meet, in *Brave New World* by the reservation in New Mexico where the Indians still live as they did in the 1930's, and in *1984* by the antique shop in whose upper room Winston Smith and the girl he loves enact their furtive personal revolution. Finally, each novel ends in defeat for the rebel, and in his punishment according to the spirit of the society in which he is trapped. D.503 is rendered surgically incapable of any further independent thought; Bernard Marx is exiled to a distant island; Winston Smith is tortured in the gleaming white cells of the Ministry of Love, betrays everything that is precious to him, and emerges a spiritual vestige of a man who waits for death in the cause of the state that has crushed him. Utopia carries on unshaken, and the pessimism of each author's conclusion is unrelieved by any hope of its collapse.

But, within this relatively complex framework of similarities, there are wide differences of character between *We, Brave New World* and *1984*; both Huxley and Orwell are clearly indebted to Zamiatin, yet each has not only written in his own individual style, but has also stressed particular aspects of the trend towards Utopia which seemed to him the most dangerous. Zamiatin was by profession an engineer; an observation of the tendency towards industrial regimentation during the 1920's gave him the idea of a world where statistics, and the mathematical outlook associated with them, become the dominant forces in shaping both the outlook of the rulers and the character of the society they establish—a crystalline, higher-mathematical order where men become merely the figures in gigantic equations. Huxley shared with Zamiatin a preoccupation with such prophets of industrial organization as Ford and Taylor but his family background also gave him a natural interest in the biological sciences in which his grandfather Thomas Henry and his brother Julian were experts, and it was natural that the possibility of the physical and mental conditioning of human beings, so much discussed by scientific popularizers during the 1920's, should have impressed him so far that it moulded the form of his personal anti-Utopia. Orwell, on the other hand, was an observant and passionate student of political affairs, and saw the great danger of the future in the ruthless elimination of opposition by means of police dictatorships and by an extension of the deliberate falsification of history and of language which has already begun in modern totalitarian states; thus, *1984* is dominated less by technological and biological factors than by the possibility of man's being turned into a mindless robot by predominantly cultural and political means.

Since Zamiatin wrote in the early 1920's, the trend of anti-Utopian writing has thus veered steadily closer to present political realities, just as present political realities have themselves moved nearer to a sardonic caricature of the visions of Plato and More. This process has been paralleled by a steady shift in the time and place of Utopia. Zamiatin saw his United State a thousand years ahead. Huxley's new world, conceived approximately a decade after *We* was completed, lay only six hundred years in the future; introducing a new edition in 1946, fifteen years later, he revised his time schedule and declared: "Today it seems quite possible that the horror may be upon us within a single century." Orwell, writing less than thirty years after Zamiatin, shifted his sights even more abruptly; finishing *1984* in the last months of 1948, he saw the final submersion of the human personality in the totalitarian nightmare as only thirty-six years ahead, and the scene as the familiar, shabby, bomb-worn London of the late 1940's, in which only the vast pyramidal strongholds of the new government agencies towered up in new and menacing indestructibility.

Brave New World shares with *We* some features which Orwell did not choose to retain in *1984*, and *vice versa*. Like Zamiatin, Huxley equates non-freedom with happiness, to preserve the latter quality, the World Controllers throw away everything that might provoke thought or passion. Humanity lives on the level of petty enjoyment and unconscious obedience. "The world's stable now," says the Controller, Mustapha Mond. "People are happy; they get what they want, and they never want what they can't get. They're well off; they're safe; they're never ill; they're not afraid of death, they're blissfully ignorant of passion and old age; they're plagued with no mothers or fathers; they've got no wives, or children, or lovers to feel strongly about; they're so conditioned that they practically can't help behaving as they ought to behave." Another element that *Brave New World* shares with *We* is the emphasis on a passionless sexual promiscuity as a means of breaking down individuality. "Every one belongs to every one else," is one of the basic slogans of the new world, and so Huxley, like Zamiatin, carries into Utopia the orgiastic vision of the Marquis de Sade.

But the really striking difference between Huxley's anti-Utopia and those of both Zamiatin and Orwell is the absence of violence and overt repression. "In the end," says Mustapha Mond, "the Controllers realised that force was no good. The slower but infinitely surer methods of ectogenesis, neo-Pavlovian conditioning, and hypnopaedia . . ." Men are so conditioned from the time when the spermatozoon enters the egg in the Hatchery that there is little likelihood of their breaking into rebellion, and when they do become discontented there are always drugs that waft them into the heavens of restorative illusion. Thus the Controllers are able to govern with a softly firm hand; the police use whiffs of anaesthetic instead of truncheons, and those few over-brilliant individuals who do not fit into the established pattern are allowed to indulge their heretical notions in the intellectual quarantine of exile.

Yet, despite this lack of physical brutality, the society of *Brave New World*, were "infantility" is the desired norm of behavior, is just as horrifying in its systematized futility as that of *We* in its forcible regimentation, and the prospect that eventually there may be no need to force man to abandon his freedom is made all the more disquieting by the fanciful ingenuity with which Huxley describes the complicated and brainless diversions in which the men of the future fritter away the meaningless years between decanting and death.

In strict detail, Orwell probably borrows more than Huxley from Zamiatin. Like the United State of *We*, his Oceania is governed by terror. Life is run on rigid time schedules, there are telescreens everywhere which allow the citizens to be observed as closely as through the glass walls of Zamiatin's city, and the place of the guardians is taken by an ubiquitous Thought Police, who operate by scientific methods of torture. Just as "fancy" is the great crime in the United State, so "thoughtcrime" is the unforgiveable felony in Oceania; there is no need to act against the state, for the slightest hint of a lapse from the required ways of thinking is sufficient to open up to the offender the dreaded secrets of Room 101 in the Ministry of Love.

Yet in one basic respect *1984* differs from both *We* and *Brave New World*, and generates a pessimism which neither of the earlier books can equal. Both Zamiatin and Huxley preserved the old assumption that Utopian organization would aim at what the rulers thought to be the good of their subjects. The loss of freedom and spontaneity, of literature and love, is a heavy price, but at least the Benefactor of the United State and the Controllers of the *Brave New World* offer in return a brainless, emotionless state of negative well-being. In *1984* even the pretence to do good is abandoned, even the promise of happiness is withdrawn.

The element which Orwell brings into the anti-Utopia is that summarized aphoristically in Lord Acton's famous saying: "Power corrupts; absolute power corrupts absolutely."* In the world of *1984* the power that was originally directed towards the doing of good, the imposition of negative happiness, has become an end in itself. It is the naked recognition of this fact by the ruling party that distinguishes Oceania from all the Utopias and anti-Utopias conceived in the past. The basic social structure of Utopia, the organizational cage of the planned society, has come into existence, but within that cage there is only the terror symbolized by the rats that face Winston in Room 101, the terror of a predatory form of power which has swallowed up the good it was meant to achieve and has become an end in itself. So, in Orwell's vision, even the negative pleasures promised by Zamiatin and Huxley no longer exist; life is shabby and austere,

*Sir John Emerich Edward Dalberg-Acton (1834–1902), professor of modern history, Cambridge University. [ed.]

science is diverted to producing refined instruments of torture, industry feeds a perpetual war that engenders the hatred on which power rests. In the terrible speech which O'Brien, of the Thought Police, makes to Winston as he stretches him on the mechanized rack, the Utopian idea reaches its nadir.

The real power, the power we have to fight for day and night, is not power over things but over men . . . Power is in tearing human minds to pieces and putting them together again in new shapes of your own choosing. Do you begin to see, then, what kind, of world we are creating? . . . In our world there will be no emotions except fear, rage, triumph and self-abasement. Everything else we shall destroy—everything. Already we are breaking down the habits of thought which have survived from before the Revolution. We have cut the links between child and parent, and between man and man, and between man and woman. No one dares trust a wife or a child or a friend any longer. But in the future there will be no wives and no friends. Children will be taken from their mothers at birth, as one takes eggs from a hen. The sex instinct will be eradicated. Procreation will be an annual formality like the renewal of a ration card. We shall abolish the orgasm. Our neurologists are at work upon it now. There will be no loyalty, except loyalty toward the Party. There will be no love, except the love of Big Brother. There will be no art, no literature, no science. When we are omnipotent we shall have no more need of science. There will be no distinction between beauty and ugliness. There will be no curiosity, no employment of the process of life. All competing pleasures will be destroyed. But always . . . there will be the intoxication of power, constantly increasing and constantly growing subtler. Always, at every moment, there will be the thrill of victory, the sensation of trampling on an enemy who is helpless. If you want a picture of the future, imagine a boot stamping on a human face—forever.

The horror of this vision rests, not merely in its pessimism, but also in its immediacy. For the foot that stamps and the face on which it stamps belong, not to men bred like Huxley's people out of bottles, nor to men lobotomized out of consciousness like Zamiatin's "numbers," but to physiologically unchanged human beings whose minds have become so dominated by cultural conditioning that they accept this travesty of existence without question; in a world where language itself has become so changed that the idea of freedom can no longer be expressed, they neither know nor imagine anything different.

But there is another reason why *1984* impresses us more sharply than its anti-Utopian predecessors. It is, indeed, so immediately horrifying because it is not merely an anti-Utopia. Orwell presents an indictment of the Utopian ideal, but also, like Swift, he exposes the faults of the world he sees around him. Had it not been for the acts perpetrated by political fanatics in the cellars of the Lubianka prison and the gas chambers of the Nazi camps, the horrors of Orwell's Ministry of Love could possibly have been imagined, but they would hardly have been described with such circumstantial conviction or have made such a direct impression upon the reader. The Party which governs Oceania is not merely a guess at what may happen in the future; it is also a portrait in satirical terms of modern totalitarian parties, and all its actions stem from the logical extension of methods practiced by the Communists and, in a less ordered way, by the Nazis.

Already, in banning Zamiatin's *We* a generation ago, the Communists showed their realization that the development of the anti-Utopian novel must end in a direct attack on their own methods and aims. In *1984* that stage has been reached; what in Zamiatin was remote satire on the Communists has now become direct. But *1984* is not merely a satire on the Communists; for Orwell indicates a general tendency towards the Utopian form of society, a tendency of which Communism is merely an extreme form in our time, and it is this that constitutes the anti-Utopian aspect of his work. But the two aspects—the satirical and the prophetic—are complementary; history has brought the indictment of the present and the warning for the future so close in time and place and spirit that it is no longer possible to divide them. Orwell, like Huxley, is greatly influenced by Zamiatin and, less directly, by the whole Utopian tradition against which he reacts; but what gives *1984* its peculiar force is the way in which it accepts Zamiatin's hints of the continuity between the present and the possible Utopian future, and shows that these may be not merely signs of direction, but actual parts of a new social structure even now forming around us.

George Orwell
Otto Freidrich

Orwell's politics present a paradox to both admirers and detractors, despite his repeated avowals of commitment to democratic socialism throughout his life. Otto Friedrich draws a clear line through this controversy in analyzing Orwell's political motivation and intent in writing *Animal Farm* and *Nineteen Eighty-Four*. To get at the essential politics of the two books, he refers to two earlier works: one, Orwell's own political manifesto, *The Lion and the Unicorn* (1941); the other, a highly influential book by the editor of the *National Review*, James Burnham, entitled *The Managerial Revolution* (1941). In the former, Orwell clearly states his conviction that the fulfillment of England's promise lay in democratic socialist revolution. And in an essay decrying the predictions made by Burnham in the latter book, Orwell takes a firm stand against what Burnham characterizes as an irresistible drift toward totalitarian government and the emergence of superstates run by a new class of political elites.

Friedrich thus takes to task those who find an easy interpretation of Orwell's two most memorable novels as satires of Soviet Stalinism, as well as those who see *Nineteen Eighty-Four* as Orwell's prophecy of the future of the Western world. As Friedrich states, "While *Animal Farm* warns of the dangers inherent in all revolutions, *1984* warns of the dangers inherent in all modern politics." The dangers, Orwell believed, lay not so much in the political strategies employed by a ruling elite to attain and maintain power, but in our betrayal of our own best attribute of humanity—common decency.

The belated outburst of critical acclaim for the last works of George Orwell provided an ironic ending to his abbreviated life, for it was based on such a widespread misunderstanding that it sounded like a chorus of trumpets proudly blaring forth a wrong note.

Politically minded criticism has become so uniform that conservative believers in free enterprise have joined ex-Communist authoritarians in falsely claiming converts to the great crusade against Communism or else in criticizing everyone still unconverted. Thus reviewers of every faction joined in misinterpreting the pre-eminently honest and clear-headed Orwell as a prophet of this crusade. *Animal Farm* and *1984* were saluted as "satires on Russia" and more recently *Homage to Catalonia* was welcomed largely as an anti-communist tract.

To the Luce publications, which splashed a cartoon version of *1984* across several pages, one might point out Orwell's indignation during the Battle of Britain over a system where "common soldiers risk their lives for two and sixpence a day (while) fat women ride about in Rolls-Royce cars, nursing Pekingeses." One might also point out his declaration that "it is only by revolution that the native genius of the English people can be set free."

To the vaguely leftist intellectual review that called one scene in *1984* "as great" or "greater" than the Grand Inquisitor scene in *The Brothers Karamazov*, one might recall that Orwell described one of its editorial advisers as suffering from a "major mental disease" of which the "roots lie partly in cowardice and partly in the worship of power."

Orwell achieved this first large-scale success in 1945 with *Animal Farm*, a short fable that quickly ran into more than 800,000 copies in English and

14 foreign languages. This moving story about an idealistic revolution that ended in slavery was apparently misunderstood from the beginning. The cover blurbs on one edition describe it as "this good-natured satire" and "this satire on Soviet Russia" and an excerpt from the generally sensible Manchester Guardian calls it "a very amusing and intrinsically wise book." To call this story of betrayed hopes and wasted lives, of terrorism and enslavement, an amusing and good-natured satire on Soviet-Russia is about as accurate as to describe Goya's pictures on war as an amusing and good-natured satire on the Napoleonic army's visit to Spain.

Critics who are determined to make *Animal Farm* fit the events of the Russian revolution have no difficulty in establishing that the pigs represent the Communists, first organizing the revolution, then managing the farm and finally enslaving the other animals. By this analogy, Lenin is Major, the old boar who first inspires the revolt; Stalin is Napoleon, who trains the puppies into fierce hounds and makes himself dictator; Trotsky is Snowball, the "intellectual" pig who leads the revolt but is driven out by Napoleon's hounds and becomes the central figure in the perpetual series of mythical plots against the farm. By the same analogy, one sees the typical Stakhanovite in Boxer, the dumb but industrious horse whose only mottoes are "Napoleon is always right" and "I will work harder." One sees the "unpolitical intellectual" in Benjamin the mule, who knows the other animals are being betrayed but is convinced that there is no point in doing anything because everything will come to a bad end anyway. This meager sort of criticism, however, accomplishes little except to limit *Animal Farm* to the glibness of some routine newspaper cartoon where a figure labelled "John Q. Public" is shown chasing a runaway automobile labelled "High Cost of Living." Such a reader, finishing the book with no reaction other than that "the pigs are the Communists." will naturally find *Animal Farm* "amusing."

This is not intended to deny that *Animal Farm* to a large extent is modelled on the development of the Russian Revolution. This was natural, since the Russian Revolution is indeed "the revolution of our time." More than any other upheaval in this century, it follows what historians long ago pointed out as the pattern of revolution—the overthrow of the old regime by the oppressed lower classes, the period of confusion and reorganization, the increasingly authoritarian rule of the revolutionary party, the struggle for power within the party, the reign of terror, and finally the emergence as dictator of the men who won control of the army and the police. It is unnecessary to exclaim over the fact that virtually all revolutions have ended with the "intellectuals" killed off or suppressed, the lower-classes at least as badly off as before, and the revolutionary leader pinning medals on his own uniform. Need one point out that the pig Napoleon is the namesake of the man who ended a revolution to overthrow a king by himself becoming emperor? Although Russia provides a case history, we shall see that Orwell's message was directed toward the revolution that failed in Britain, and his experience was drawn from the revolution that failed in Spain.

It would be equally wrong, however, for the complacent "moderate" to consider *Animal Farm* an "attack" on all revolutions and consequently an argument in favor of the status quo. Through one betrayal after another, each serving to enslave the animals more and more, Orwell saves his cruellest blow for the very last lines. The pigs have eliminated every law protecting the democracy of the animal farm. They live like gluttons in the farmer's house, they walk on their hind legs with whips held in their trotters, and all the commandments of "Animalism" have been replaced by one all-encompassing law: "All animals are equal but some are more equal than others." But the worst betrayal comes at the very end, when the enslaved animals peer through the window of the farmhouse where the pigs and their human neighbors are quarrelling drunkenly over a card game. "The creatures outside looked from pig to man, and from man to pig, and from pig to man again; but already it had become impossible to say which was which." This is the final betrayal because it is the final proof that nothing has changed, that the revolution is no revolution. But if the pigs have become indistinguishable from the humans, the reverse if also true. If one returns to the general analogy of Russia, one realizes the relationship Orwell saw between the whip-bearing Communists and the "fat lady in the Rolls-Royce car."

To get a clearer idea of what Orwell meant, what he was for and against, we must turn back to an earlier book, *The Lion and the Unicorn*, published in 1941. This Socialist manifesto has all the merits and all the shortcomings of a political pamphlet. It has all the directness and all the savagery of its Marxian ancestor, *The Communist Manifesto*; it also recalls an older tradition of British polemical writing that goes back to Defoe, Milton and Knox, a tradition Orwell later analyzed and praised in his introduction to *The British Pamphleteers*.

The Lion and the Unicorn begins with an effort to analyze the "British character" with emphasis on the workers and the lower middle classes. Orwell writes at length of "their old-fashioned outlook, their graded snobberies, their mixture of bawdiness and hypocrisy, their extreme gentleness, their deeply moral attitude toward life. . . . In England, such concepts as justice, liberty and objective truth are still believed in. They may be illusions, but they are very powerful illusions."

From a description of the English, Orwell moves on into a description of the English regime—"the ruling classes will rob, mismanage, sabotage, lead us into the muck." Orwell stresses the way the war has speeded up the downfall of the old order. "What this war has demonstrated is that private capitalism—that is, an economic system in which land, factories, mines and transport are owned privately and operated solely for profit—*does not work* . . . England fights for her life, but business must fight for profits. . . . The ruling classes are fighting for their own privileges, which cannot possibly be reconciled with the public interest."

Orwell backs up his fierce denunciations with examples—not only the sale of war materials to Germany until the very outbreak of the war, not only the picture of Conservative members of Parliament standing and cheering at the news that a ship bringing relief to the Spanish government has been sunk, but the fact that during the darkest days of the war "at the same time as factory workers are asked to put up with longer hours, advertisements for 'Butler. One in family, eight in staff' are appearing in the press."

From here, Orwell begins to set forth his own view on what must be done. "It is only by revolution that the native genius of the English people can be set free. Revolution does not mean red flags and street fighting, it means a fundamental shift of power. . . . We cannot win the war without introducing Socialism, nor establish Socialism without winning the war."

Orwell believed an English Socialist revolution was both necessary and inevitable. "There will be a bitter political struggle, there will be conscious and half-conscious sabotage everywhere. At some point or other it may be necessary to use violence. . . . We shall have to fight against bribery, ignorance and snobbery. The bankers and larger businessmen, the land owners and dividend drawers, the officials with their prehensile bottoms, will obstruct for all they are worth. . . . The chances are that the will of the majority will prevail."

Orwell's definition of Socialism included not only the nationalization of industry but "approximate equality of incomes, political democracy and abolition of hereditary privilege, especially in education." In an earlier book, *The Road to Wigan Pier* (1937), he developed another important aspect of what he meant by Socialism: "No genuine working man grasps the deeper implications of Socialism. Often, in my opinion, he is a truer Socialist than the Orthodox Marxist, because he does remember, what the other so often forgets, that Socialism means justice and common decency."

In *The Lion and the Unicorn*, Orwell was more specific in saying what was necessary for the "fundamental shift of power" that the English revolution was to achieve. "I) Nationalization of land, mines, railways, banks and major industries. II) Limitation of incomes on such a scale that the highest tax-free income in Britain does not exceed the lowest by more than ten to one. III) Reform of the educational system along democratic lines . . ." As one reads the manifesto, one sees how closely it fits what was to become the policy of the Labor government that won the support of the majority of British voters in all three general elections since the war. Indeed, the failure of the Labor government was its hesitation in carrying out this revolution. Land has not been nationalized, incomes have not been equalized, and old women still nurse Pekingeses on their laps as they roll through "austerity" London in Rolls-Royce cars.

But if we remember that *Animal Farm* was written in 1944, the year before the Labor Party was voted into power, we realize that Orwell was writing it as England stood on the threshold of the revolution he had demanded so urgently a few years before. Orwell was a patriotic Englishman, who felt very deeply about his country and about the freedom of its people; at the same time, he was a rather anarchistic socialist who had seen the alliance of Communists and "liberals" betray the cause he had fought for in Spain. It was natural, therefore, that the success of the English Socialist revolution and the danger of its betrayal by "sabotage, bribery, ignorance and snobbery" should dominate his mind as he wrote *Animal Farm*.

The real danger to the revolution came not from either the Communists as a party or the Conservatives as a party but from the repetition of the same mistakes that had turned the Russian workers' and peasants' hopes for bread, land and peace into the reality of secret police, concentration camps and huge armed forces. In *Animal Farm*, Orwell is condemning not only the indistinguishably criminal capitalists and Communists; he is also pointing out where the revolution went wrong and why it failed. It was the animals themselves who let themselves be betrayed. It was Benjamin the mule, who knew what was happening but did nothing. It was Boxer the horse who was too stupid to see that Napoleon was not always right. It was the sheep who did nothing but bleat "Four legs good, two legs bad" until the pigs learned to walk on their hind legs and taught the sheep to bleat "Four legs good, two legs better." *Animal Farm* is neither an attack nor a "satire" so much as a warning; it is not a warning about the Communists so much as a warning about the stupidity and foolishness by which the people betray themselves.

The world of *1984* is an historical continuation of the animal farm. Snowball, the intellectual revolutionary and master-spy, has become Goldstein, object of the universal "hate week." Napoleon, who became more and more withdrawn toward the end of *Animal Farm*, has become Big Brother, who is never seen at all. The ferocious dogs have become the Thought Police of the Ministry of Love. The largely fictitious machinations of the neighboring farms have become the eternal wars against Eastasia or Eurasia. The ultimate commandment that "Some animals are more equal than others" has become O'Brien's celebrated declaration: "The object of power is power."

Like *Animal Farm*, *1984* took the analogy of Russia as a point of departure, but as the Russian Revolution is the revolution of our times, so the Soviet Union is the tyranny of our times. By 1948, when the book was being written, the Nazi machine had been wiped out, the alternative regimes in China were still at war, the governments of Spain, South Africa and Argentina were relatively inefficient. In the Western world, the rise of totalitarian dictatorship remained less an observable reality than an ominous possibility, foreshadowed by a constant increase in regimentation, coercion and fraud. While *Animal Farm* warns of the dangers inherent in all revolutions, *1984* warns of the dangers inherent in all modern politics. Any critic who limits these dangers to the Soviet Union must wilfully ignore the fact that Oceania is not Russia but a superstate made up mainly of Britain, Canada and the United States; he must ignore the more important fact that it is not Communism that rules Oceania but *Ingsoc*, the *newspeak* word for English Socialism. Most important of all, he must ignore the fact that the most powerful dictatorships are not superimposed by foreign countries but spring from the national characteristics and circumstances of any given country. They take the most successful methods and the most useful principles from foreign or past dictatorships and adapt them to the needs of their own time and place.

In describing the world of 1984, Orwell extended many of today's political and social phenomena only slightly beyond their present stage. Newspeak is already here; it is only a short linguistic jump from NATO to Minipax, from the Department of Defense to the Ministry of Peace. *Doublethink* is already here; the 1939 convulsion of Communist "beliefs" that followed the Hitler-Stalin treaty was not much more extreme than the American switch from mass hatred of the Japanese to mass approval of the recent peace treaty. The versimilitude extends down to the details of everyday life. It can scarcely be long before some anonymous inventor spans the narrow gap between the television set and the two-way *telescreen* that cannot be turned off. The victory gin that burns your throat, the victory cigarettes that fall apart, the voluntary subscriptions for pointless causes, the meals of ersatz food in grimy canteens—all the details of the shabby life leave the reader wondering whether he really has another thirty years of grace before the coming of the new order.

1984 is a good book despite the fact that it is a bad novel. The love scenes are pallid and the torture scenes are exaggerated, but Orwell's strength was his combination of intelligence and honesty, and the book's strength is its political insight. The fact which Orwell saw most clearly and analyzed most fully is that coercion alone is not enough to hold a slave state together; it needs the stronger method of deception. It needs the falsification of history so that there are no facts to cast doubt on the "eternal" truth of whatever the party decrees. The alteration of fact demands the alteration and eventually the abolition of thought. This in turn demands the abolition of language as a method of expressing and communicating ideas.

"The organized lying practised by totalitarian states is not, as is sometimes claimed, a temporary expedient of the same nature as military deception," Orwell wrote in an essay called *The Prevention of Literature.* "It is something integral to totalitarianism, something that would still continue even if concentration camps and secret police forces had ceased to be necessary. . . . A totalitarian state is in effect a theocracy, and its ruling caste, in order to keep its position, has to be thought of as infallible. . . . Totalitarianism demands, in fact, the continuous alteration of the past, and in the long run probably demands a disbelief in the very existence of objective truth."

In *1984,* this becomes doublethink, the act of believing unreservedly in two opposites at the same time and of seeing no contradiction; to understand doublethink is an act of doublethink. Since doublethink implies the abolition of all rational thought, it requires newspeak, which eliminates speech as a means of thought and is destined finally to eliminate speech itself, replacing it by *duckspeak*, where words flow automatically from the larynx while the brain atrophies.

"The whole aim of newspeak is to narrow the

range of thought," gloats a compiler of the new-speak dictionary. "In the end we shall make *thoughtcrime* literally impossible, because there will be no words in which to express it . . . The revolution will be complete when the language is perfect. Newspeak is Ingsoc and Ingsoc is newspeak."

In an essay called *Politics and the English Language*, apparently written about the same time as *1984*, Orwell made an extensive analysis of the ways present-day political language is deliberately or unconsciously turned into a means of falsifying facts.

"In our time," he concludes, "political speech and writing are largely the defense of the indefensible. Things like the continuance of British rule in India, the Russian purges and deportations, the dropping of the atom bombs on Japan, can indeed be defended, but only by arguments which are too brutal for most people to face, and which do not square with the professed aims of the political parties. Thus political language has to consist largely of euphemism, question-begging and sheer cloudy vagueness. . . .

"The great enemy of clear language is insincerity. When there is a gap between one's real and one's declared aims, one turns as it were instinctively to long words and exhausted idioms, like a cuttlefish squirting out ink. In our age, there is no such thing as 'keeping out of politics.' All issues are political issues, and politics itself is a mass of lies, evasions, folly, hatred and schizophrenia."

The fundamental issue in *1984* thus becomes the "right" to know that two plus two makes four. As a specific issue, it may not seem very important; indeed it can probably be mathematically proved that it is the right to believe in the permanence of a given fact and to state it precisely. From the right to know that two always makes four, no matter what war is being fought or what the present government policy is, one can infer even the right to try to prove that two plus two makes five, because one can infer the right to common sense and the right to think.

"Freedom," writes the thought criminal Winston Smith in his forbidden diary, "is the freedom to say that two plus two makes four. If that is granted all else follows."

This is banal, but in a world where shoe production quotas are constantly being overfulfilled by thousands of non-existent pairs, in a world where the radio reports spontaneous demonstrations to thank Big Brother for raising the chocolate ration only two days after it has been reduced, in the world of the slave state "the obvious, the silly and the true had got to be defended. Truisms are true. . . . The solid world exists, its laws do not change. Stones are hard, water is wet, objects unsupported fall towards the earth's center. . . . In the end, the party would announce that two and two made five and you would have to believe it. . . . The logic of their position demanded it. Not merely the validity of experience but the very existence of external reality was tacitly denied by their philosophy. The heresy of heresies was common sense."

Common sense is the termite in the structure of the slave state. It must be replaced by doublethink and newspeak, the two methods of orthodoxy, or *rightthink*. Ultimately, newspeak must be supplanted by duckspeak and doublethink must be supplanted by a perpetual state of *bellyfeel*. Thus the superstate crunches onward into the future.

For anyone like Benjamin the mule who takes the view that world politics are inherently evil and getting worse all the time, the world of 1984 represents an almost gratifying confirmation of all one's gloomiest forebodings. In this connection, it is interesting to compare Orwell's description of Oceania with his description of James Burnham's *The Managerial Revolution.*

"These people (the 'managers') will eliminate the old capitalist class, crush the working class, and so organize society that all power and economic privilege remain in their own hands. Private property will be abolished but common ownership will not be established. The new managerial societies will not consist of a patchwork of small independant states, but of great superstates grouped around the main industrial centres of Europe, Asia and America. These superstates will fight among themselves for possession of the remaining uncaptured portions of the earth but will probably be unable to conquer one another completely. Internally, each society will be hierarchical, with an aristocracy of talent at the top and a mass of semi-slaves at the bottom."

This is in effect the world of *1984,* just as it is the world of Russia and Nazi Germany. "Burnham's theory is not, strictly speaking, a new one," Orwell comments. ". . . As an interpretation of what *is happening* (it) is extremely plausible, to put it at the lowest . . . Where Burnham differs from most other thinkers is in trying to plot the course of the 'managerial revolution' accurately on a world scale, and in assuming that the drift towards totalitarianism is irresistible."

Orwell, who had spent much of his life fighting against this drift and more particularly against the assumption that the drift was irresistible, severely criticizes Burnham for the power worship that obsesses so many modern intellectuals throughout all their shifts of allegiance from one power to another.

"It was only *after* the soviet regime became unmistakably totalitarian that English intellectuals, in large numbers, began to show interest in it," Orwell wrote. "Burnham, although the English Russophile intelligentsia would repudiate him, is really voicing their secret wish: the wish to destroy the old equalitarian version of Socialism and usher in a hierarchical society where the intellectual can at last get his hands on the whip."

Orwell points out Burnham's catastrophic series of wrong predictions—that Germany would not attack Russia until after defeating Britain (1940), that Germany would defeat Russia and Russia would break up (1942), that Russia would gang up with Japan against the United States (1944), and that Russia would dominate all Germany (later in 1944).

"It will be seen that at each point Burnham is predicting a *continuation of the thing that is happening.* Now the tendency to do this is not simply a bad habit like inaccuracy or exaggeration, which one can correct by taking thought. It is a major mental disease, and its roots lie partly in cowardice and partly in the worship of power, which is not fully separable from cowardice.

"So long as they were winning," Orwell concluded, "Burnham seems to have seen nothing wrong with the methods of the Nazis. Such methods, he says, only appear wicked because they are new. . . . This implies that literally anything can become right or wrong if the dominant class of the moment wills it. It ignores the fact that certain rules of conduct have to be observed if human society is to be held together at all. Burnham, therefore, was unable to see that the crimes and follies of the Nazi regime *must* lead by one route or another to disaster. So also with his new-found admiration for Stalinism. . . . The huge everlasting slave empire of which Burnham appears to dream will not be established, or if established will not endure, because slavery is no longer a stable basis for human society."

The artice called *Second Thoughts on James Burnham* provides an interesting footnote to *1984*, for a number of critics have attacked Orwell precisely because of the apparent hopelessness of his last novel. Apart from the fact that these critics are usually the ones who speak with defensive belligerence in favor of a "good story" and a "satisfying ending," one has only to read the bulk of Orwell's books to see how unwarranted the accusation is. In one of his earliest works, *A Clergyman's Daughter* (1935), he wrote that "the sense of futility" is "the subtlest weapon of the devil" and concluded "the solution to her difficulty lay in accepting the fact there was no solution; that if one gets on with the job that lies to hand, the ultimate purpose of the job fades into insignificance; that faith and no faith are very much the same provided that one is doing what is customary, useful and acceptable." In *The Road to Wigan Pier* (1937), he declared that "the job of the thinking person is not to reject Socialism but to humanize it," to concentrate on the two essential facts, one "that the interests of all exploited people are the same; the other, that Socialism is compatible with common decency." In *The Lion and the Unicorn*, he outlined his hopes for England, and in *Animal Farm* he warned of the dangers that could betray them. In his essays he criticized not only Burnham's power worship but Arthur Koestler's "tract purporting to show that revolutionary creeds are rationalizations of neurotic impulses."

1984 is certainly the gloomiest of Orwell's books,

partly because Orwell was dying. "I made it more pessimistic than I meant to," he told a friend, "probably because I was so ill at the time I wrote it." Even *1984*, however, does not make the mistake of treating the drift towards totalitarianism as irresistible. But if the slave empire will not endure, what hope then is there for the slaves of Oceania?"

"If there is hope," Winston Smith wrote in his diary, "it lies in the proles."

The prole(tarian)s are not even considered worth regimenting beyond a certain degree. They are merely supposed to work, breed and die. For the most part, the state stands secure in the conviction that the proles will remain perpetually indifferent. As he wrote *1984*, Orwell was not only dying, but he was dying in the midst of the failure of the Socialist government, a failure for which the indifference of the working people was largely to blame. In *The Road to Wigan Pier*, Orwell recalled the way the common people had been aroused by a swindle in the football pools, while they ignored the simultaneous march of the Nazis into the Rhineland. In 1984 as in 1948, "the lottery, with its weekly payout of enormous prizes, was the one public event to which the proles paid serious attention. It was probable that there were some millions of proles for whom the lottery was the principle if not the only reason for remaining alive. It was their delight, their folly, their anodyne, their intellectual stimulant. Where the lottery was concerned, even people who could barely read and write seemed capable of intricate calculations and staggering feats of memory. There was a whole tribe of men who made a living simply be selling systems, forecasts and lucky amulets . . . The prizes were largely imaginary. Only small sums were actually paid out, the winners of the big prizes being non-existent persons."

Winston Smith, the rebellious party member, will be captured, tortured, and the ultimate triumph of doublethink will be the expression of his total defeat as total victory—"He had won the victory over himself. He loved Big Brother." But the proles go on and on, "living and partly living"; they are the slumbering mass that no ruler can ever either eliminate or withstand, that no ruler can ever truly rule. It is banal to say that the working people have a right to earn a decent wage and live in peace and freedom, but it is the same important banality of two plus two making four, and one of the finest things about Orwell is his persistence in these half-forgotten banalities. In these hysterical times, when the dictator Franco is the hero of the right and the dictator Tito is the hero of the left, and when the common working people of England have botched one of their greatest chances, Orwell's determined faith in these common working people with their football pools reminds one of a fine man's love for a thoroughly foolish woman.

"Only there, in those swarming disregarded masses, eighty-five percent of the population of Oceania, could the force to destroy the party ever be generated," Orwell wrote in that strange tone of mixed bitterness and faith that comes from a sense of unnecessary failure. "The party could not be overthrown from within . . . But the proles, if only they could somehow become conscious of their own strength, would have no need to conspire. They needed only to rise up and shake themselves like a horse shaking off flies. If they chose they could blow the party to pieces tomorrow morning. . . .

"But if there was hope, it lay in the proles. You

had to cling on to that. When you put it in words, it sounded reasonable; it was when you looked at the human beings passing you in the street that it became an act of faith."

Halfway to 1984
Lawrence Malkin

This piece appeared originally in 1970, and, as its title suggests, it looks both backward to Orwell's writing as well as forward to the year of his fictional prophecy. But Malkin's cogent examination of Orwell, his milieu, and the nominal sources for several elements in the novel warrants inclusion of the article with the origins of *Nineteen Eighty-Four*.

Malkin recounts in brief the troubles Orwell had finding a publisher for *Animal Farm*, and later, after Frederic Warburg had published that book and then *Nineteen Eighty-Four*, Orwell's problems with reviewers and critics, whose numerous misinterpretations of *Nineteen Eighty-Four*, prompted Orwell to dictate a press release stating what the novel was *not* about. (Ironically, even Warburg mistook the book for a critique of British Labour Party government in the post-World War II years.)

While the examples Malkin cites from politics and affairs of the day have passed into recent history, it's evident that *Nineteen Eighty-Four* retains undiminished relevance as a touchstone for the tumultuous and increasingly precarious global situation in which we find ourselves today. In reaching 1984, there's no small cause to feel that Orwell's projection may have simply fallen some years short of the mark.

I never think of 1984, either the book or the year, without a slight shudder of foreboding. This can be no accidental idiosyncrasy. George Orwell set out to shock by the juxtaposition of fact and fancy.

He combined the stylistic skills of the modern polemicist with the wry detachment of the classical moralist. He stood the year of the book's completion on its head to sum up his negative vision of the future in a single stroke. He had considered entitling it *The Last Man in Europe*, which lacks the stinging immediacy of his final choice but gives a stronger clue to his humanist aspirations. Had he been less a propagandist (and he said every artist was a propagandist for his own vision of life), I would not be writing this now. This curious, uncomfortably honest, and painfully decent man wanted to reach his readers primarily for political purposes; by the end of his life as a writer he had come to believe that people didn't make aesthetic judgments at all, only political ones. He wanted to be a popular author without surrendering his particular vision of the world. In all this he succeeded. Since World War II no political book, whether fiction or nonfiction—and the essence of Orwell's success is that no one is ever sure whether *1984* is one or the other—has passed more thoroughly into the English language and the popular consciousness of the Western world than Orwell's dark masterpiece.

Various insights expressed in this short, prophetic tract (Orwell described it as "a Utopia in the form of a novel") have secured a hold on individuals and groups of amazing diversity. *Life* published the first excerpts in 1949 with cartoon illustrations by Abner Dean; readers were offered the interpretation that "in the year 1984 left-wing totalitarianism rules the world." Michael Harrington wrote that Orwell had discovered that a technology of abundance would disenfranchise the victims of poverty and racism to maintain a permanent menial class. The John Birch Society of Westchester County offered *1984* for sale, and its

Washington branch adopted 1984 as its telephone number. Writers of the Budapest Petöfi Club read *1984* before the 1956 Hungarian uprising, and the BBC's Overseas Service receives reports of the book's continuing popularity in Eastern Europe. Various members of Congress have invoked the image of Big Brother against wiretapping, government personality testing, and plans for a computerized central data bank. The liberal critic Harold Rosenberg said *1984* had set the tone of the postwar imagination by first describing the organization man as "the victim of the dehumanized collective that so haunts our thoughts."

The message that these and many, many others most commonly extract from *1984* lies in its most obviously frightening level: the totalitarian threat to individual freedom from collectives of the right or left. Any book that becomes such common intellectual currency risks being turned into debased coinage, especially when minted by such a critical and nonsystematic intelligence as Orwell's. But equally, any book that can strike such a responsive chord among such natural enemies must say something about the world in which they all live.

What the Orwell cultists cannot take in is his description of the most pervasive development of postwar political thought: the bankruptcy of liberal rationalism. Most of us have been raised on the comforting meliorist belief that if only the weight of human institutions is more equitably distributed, man will at last behave decently and rationally. We may disagree, as Mr. Rosenberg, say, disagrees with the John Birch Society, on where the balance of equity lies. But we still believe that ideas can make a more perfect society. Orwell says this simply is not true, or at the very best it is not possible. We have been schooled to believe that the best defense against totalitarian invasions of the privacy of the human spirit must be centered around rationally perfectible institutions. Orwell maintains they are no defense. He warns that the rationalist spirit of progress represents in fact the first step toward the very thing it aims to prevent, because it means giving me the power to enforce my ideas on you.

According to Orwell's timetable, by 1984 institutions of social and political control will have been invented that could, if those guiding them only desired it, solve the problems of mankind by issuing a few orders of the day. But those in power simply refuse to do so. "Sensible men have no power," Orwell said in dismissing the dream of a well-ordered world government. "The energy that actually shapes the world springs from emotions—racial pride, leader-worship, religious belief, love of war—which liberal intellectuals mechanically write off as anachronisms, and which they have usually destroyed so completely in themselves as to have lost all power of action." Orwell wrote those lines in 1941 in an attack on the utopianism of H.G. Wells. Had he lived into another generation, and watched the rise and sometimes tragic fall of American political dynasties with their attendant courts of pundits and professors, I doubt that he would have concluded the sentence as he did. No one could accuse the Kennedy Mafia or Johnson's Texans of forgetting race, leadership, religion, or war. Their overriding concern, however, was the pursuit of politcal power for its own sake, a pursuit followed at the cost of their sense and their sensibilities.* Orwell's most important discovery

---

*Had this essay been written more recently, Mr. Malkin would have no doubt mentioned the Nixon White House as a flagrant example of this point. [ed.]

was that the managers of our society, far from being sensible men, share the irrational drives of their fellows, and these include power. This is really what frightens us as we watch the liberal imagination turn into a totalitarian nightmare.

As a novel, *1984* is not particularly good. It is more fable than fiction and more fantasy than both. Big Brother is the only character anyone seems to remember, and he probably doesn't even exist. This is quite proper. Big Brother is the symbol and apex of an all-embracing and self-perpetuating state machine called the Party. It is split into an Inner Party (the decision makers) and an Outer Party (middle management). The mass of citizens, called the proles, simply do not count at all in the political scheme. Their lives are dominated by work and poverty, but their emotions are still free.

The plot of *1984* concentrates on the life of Winston Smith, a member of the Outer Party who cannot bear his job of rewriting the past to conform to the Party's directives and simply wants to be left alone. This desire for privacy, is of course, a crime; in every Party member's home stands a two-way telescreen to regulate his behavior and his thoughts. Winston is the last in a consistent line of Orwell's anti-heroes starting with Flory in his novel *Burmese Days*, who said, "Be as degenerate as you can. It all postpones Utopia." Winston's degeneracy consists first in keeping a diary of his private thoughts, then in having a love affair. In *1984* hate is the common emotion; the Two Minutes Hate against the Party's enemies, real or imagined, is a daily ritual. Nevertheless, Julia, a dissident member of the Junior Anti-Sex League, makes clandestine contact with Winston, and they fall in love. All this is watched by the Thought Police. The guilty couple are tricked into a mock conspiracy against the state by O'Brien, a member of the Inner Party and a supremely rational ideologist. He finally tortures Winston into betraying Julia, and at the book's end, into loving Big Brother instead.

Winston's pitiful retreat into privacy, his blowzy love affair, his melodramatic detection, torture, and extinction as even a pallid individual by the apparatus of the Party, are unworthy of second-rate science fiction. Yet here we are more than halfway to 1984, and the book is still selling in the tens of thousands each year. To find a literary parallel, one would have to reach back beyond the nineteenth-century English novel with its romantic conception of a man as a problem solver and into the eighteenth century, where life is larger than man and the world is a wicked place. Winston is a descendant of that almost faceless traveler in strange lands, Lemuel Gulliver.

The book tells us more, much more, about the quality of modern life than about the people in it. Orwell's style, a mixture of ideological fantasy and grubby realism, grows naturally from his beliefs. He confronts ideas with the rough edge of fact. He once wrote of Shakespeare: "he loved the surface of the earth and the process of life," and he could have been writing about himself. By 1984 life has been streamlined to a drab uniformity and the surface of the earth has been paved over, although not without cracks. People have been turned into mere ciphers in a topsy-turvy equation of ideas. The state is organized for war, but War is Peace. A fantastic communications system has been developed (even a "speakwrite" machine), but the Party uses it only to disseminate its own ideas, so Ignorance is Strength. Society has been organized into an immutable hierarchy that frees the individual from even considering his position in it, so Freedom is Slavery. These are the slogans of Oceania. People live by them with an unthinking drudgery. The plastic food has stirring names ("Victory Coffee"). Clothing has no style. Houses are collapsing, and people are crowded into them. Most important, the past is being systematically expunged as part of a process of controlling thought; without human experience, ideas thus can exist in a vacuum. Privacy, individuality, history, tragedy, have vanished. As Winston realizes:

> The terrible thing that the Party had done was to persuade you that mere impulses, mere feelings, were of no account, while at the same time robbing you of all power over the material world. When once you were in the grip of the Party, what you felt or did not feel, what you did or refrained from doing, made literally no difference. Whatever happened you vanished, and neither you nor your actions were ever heard of again. You were lifted clean out of the stream of history. And yet to the people of only two generations ago, this would not have seemed all-important, because they were not attempting to alter history. They were governed by private loyalties which they did not question. What mattered were individual relationships, and a completely helpless gesture, an embrace, a tear, a word spoken to a dying man, could have value in itself. The proles, it suddenly occurred to him, had remained in this condition. . . . they were loyal to one another. . . . The proles had stayed human.

This is not a very helpful view of society for those trying to order it to some predetermined outline. It has never been fashionable for the modern intelligence to consider such human qualities as important *by themselves*. For Orwell, they were the main reason for living. For modern social engineering, human feelings represent unfortunate variables that somehow must be fitted into projections of gross

national product (which sound increasingly like
those phony figures of rising standards of living
blared over the loudspeakers in *1984*); conditioned
politically and psychologically for ideological wars
in some obscure corner of the world (in *1984* the
telescreen carries gruesome pictures of carnage from
Malabar—is it?—and announcements of victories
that never bring peace any nearer); adjusted willy-
nilly for the huge structures of human beings organized to produce, to dwell, and to play together
(and you better like it and look the part, for by
1984 you may be guilty of an offense known as
"facecrime").

Orwell deliberately ignored the two major areas
of the social sciences where the twentieth century
has made its strongest advances (if that is what
they are): economics and psychology. "Economic
injustice will stop the moment we want it to stop,
and no sooner," he wrote in *The Road to Wigan
Pier*, "and if we genuinely want it to stop the
method adopted hardly matters." Richard Rees, a
friend and colleague for twenty years, never once
heard Orwell mention Freud, Jung, Kafka, or
Dostoevsky. He was not a modern man, and he
abhorred systematic (which is not to say critical)
thought. By his own admission, he liked gardening,
cheese, and even English food. He liked the combination of stolidity and irreverence that marks the
English working class, although he never felt at
home with them. He was half Eric Blair of Eton
and the Imperial Burmese Police, and half down-
and-out tramp revolutionary-socialist, a literary
propagandist and apocalyptic allegorist who became known as George Orwell. His friends addressed him by the name under which they had
first known him; he always meant to change his
name legally but never got around to it. In the
same way he never really decided who he was,

although there was no doubt that his loyalties lay on the left. This constant confrontation of values, shaped by a personal honesty that is unique in modern letters, made Orwell what he was. In a way the nagging dilemma came to a head during the war, when the pacifist and intellectual left revolted him and the rest of England got out and fought. He wrote in 1943: "As to the real moral of the last three years—that the Right has more guts and ability than the Left—no one will face up to it." Indeed, an uncomfortable man to know.

Because *1984* appeared when the postwar Labor government was on its last legs, and because the society it describes lives under a system of government called Ingsoc, the book is often interpreted as the pained protest of a disillusioned socialist. Admittedly, the postwar world of London, with rationing, shortages, and the endless exhortations of the first ideological government England had ever known, provided much color for the book. But Orwell was a far more complex man than that. "I am not a real novelist," Orwell once wrote his friend Julian Symons. "One difficulty I have never solved is that one has masses of experience which one passionately wants to write about . . . and no way of using them up except by disguising them as a novel."

Orwell got the idea for *1984* while working on wartime propaganda for the BBC. He was appalled by the entanglement, perversion, and eventual swallowing up of ideas in the BBC bureaucracy and described the place as "a mixture of a whoreshop and a lunatic asylum." He resigned in 1943 to recover his freedom as a political commentator; just before quitting he wrote a friend: "At present I'm just an orange that's been trodden on by a very dirty boot." (O'Brien says in *1984*: "If you want a picture of the future, imagine a boot stamping on a human face—forever.") The BBC canteen, windowless and underground, was a model for the *1984* cafeteria in the Ministry of Truth (i.e., the propaganda ministry). A wartime colleague tells me that while Orwell survived the stale fish and cabbage smells with less grumbling than most, his imagination dwelt on what the BBC would be like if it were run by a Stalin instead of the liberal muddlers of Broadcasting House.

Orwell was dying of tuberculosis when he wrote the book; the disease killed him in January, 1950, seven months after *1984* was published. It was reviewed on the BBC by Malcolm Muggeridge and Tosco Fyvel, two friends and sometime literary colleagues. Discussing the climactic scene in which Winston breaks down and betrays Julia under threat of having his face chewed by rats, they compared it to the worst imaginings of a pair of prep-school boys trying to scare each other after lights out. Orwell was listening in his hospital bed and laughed out loud. But Orwell refused to accept the thesis of another friend, Arthur Koestler, that political reformism springs from infantile neurosis. His strength lies in his insistence that politics rests on a moral foundation outside the individual and that truth rests in experience outside any system the individual can construct. An individual's search for truth in political life is not purely a function of intellect but of something with an old-fashioned name. The English call it character.

It is no accident that after a lifetime as a political essayist and a writer of starkly realistic novels, Orwell suddenly shifted to allegory in *Animal Farm* and *1984*. It is the literary form best suited to pointing up the contradictions between idea and reality. For Orwell it became the vehicle for explaining the major intellectual event of the first half of this century, the failed utopia—in Russia and elsewhere. The raw material consists of the curiously dated sectarian quarrels of the left in the 1930's, which Orwell freezes forever in the brilliant amber of *Homage to Catalonia*. But the issue described there is still real: freedom vs. power. In a time of social change, how much freedom can be allowed the individual to adjust to it, and at what rate must he adjust? His own or theirs? Totalitarianism insists on controlling the speed of change without reference to individual needs and finally must insist on trying to mold those very needs to fit its predetermined utopia.

Winston, in his subversive notebook, casts utopia aside and insists on following the instincts of his senses—"stones are hard, water is wet"—and finally: "Freedom is the freedom to say that two plus two make four. If that is granted, all else follows." But the catch phrase becomes perverted into the symbol of his humiliating subservience to the Party beyond the bounds of common sense. O'Brien forces him to admit that if the Party decrees it, "two plus two make five." This innumerate slogan has a revealing genesis. In *Assignment in Utopia*, which Orwell read soon after its publication in 1937, at the height of the Soviet purge trials, Eugene Lyons reports that electric signs were affixed to Moscow buildings with the slogan "2 + 2 = 5," exhorting the populace to work hard and complete the then current five-year plan in four years.

"The real answer," Orwell once wrote, "is to dissociate Socialism from Utopianism." The myth of utopia lies as deep in Western culture as that of the Garden of Eden, but it did not come alive politically until Thomas More added topical realism to it in the sixteenth century. As an early humanist, More raised the question of whether utopia could be transferred from the next world to this. As a Christian, he realized that after the Fall and before salvation the answer would have to be no. A utopia of happiness and boredom was literally no place, because of the nature of man and his exposure to the Christian experience—but by 1984 rational idealism has eradicated experience. All ideologies are to some degree utopian, from Pauline Christianity to Bolshevism to the Great Society. To the extent that they are rational and programmatic—and they cannot escape that any more than water can escape being wet—they are subject to disillusion and to perversion by power for its own sake. When More's *Utopia* is translated from the original Latin into modern English, it contains more than a hint of *1984*. Here is a random passage: "wherever you are, you always have to work. There's never any excuse for idleness. There are also no wine-taverns, no ale-houses, no brothels, no opportunities for seduction, no secret meeting-places. Everyone has his eye on you, so you're practically forced to get on with your job, and make some proper use of your spare time." More finally concludes: "Pride would refuse to set foot in paradise, if she thought there'd be no under-privileged classes there to gloat over . . ."

More was a humanist trying to preserve Christian values, Orwell a socialist trying to preserve libertarian values. Later utopians, especially those late Victorians bemused by the deceptively liberating potentialities of technology, were not so wise. They failed to realize that human experience and philosophical perfection are incompatible. Orwell did, and he turned utopia into "dystopia." Like that other eccentric and pseudonymous English allegorist of modern life, Lewis Carroll, he stepped through the looking glass and parodied rational beliefs to their logical conclusions. Technology, especially the new technology of communications and management, becomes a tyrannical instead of a liberating force in *1984*.

The utopia from which Orwell borrowed most closely was Evgeny Zamyatin's *We*. Zamyatin, a Russian novelist, underwent the enlightening experience of being imprisoned by the czar's police in 1906 and by the Bolsheviks in 1922—in the same corridor of the same prison. He seems, however, to have looked all the way back to Bakunin, the father of anarchism. "I do not want to be I, I want to be We," Bakunin said, alluding to the anarchist's sense of community as a defense against centralized state power. Zamyatin foresaw the collapse of even the community into the state. His book was written in 1923 and set in the year 2600. People have numbers instead of names, and "The Benefactor" rules the "United State." The narrator, D-503, is the mathematician-designer of the first spaceship, soon to be launched carrying the message: "Long live the United State. Long live the Numbers. Long live the Benefactor." D-503's only problem in this well-ordered state is that he suffers from the serious mental disease of imagination. Eventually, after committing the crime of falling in love with beautiful young I-330 and joining her in a rebellion against the "reason" of the United State, he is forced to submit to X-ray treatment that removes the brain center responsible for imagination. He then betrays I-330. Afterward, this chastened number writes: "No more delirium, no absurd metaphors, no feelings—only facts. For I am healthy —perfectly, absolutely healthy . . . I am smiling." In the end D-503 throws in his lot with law and order: "I am certain we shall win. For Reason must prevail."

Orwell first read Zamyatin's book in 1945, when

he was already making notes for *1984*. "What Zamyatin seems to be aiming at," Orwell wrote in a review, "is not any particular country but the implied aims of industrial civilization. . . . It is in effect a study of the Machine, the genie that man has thoughtlessly let out of its bottle and cannot put back again." Aldous Huxley also seems to have borrowed from *We*, for *Brave New World*. Zamyatin's, Huxley's, and Orwell's books all make similar assumptions about a technological utopia—that it has at last become possible, but that it also will be collectivist, elitist, and incompatible with the ideas of freedom.

In none of these dystopias is physical force the effective agent of control. It is, of course, the ultimate threat—as it must be even in a truly democratic state but not the proximate one. In the first two the citizens are held down largely by a sort of synthetic happiness, a myth of contentment reinforced by material well-being. For this they have exchanged their freedom. By 1984 the citizens of Oceania have not only lost their freedom but have not even gained happiness for it. Those who wish to retrieve their freedom are subjected to humiliation, loss of identity, and in the last resort, pain. "We shall meet in the place where there is no darkness," O'Brien tells Winston, as he tricks him into disclosing himself as a rebel. This promised utopia turns out to be the torture chambers of the windowless Ministry of Love.

In Orwell's dystopia the proximate agent of control is language. The myths of freedom and peace are kept alive by a hollow language that has completely lost its meaning. In Newspeak, Orwell's most brilliant and culturally incisive creation, language, like personality, has been leached of all flavor. It is "objective," without the subtlety or irony that reflects experience. Newspeak is a caricature of C.K. Ogden's Basic English, in which the inventor hoped to compress the English language into 850 words. Orwell at first became interested in it as a possible corrective to official euphemism and as a cleansing agent at a time when, he said, most political writing consisted of phrases bolted together like a child's erector set. But he later realized its sinister possibilities when the British government bought the world rights. Syme, a compiler of a Newspeak dictionary in *1984* (he is a bit too clever and is eventually vaporized), knows what it is all about. His team is destroying words by the hundreds every day: "Don't you see that the whole aim of Newspeak is to narrow the range of thought? In the end we shall make thoughtcrime literally impossible, because there will be no words in which to express it. . . . Every year fewer and fewer words, and the range of consciousness always a little smaller." Newspeak accomplishes this, as Orwell explains in an appendix, by divorcing language from thought. Such words as remain express acceptable ideas or condemn unacceptable ones out of hand. Even by 1984 the process has not been completed, but it is well under way. . . .

In truth, everything in 1984 is controlled, ordered, managed. But who shall guard the guardians? In 1984, as ever, no one. Although the concept of an Inner Party can be traced back to Plato, Orwell's most immediate source was the American writer James Burnham, and his book *The Managerial Revolution*. It provided the ideological stalking horse for *1984* by predicting the rise of a new managerial class that would not be different from one superstate to another. (Milovan Djilas calls it the New Class in the Communist world.) Burnham foresaw the division of the world into power blocs centered around Europe, Asia, and America, another concept Orwell took over. These managers are described in the theoretical center of *1984*, the book-within-a-book that describes the principles of Ingsoc. Naturally it is forbidden, as is any truthful book. It says:

> The new aristocracy was made up for the most part of bureaucrats, scientists, technicians, trade-union organizers, publicity experts, sociologists, teachers, journalists, and professional politicians. These people, whose origins lay in the salaried middle class and the upper grades of the working class, had been shaped and brought together by the barren world of monopoly industry and centralized government. As compared with their opposite numbers in past ages, they were less avaricious, less tempted by luxury, hungrier for pure power, and, above all, more conscious of what they were doing and more intent on crushing opposition.

It would be invidious to put names on this rogues' gallery of twentieth-century American types; I should imagine that for any casual student of the daily newspapers no names would be needed. The essence of Orwell's quarrel with Burnham, and he explains it in two detailed essays, is not that Burnham's description is incorrect but that, having worked it out, he has become fascinated by it and has accepted it as inevitable and therefore even desirable. Orwell labels this, with a kind of political prophecy, "realism." Burnham for a time accepted Nazism as a viable social order—until it began to lose. In England Orwell found that the middle-class managers accepted the Soviet regime, but only *after* it became totalitarian: "Burnham, although the English Russophile intelligentsia would repudiate him, is really voicing their secret wish: the wish to destroy the old, equalitarian version of socialism and usher in a hierarchical society where the intellectual can at last get his hands on the whip."

It is not surprising that when success finally came to Orwell, it was far from sweet and did strange things to this critic of the modern world. After his wife died suddenly in 1945, he retired with their adopted child to the barren and primitive Hebrides to write *1984* in surroundings simpler and more stark than the intellectual hothouse of London liberal society. The move helped break his health. He never bothered to conceal his views; quite the contrary, he exaggerated them to the point of personal abrasion. Michael Ayrton, then a young artist, recalls that whenever Orwell, wrapped in his old raincoat and scarf, appeared in the local pub, the young people would bemoan the arrival of "Gloomy George." But he loved to entertain friends in his flat for a high tea with English jams and pickles, and when he struck pay dirt with *Animal Farm*, he told his publisher: "At last I can take you out to lunch." Before his death this committed socialist was in the process of turning himself into a limited company to escape England's high income-tax rates.

Animal Farm, the anti-Stalinist satire in which Orwell said he had for the first time managed to fuse artistic and political purpose, had "a hell of a time" finding a publisher. Victor Gollancz, the epitome of the left-wing British intellectual between the wars, refused to publish it although Orwell was under contract to him. "We couldn't have published it then," Gollancz told me several years ago. "Those people were fighting for us, and they had just saved our necks at Stalingrad." T. S. Eliot turned it down for Faber, but on the debatable critical ground that Orwell had failed to bring off the satire. Some Nice Nelly at the Ministry of Information or the publisher Jonathan Cape, Orwell wasn't quite sure which, objected to the use of pigs as a symbol for Bolsheviks. Ironically, Frederic Warburg, no less a middle-class, Oxford-educated Jewish liberal intellectual than Gollancz, took on *Animal Farm* and became Orwell's publisher and friend. In the United States Orwell's last books encountered initial misunderstanding that has dogged them ever since. Dial Press wrote Orwell that *Animal Farm* would not do for the American market because it is "impossible to sell animal stories in the USA." A year later, after Harcourt, Brace had accepted it, Dial wrote back and said someone had made a horrible mistake.

Going through the original reviews of *1984* seems to justify the complaint of the Trotskyite historian Isaac Deutscher: "The novel has served as a sort of an ideological super-weapon in the cold war." Scores of American newspaper reviews hailed it as a warning of the menace of "creeping Socialism." In the more liberal big-city press there was an almost grudging admission that tyrannies other than left-wing ones might be involved. Saddest of all is the *New Republic*'s review. "The only thing to guard against is taking it too seriously," wrote Robert Hatch, who refused to believe—and this, in the same decade as Hitler's gas chambers—that men could sink to such depths as to be unable to solve their problems by reason. The English reviewers, less hysterical, more thoughtful and questioning, got closer to the book's human values. They may be summed up by V. S. Pritchett's remark: "The heart sinks but the spirit rebels as one reads Mr. Orwell's opening page."

I don't think Orwell was the least surprised by such massive misunderstandings. ("Of course not," Warburg comments. "He regarded the world as a wicked place.") Orwell meant the book to go into the political arena like all his works and was quite prepared for it to take its lumps there. From his hospital bed he fought back as best he could. He wrote a friend: "I am afraid some of the US Republic papers have tried to use *1984* as propaganda against the Labor Party, but I have issued a sort of démenti which I hope will be printed."

On June 15, 1949, Warburg dictated a memo containing a statement that Orwell approved. It begins by saying that *1984* is a parody; Orwell does not believe that its details will come true in the Western World but "Something like 1984 could happen." It continues: "This is the direction in which the world is going at the present time, and the trend lies deep in the political, social and economic foundations of the contemporary world situation. Specifically, the danger lies in the structure imposed on Socialist and Liberal capitalist communities by the necessity to prepare for total war with the USSR and the new weapons, of which of course the atomic bomb is the most powerful and the most publicized. But the danger lies also in the acceptance of a totalitarian outlook by intellectuals of all colors. The moral to be drawn from this dangerous nightmare situation is a simple one: *Don't let it happen to you. It depends on you.*" The memo then cites the dangers of superstates and adds: "The superstates will naturally be in opposition to each other or (a novel point) will pretend to be much more in opposition than they in fact are . . . it is obvious that the Anglo-Americans will not take the name of their opponents and will not dramatize themselves on the scene of history as Communists. The name suggested in 1984 is of course Ingsoc, but in practice a wide range of choices is open. In the USA the phrase 'Americanism' or '100 per cent Americanism' is suitable and the qualifying adjective is as totalitarian as anyone can wish."

As a prophet of specific events, Orwell has a less than perfect record, but only those who want to turn him into the original anti-Communist ideologue could complain of that. Orwell had long before written off the Communist experiment as a brutal failure. He was more immediately concerned with preserving deeper individual values. Ingsoc does not rule the English-speaking world, and we have not been smothered by a blanket of collective thought, at least not yet. Even in the Communist world the plants of individualism keep putting up flowers, if only to be tragically lopped off as soon as they bloom. In any society Orwell's message is what carries the relevance: it still "depends on you" whether or not 1984 comes true. I prefer to think of Julia as the precursor of the slogan that helped ignite a generation: "Make love, not war."

It is comforting to feel that more than halfway to 1984 we have no real Big Brother, and in fact the letters. B.B. are more commonly understood nowadays to refer to a French movie star. London today is not the shabby metropolis of *1984*. It has given birth to a species of pop culture that, although it may be excessively channeled into the pleasures of personal adornment and self-expression, has at last turned its back on the pretentious mock-aristocratic manners of the middle class that Orwell detested.

On a cool and luscious June day I visited No. 27B Canonbury Square; Orwell's fifth-floor wartime walkup there was the model for Winston Smith's "Victory Mansions." Poor Winston would never have recognized it. The neighborhood is festooned with greenery. Trees line the streets. Children play in the square; old folks sun themselves in it. Across the street, in a beautifully proportioned eighteenth-century mansion rented from the Marquis of Northampton, lives the London correspondent of *The New York Times*. The garden, the brickwork, and even the plumbing of Orwell's old house are in excellent order. Around the corner is an outdoor pub, a rarity in London. It is frequented by a mixture of working-class couples and the chic middle class (Orwell avoided the place because it used to be a hangout for Stalinist intellectuals). The whole neighborhood is urban landscape at its best, but of course property values have skyrocketed. I met a delightful London type tending the garden who could have been the model for the singing prole woman hanging her washing on the line in *1984*. Of course she remembered Mr. Blair, the writer; she used to work as a housekeeper for the woman who eventually became his second wife. Now she was a pensioner, and her chief worry was that the building had just been sold to some faceless property company. She hadn't even been told its name, and she was afraid she would be evicted and housed in some anonymous government redevelopment scheme far from her old neighborhood. So perhaps Big Brother, unseen as always, is not so distant from Orwell's old back yard after all.

It is easy to draw pictures of bogeymen; the caricature is too quickly adopted as imminent reality, and that is what has happened to Orwell's *1984*. I think Orwell underestimated the strength of European culture in resisting the encroachments of the machine age. The shared experiences that the Party would rub out in 1984 are still very much alive. Surely his own country still contains the sanest, kindest, and probably the most civilized people in Europe or possibly anywhere. Their mature self-awareness expresses itself in an articulate culture that exalts the individual and tolerates his eccentricities. Despite the erosions of two world wars, they cling to a hierarchic social order that encourages self-development, but only within boundaries so comfortably defined that everyone knows the rules of the game stop at actually winning it.

But the threat of 1984 has roosted, like a vulture in a tree, most firmly in the American consciousness. The myths of our competitive culture are coming up against the rough edge of human experience, and the culture itself is shuddering under the strain. The sleek society of managers, the streamlined men whose values lie in sheer accomplishment by control of their environment, has dehumanized itself as Orwell foresaw. Values imposed by work have tended to transcend and sometimes obliterate those that grow naturally from human contact. The community is a place to *do* something—to work, to play, to sleep—rather than to *be* someone. Synthetic personal contacts through the telescreen ("Good night, David. . . . Good night, Chet.") are more real than everyday life.

The trouble with literary dystopias is that they are essentially negative. Orwell says that "hopes lies with the proles"—hope lies with human experience—but it will take a long time. To find a more concrete way out one has to look elsewhere in Orwell's work. It simply will not do to try to turn Orwell into a prophet of anti-Communism or some kind of New Conservative. He simply refuses to get into bed with the left or the right, or any other programmatic apostle. Just before leaving Spain in 1937 he wrote Cyril Connolly: "I have seen wonderful things and at last really believe in Socialism, which I never did before." If his words mean anything, Orwell remained a socialist to his death. But to him socialism was not a programmatic ideology of social and economic change. It dwelt more deeply in the transcendent values of justice, liberty, equality, and the community of feeling (the brotherhood perverted into Big Brother) in which material values play their role alongside human ones. Its primary motives are surely neither rational nor public. Life is held together by family, community, and the shared values and experiences that constitute culture. For the rest of his life Orwell stressed the human and individual quality of this type of socialism. His critics find him gloomy because he returned to classical stoicism and abandoned progress. But without the relativism of ideology to organize human affairs, only the stark absolutes of human character remain. What Orwell is saying is that, now or in 1984, they are the things that really matter.

THE RESPONSE TO
NINETEEN EIGHTY-FOUR

Nineteen Eighty-Four was published on June 8, 1949, by Secker & Warburg in England and on June 13 by Harcourt, Brace in the United States. By that time, Orwell was well-established as a popular author with the success of *Animal Farm*, especially on this side of the Atlantic. The response to *Nineteen Eighty-Four* was widespread and immediate. Most critics and reviewers were unanimous in their agreement about the book's importance and impact. But, as the selection of reviews that follow reveal, there was a considerable range of opinion about Orwell's intent and about the overwhelming pessimism of the book. Both of these topics will receive close attention in the essays that follow these reviews.

Also, Aldous Huxley's letter to Orwell accents the differences in outlook between the two authors, as mentioned by George Woodcock; while giving Orwell his due credit, Huxley holds firm to his belief in behavior conditioning as the perfection of social control. Orwell, of course, preferred the image of a boot crushing a human face—forever.

"Power and Corruption"

Julian Symons

Times Literary Supplement, June 10, 1949

It is possible to make a useful distinction between
novelists who are interested primarily in the emotional relationships of their characters and novelists for whom characters are interesting chiefly as
a means of conveying ideas about life and society.
It has been fashionable for nearly half a century to
shake a grave head over writers who approach
reality by means of external analysis rather than
internal symbolism; it has even been suggested
that the name of novelist should be altogether
denied to them. Yet it is a modern convention that
the novel must be rather visceral than cerebral.
The novel in which reality is approached through
the hard colours of outward appearance (which is
also, generally, the novel of ideas) has a respectable lineage, and distinctive and distinguished modern representatives. Among the most notable of
them is Mr. George Orwell; and a comparison of
Nineteen Eighty-Four, his new story of a grim
Utopia, with his first novel *Burmese Days* (published
originally fifteen years ago and recently reissued)
shows a curious and interesting journey of the
mind. It is a queer route that Mr. Orwell has taken
from Burma to the Oceania of *Nineteen Eighty-
Four*, by way of Catalonia and Wigan Pier.

Burmese Days tells the story of a Flory, a slightly
intellectual timber merchant, marooned among a
group of typical Anglo-Indians in a small Burmese

town. Bored by his surroundings and disgusted by his companions, Flory becomes friendly with an Indian doctor; but he is for a long time too timid to risk offending the opinion of the white men he despises by proposing the doctor as a member of the European Club. This problem in social relationships is one of the narrative's two poles of interest: the other is Flory's unhappy, self-deceiving love for Elizabeth, niece of one of the Anglo-Indians. Elizabeth is a thoroughly commonplace girl, perfectly at home in the European Club, but Flory invests her with qualities that exist only in his tormented imagination. When he has been robbed of all illusion about Elizabeth, and thus about his own possible future, Flory shoots himself; Elizabeth marries the Deputy Commissioner of the district; the Indian doctor, robbed of Flory's support, is the victim of a plot to disgrace him made by U-Po-Kyin, a rascally Burman, who—a last ironical stroke—obtains membership of the European Club.

What is particularly noticeable about *Burmese Days* is that the two poles of its narrative are very unequal in strength. The passages dealing with conflicts between whites and natives, and with the administrative problems facing the British, are written with subtlety; and Mr. Orwell's attitude is remarkable, both in its avoidance of false idealism about the British and of false sentimentality about the Burmese. The part of the book that explores Flory's relationship with Elizabeth is in comparison crude and naive; and this is because Mr. Orwell is already a novelist interested in ideas, rather than in personal relationships. When he is forced to deal with them, here and in later books, he does so often in terms of a boys' adventure story. When Flory first meets Elizabeth, for example, she likes him because he drives away some harmless water-buffaloes, of which she is terrified. Friendship ripens when they go out shooting, and he is successful in killing a leopard. Her final rejection of him is symbolized by the fact that he is thrown from a pony when about to show off in front of her, by spearing a tent peg. It is true that other motives influence Elizabeth's conscious rejection of Flory; but it is obvious that this very simple underlying symbolism is important for Mr. Orwell himself. He shows great insight into the political and ethical motives of his characters; he seldom puts a word wrong when he looks at very varied facets of external reality; but his view of man as an emotional animal is often not far away from that of the boys' weeklies about which he has written with such penetration. It is such a mingling of subtlety and simplicity that makes *Animal Farm* a perfect book in its kind: in that fairy-story with an unhappy ending there are no human relationships to disturb the fairy-tale pattern and the political allegory that lies behind it.

It is natural that such a writer as Mr. Orwell should regard increasingly the subject rather than the form of his fictional work. *Burmese Days* is cast fairly conventionally in the form of the contemporary novel; this form had almost ceased to interest Mr. Orwell in 1939, when, in *Coming Up For Air*, the form of the novel was quite transparently a device for comparing the England of that time with the world we lived in before the First World War. In *Coming Up For Air*, also, characterization was reduced to a minimum: now, in *Nineteen Eight-Four*, it has been as nearly as possible eliminated. We are no longer dealing with characters, but with society.

The picture of society in *Nineteen Eighty-Four* has an awful plausibility which is not present in other modern projections of our future. In some ways life does not differ very much from the life we live to-day. The pannikin of pinkish-grey stew, the hunk of bread and cube of cheese, the mug of milkless Victory coffee with its accompanying saccharine tablet—that is the kind of meal we very well remember; and the pleasures of recognition are roused, too, by the description of Victory gin (reserved for the privileged—the 'proles' drink beer) which has 'a sickly oily smell, as of Chinese rice-spirit' and gives to those who drink it 'the sensation of being hit on the back of the head with a rubber club.' We can generally view projections of the future with detachment because they seem to refer to people altogether unlike ourselves. By creating a world in which the 'proles' still have their sentimental songs and their beer, and the privileged consume their Victory gin, Mr. Orwell involves us most skilfully and uncomfortably in his story, and obtains more readily our belief in the fantasy of thought-domination that occupies the foreground of his book.

In *Nineteen Eighty-Four* Britain has become Airstrip One, part of Oceania, which is one of the three great world-States. The other two are Eurasia and Eastasia, and with one or the other of these States Oceania is always at war. When the enemy is changed from Eurasia to Eastasia, the past is wiped out. The enemy, then, has always been Eastasia, and Eurasia has always been an ally. This elimination of the past is practised in the smallest details of administration; and incorrect predictions are simply rectified retrospectively to make them correct. When, for instance, the Ministry of Plenty issues a 'categorical pledge' that there will be no reduction of the chocolate ration, and then makes a reduction from thirty grammes to twenty, rectification is simple. 'All that was needed was to substitute for the original promise a warning that it would probably be necessary to reduce the ration at some time in April.' The appropriate correction is made in *The Times*, the original copy is destroyed, and the corrected copy placed on the files. A vast organization tracks down and collects all copies of books, newspapers and documents which have been superseded. 'Day by day and almost minute by minute the past was brought up to date.'

To achieve complete thought-control, to cancel the past utterly from minds as well as records, is the objective of the State. To this end a telescreen, which receives and transmits simultaneously, is fitted into every room of every member of the Party. The telescreen can be dimmed but not turned off, so that there is no way of telling when the Thought Police have plugged in on any individual wire. To this end also a new language has been invented, called 'Newspeak,' which is slowly displacing 'Oldspeak'—or, as we call it, English. The chief function of Newspeak is to make 'a heretical thought—that is, a thought diverging from the principles of Ingsoc (English Socialism in Oldspeak) —literally unthinkable.' The word 'free,' for example, is still used in Newspeak, but not in the sense of 'politically free' or 'intellectually free,' since such conceptions no longer exist. The object of Newspeak is to restrict, and essentially to order, the range of thought. The end-objective of the members of the Inner Party who control Oceania is expressed in the Newspeak word 'doublethink,' which means:

> To know and not to know, to be conscious of complete truthfulness while telling carefully-constructed lies, to hold simultaneously two opinions which cancelled out, knowing them to be contradictory and believing in both of them: to use logic against

logic, to repudiate morality while laying claim to
it, to believe that democracy was impossible and
that the Party was the guardian of democracy; to
forget whatever it was necessary to forget, then to
draw it back into memory again at the moment
when it was needed, and then promptly to forget it
again: and, above all, to apply the same process to
the process itself.

The central figure of *Nineteen Eighty-Four* is a
member of the Outer Party and worker in the
records department of the Ministry of Truth, named
Winston Smith. Winston is at heart an enemy of
the Party; he has not been able to eliminate the
past. When, at the Two Minutes' Hate sessions the
face of Emmanuel Goldstein, classic renegade and
backslider, appears on the telescreen mouthing
phrases about party dictatorship and crying that
the revolution has been betrayed, Winston feels a
hatred which is not—as it should be—directed entirely against Goldstein, but spills into heretical
hatred of the Thought Police, of the Party, and of
the Party's all-wise and all-protecting figurehead,
Big Brother.

Winston's heresy appears in his purchase of a
beautiful keepsake album which he uses as a
diary—an activity likely to be punished by twenty-
five years' confinement in a forced labour camp—
and in his visits to the 'proles'' areas, where he
tries unsuccessfully to discover what life was like
in the thirties and forties. He goes to the junk shop
where he found the album and buys a glass paper-
weight; and he is queerly moved by the old proprietor's quotation of a fragment of a forgotten
nursery rhyme: 'Oranges and lemons, say the bells
of St. Clement's.' Sexual desire has been so far as
possible removed from the lives of Party members;
and so Winston sins grievously and joyously with
Julia, a member of the Junior Anti-Sex League.

The downfall of Winston and Julia is brought about through O'Brien, a friendly member of the Inner Party, who reveals that he, too, is a heretic. They are admitted to membership of Goldstein's secret organization 'the Brotherhood,' which is committed to the overthrow of the Party. But O'Brien is not in fact a member of 'the Brotherhood'—if indeed that organization is not simply an invention of the Inner Party—and the benevolent-seeming proprietor of the junk shop belongs to the Thought Police. Winston is arrested and subjected by O'Brien to physical and mental coercion; its effect is to eradicate what O'Brien calls his defective memory. The past, O'Brien tells him, has no real existence. Where does it exist? In records and in memories. And since the Party controls all records and all memories, it controls the past. At last Winston is converted to this view—or rather, his defective memory is corrected. Our last sight of Winston shows him sitting in the Chestnut Tree café, haunt of painters and musicians. A splendid victory has been announced, and Winston hears of it not with scepticism but with utter belief. He looks up at the great poster of Big Brother.

> Two gin-scented tears trickled down the sides of his nose. But it was all right, everything was all right, the struggle was finished. He had won the victory over himself. He loved Big Brother.

The corrosion of the will through which human freedom is worn away has always fascinated Mr. Orwell; *Nineteen Eighty-Four* elaborates a theme which was touched on in *Burmese Days*. Flory's criticism of Burma might be Winston Smith's view of Oceania: 'It is a stifling, stultifying world in which to live. It is a world in which every word and every thought is censored. . . . Free speech is unthinkable.' And Flory's bitter words: 'Be as degenerate as you can. It all postpones Utopia,' is a prevision of Winston saying to Julia in his revolt against Party asceticism: 'I hate purity, I hate goodness! I don't want any virtue to exist anywhere.' But in *Nineteen Eighty-Four* the case for the Party is put with a high degree of sophistical skill in argument. O'Brien is able easily to dispose of Winston in their discussions, on the basis that power is the reality of life. The arrests, the tortures, the executions, he says, will never cease. The heresies of Goldstein will live for ever, because they are necessary to the Party. The Party is immortal, and it lives on the endless intoxication of power. 'If you want a picture of the future, imagine a boot stamping on a human face—for ever.'

Mr Orwell's book is less an examination of any kind of Utopia than an argument, carried on at a very high intellectual level, about power and corruption. And here again we are offered the doubtful pleasure of recognition. Goldstein resembles Trotsky in appearance, and even uses Trotsky's phrase, 'the revolution betrayed'; and the censorship of Oceania does not greatly exceed that which has been practised in the Soviet Union, by the suppression of Trotsky's works and the creation of 'Trotskyism' as an evil principle. 'Doublethink,' also, has been a familiar feature of political and social life in more than one country for a quarter of a century.

The sobriety and subtlety of Mr Orwell's argument, however, is marred by a schoolboyish sensationalism of approach. Considered as a story, *Nineteen Eighty-Four* has other faults (some thirty pages are occupied by extracts from Goldstein's book, *The Theory and Practice of Oligarchical Collectivism*): but none so damaging as this inveterate schoolboyishness. The melodramatic idea of the Brotherhood is one example of it; the use of a nursery rhyme to symbolize the unattainable and desirable past is another; but the most serious of these errors in taste is the nature of the torture which breaks the last fragments of Winston's resistance. He is taken, as many others have been taken before him, to 'Room 101.' In Room 101, O'Brien tells him, is 'the worst thing in the world.' The worst thing in the world varies in every case; but for Winston, we learn, it is rats. The rats are brought into the room in a wire cage, and under threat of attack by them Winston abandons the love for Julia which is his last link with ordinary humanity. This kind of crudity (we may say with Lord Jeffrey) will never do; however great the pains expended upon it, the idea of Room 101 and the rats will always remain comic rather than horrific.

But the last word about this book must be one of thanks, rather than of criticism: thanks for a writer who deals with the problems of the world rather than the ingrowing pains of individuals, and who is able to speak seriously and with originality of the nature of reality and the terrors of power.

"An Indignant and Prophetic Novel"
Mark Schorer
The New York Times Book Review, **June 12, 1949**

James Joyce, in the person of Stephen Daedalus, made a now famous distinction between static and kinetic art. Great art is static in its effects: it exists in itself, it demands nothing beyond itself. Kinetic art exists in order to demand: not self-contained, it requires either loathing or desire to achieve its function. The quarrel about the fourth book of "Gulliver's Travels" that continues to bubble among scholars—was Swift's loathing of men so great, so hot, so far beyond the bounds of all propriety and objectivity that in this book he may make us loathe them and indubitably makes us loathe his imagination?—is really a quarrel founded on this distinction.

It has always seemed to the present writer that the fourth book of "Gulliver's Travels" is a great work of static art; no less, it would seem to him that George Orwell's new novel, "Nineteen Eighty-Four," is a great work of kinetic art. This may mean that its greatness is only immediate, its power for us alone, now, in this generation, this decade, this year, that it is doomed to be the pawn of time. Nevertheless it is probable that no other work of this generation has made us desire freedom more earnestly or loathe tyranny with such fulness.

"Nineteen Eighty-Four" appears at first glance to fall into that long-established tradition of satirical fiction, set either in future times or in imagined places or both, that contains works so diverse as "Gulliver's Travels" itself, Butler's "Erewhon," and Huxley's "Brave New World." Yet before one has finished reading the nearly bemused first page, it is evident that this is fiction of another order, and presently one makes the distinctly unpleasant discovery that it is not to be satire at all.

In the excess of satire one may take a certain comfort. They provide a distance from the human condition as we meet it in our daily life that preserves our habitual refuge in sloth or blindness or self-righteousness. Mr. Orwell's earlier book, "Animal Farm," is such a work. Its characters are animals, and its content is therefore fabulous, and its horror, shading into comedy, remains in the generalized realm of intellect, from which our feelings need fear no onslaught. But "Nineteen Eighty-Four" is a work of pure horror, and its horror is crushingly immediate.

The motives that seem to have caused the difference between these two novels provide an instructive lesson in the operations of the literary imagination. "Animal Farm" was, for all its ingenuity, a rather mechanical allegory; it was an expression of Mr. Orwell's moral and intellectual indignation before the concept of totalitarianism as localized in Russia. It was also bare and somewhat cold, and without being really very funny, undid its potential gravity and the very real gravity of its subject, through its comic devices. "Nineteen Eighty-Four" is likewise an expression of Mr. Orwell's moral and intellectual indignation before the concept of totalitarianism, but it is not only that.

It is also—and this is no doubt the hurdle over which many loyal liberals will stumble—it is also an expression of Mr. Orwell's irritation at many facets of British socialism, and most particularly, trivial as this may seem, at the drab gray pall that life in Britain today has drawn across the civilized amenities of life before the war.

One hesitates to write this, to seem to equate physical discomfort with moral outrage, yet for the novelist as a practicing being, the equation is not unreal, and, in fiction, physical discomfort can give texture and body and feeling and finally force to even the gravest moral issue, and it can, apparently, give it even the fearful vitality that characterizes "Nineteen Eighty-Four."

As Winston Smith comes home for lunch from his office (we do not yet know that he works at the Ministry of Truth) on an April day thirty-five-years from now, we are first of all aware of the depressing seediness of things—the "gritty dust" in the street, the smell of "boiled cabbage and old rag mats" in the corridor, the elevator that seldom works because electricity must be saved, Winston's skin "roughened by coarse soap and blunt razor blades," the festering varicose ulcer on his ankle.

Such physical details, even as the outlines of the horrendous moral world that Smith inhabits become clear, create the texture, the immediate reality of the novel, and as the dust of broken plaster settles into the pores of his skin, as he eats his dispirited way through many tasteless, sodden, public meals, as he drinks the raw, burning stimulant called Victory Gin, he is seen in one area after another of his lonely and never private life more and more deeply submerged in the gray squalor of a world which is without joy or love and in which desultory but still destructive war is the permanent condition. It is always the atmosphere created by these details that heightens and intensifies, that signifies, indeed, the appalling moral facts.

In 1984, the world has been divided into three great super-states—Eastasia, Eurasia, and Oceania. Eurasia followed upon "the absorption of Europe by Russia," and Oceania, "of the British Empire by the United States." England is known as Airstrip One, and London is its capital. The English language is being transformed into something called Newspeak, a devastating bureaucratic jargon whose aim is to reduce the vocabulary to the minimum number of words so that ultimately there will be no tools for thinking outside the concepts provided by the state. (Mr. Orwell obligingly appends an essay on the structure and etymology of Newspeak.) All the literary classics of the past, together with all historical documents, are in the process of being "translated" into the new language, lest the future be led to believe that there was some past before the gruesome, self-perpetuating present.

Oceania is controlled by the Inner Party. The Party itself comprises 25 per cent of the population, and only the select members of the Inner Party do not live in total slavery. The bulk of the population is composed of the "proles," a depraved mass encouraged in a gross, inexpensive debauchery. For Party members, sexual love, like all love, is a crime, and female chastity has been institutionalized in the Anti-Sex League.

Party members cannot escape official opinion or official observation, for every room is equipped with a telescreen that cannot be shut off; it not only broadcasts at all hours, but it also registers precisely with the Thought Police every image and voice; it also controls all the activities that keep the private life public, such as morning calisthenics beside one's bed. It is the perpetually open eye and mouth. The dictator, who may or may not be alive but whose poster picture looks down from almost every open space, is known as B. B., or Big Brother, and the political form is called Ingsoc, the Newspeak equivalent of English socialism.

One cannot briefly outline the whole of Mr. Orwell's enormously careful and complete account of life in the super-state, nor do more than indicate its originality. He would seem to have thought of everything, and with vast skill he has woven everything into the life of one man, a minor Party member, one of perhaps hundreds of others who are in charge of the alteration of documents necessary to the preservation of the "truth" of the moment.

Through this life we are instructed in the intricate workings of what is called "thoughtcrime" (here Mr. Orwell would seem to have learned from Koestler's "Darkness at Noon"), but through this life we are likewise instructed in more public matters such as the devious economic structure of Oceania, and the nature and necessity of permanent war as two of the great superstates ally themselves against a third in an ever-shifting and ever-denied pattern of change. But most important, we are ourselves swept into the meaning and the means of a society which has as its single aim the total destruction of the individual identity.

To say more is to tell the personal history of Winston Smith in what is probably his thirty-ninth year, and one is not disposed to rob the reader of a fresh experience of the terrific, long crescendo and the quick decrescendo that George Orwell has made of this struggle for survival and the final extinction of a personality. It is in the intimate history, of course, that he reveals his stature as a novelist, for it is here that the moral and the psychological values with which he is concerned are brought out of the realm of political prophecy into that of personalized drama.

No real reader can neglect this experience with impunity. He will be moved by Smith's wistful attempts to remember a different kind of life from his. He will make a whole new discovery of the beauty of love between man and woman, and of the strange beauty of landscape in a totally mechanized world. He will be asked to read through pages of sustained physical and psychological pain that have seldom been equaled and never in such quiet, sober prose. And he will return to his own life from Smith's escape into living death with a resolution to resist power wherever it means to deny him his individuality, and to resist for himself the poisonous lures of power.

"Nineteen Eighty-Four," the most contemporary novel of this year and who knows of how many past and to come, is a great examination into and dramatization of Lord Acton's famous apophthegm, "Power tends to corrupt and absolute power corrupts absolutely."

"1984"

V.S. Pritchett

The New Statesman and Nation, June 18, 1949

Nineteen Eighty-Four is a book that goes through the reader like an east wind, cracking the skin, opening the sores; hope has died in Mr. Orwell's wintry mind, and only pain is known. I do not think I have ever read a novel more frightening and depressing; and yet, such are the originality, the suspense, the speed of writing and withering indignation that it is impossible to put the book down. The faults of Orwell as a writer—monotony, nagging, the lonely schoolboy shambling down the one dispiriting track—are transformed now he rises to a large subject. He is the most devastating pamphleteer alive because he is the plainest and most individual—there is none of Koestler's lurid journalism—and because, with steady misanthropy, he knows exactly where on the new Jesuitism to apply the Protestant whip.

The story is simple. In 1984 Winston Smith, a civil servant and Party member in the English Totalitarian State (now known as Air Strip No. 1), conceives political doubts, drifts into tacit rebellion, is detected after a short and touching period of happiness with a girl member of the Party and is horribly "rehabilitated." Henceforth he will be spiritually, emotionally, intellectually infantile, passive and obedient, as though he had undergone a spiritual leucotomy. He is "saved" for the life not worth living. In *Darkness at Noon*, death was the eventual punishment of deviation: in 1984 the punishment is lifeless life.

> Oh, stubborn self-willed exile from the loving breast! Two gin-scented tears trickled down the sides of his nose. But it was all right, everything was all right, the struggle was finished. He had won the victory over himself. He loved Big Brother.

A generation from now the world is composed of three States, Oceania, Eurasia, Eastasia in perpetual war. From time to time these States change sides, and the mass of people have little clear idea at any moment of who are their allies or their enemies. These wars are mainly fought on the frontiers away from the great cities—for atom bombing turned out to be too destructive and made useful war impossible—and their objects are, fundamentally, to use up the excessive productivness of the machine, and yet, contradictorily, to get control of rare raw materials or cheap native labour. Another important attraction of war is that it enables the new governing class, who are modelled on the Stalinists, to keep down the standard of living and nullify the intelligence of the masses who they no longer pretend to have liberated. War is peace: the party slogan indicates that war is not itself necessary; but that the collective oligarchy can operate securely only on a war footing.

It is with this moral corruption of absolute political power that Mr. Orwell's novel is concerned. London lies decaying like an old cabbage in the remains of its seedy 19th-century buildings, but high above the streets tower the four main ministries of Ingsoc: the Ministry of Truth, for the issuing of lies, that is to say, official news, official culture; the Ministry of Plenty, for the purpose of organising scarcity; the Ministry of Peace for conducting war; and the dubious Ministry of Love, windowless and surrounded by barbed wire and machine guns, where political prisoners are either executed or "rehabilitated" by the new Inquisition. A recalcitrant will enter the Ministry of Love and emerge eventually an official sponge, incapable of private life, without memory; private memory and the sexual impulse are the two deadly sins. Enjoying them, the virtues of obedience and hysteria are impossible to the citizen. In the homes of Party members—and all except the "proles" or workers have some place in this hierarchy—a telescreen is fitted, from which canned propaganda continually pours, on which the pictures of Big Brother, the leader and the ancient enemy and anti-Christ, Goldstein often appear. Also by this device the Thought Police, on endless watch for Thought Crime, can observe the people night and day. What precisely Thought Crime really is no one knows; but in general it is the tendency to conceive a private life secret from the State. A frown, a smile, a shadow on the face, a sigh may betray the citizen, who has forgotten, for the moment, the art of "reality control" or, in Newspeak, the official language, "doublethink." Winston Smith's doubts began when, accidentally, there came into his hands a complete piece of evidence of State lying. The doubts drove him to action: he bought a notebook and started a diary, that is to say, a piece of writing not directed by the State. He tried to define "doublethink":

> To know and not to know, to be conscious of complete truthfulness while telling carefully constructed lies, to hold simultaneously two opinions which cancelled out, knowing them to be contradictory and believing in both of them; to use logic against logic, to repudiate morality while laying

claim to it, to believe that democracy is impossible and that the Party was the guardian of democracy; to forget whatever it was necessary to forget, then to draw it back into memory again at the moment it was needed, and then promptly to forget again; and, above all, to apply the same process to the process itself. That was the ultimate subtlety; consciously to induce unconsciousness, and then, once again, to become unconscious of the act of hypnosis you had just performed. Even to understand the word "doublethink" involved the use of doublethink.

Newspeak, the new Basic English blessed by the scientists and the Party, is the natural offspring of Doublethink. "You think, I dare say," says Syme, the Party philologist, "that our chief job is inventing new words. But not a bit of it! We're destroying words, scores of them." And he goes on to give examples:

It is a beautiful thing, the destruction of words. Of course, the great wastage is in the verbs and adjectives, but there are hundreds of nouns that can be got rid of as well. It isn't only the synonyms; there are also the antonyms. After all, what justification is there for a word which is simply the opposite of some other word? A word contains its opposite in itself. Take "good," for instance. If you have a word like "good," what need is there for a word like "bad." "Ungood" will do just as well—better, because it is the exact opposite which the other is not. Or, again, if you want a stronger version of "good," what sense is there in having a whole string of vague, useless words like "excellent" and "splendid" and all the rest of them. "Plusgood" covers the meaning.

The aim of Newspeak is to narrow the range of thought, and to remove from the classics all the subversiveness which could pollute the minds of Party Members. The time will come when the official slogans: War is Peace, Freedom is Slavery, Ignorance is Strength, will not be required, "simply because there will be no thought as we understand it now."

Mr. Orwell's book is a satirical pamphlet. I notice that some critics have said that his prophecy is not probable. Neither was Swift's *Modest Proposal* nor Wells's *Island of Dr. Moreau*. Probability is not a necessary condition of satire which, when it pretends to draw the future, is, in fact, scourging the present. The purges in Russia and, later, in the Russian satellites, the dreary seediness of London in the worst days of the war, the pockets of 19th-century life in decaying England, the sordidness of bad flats, bad food, the native and whining streak of domestic sluttishness which have sickened English satirists since Smollett, all these have given Mr. Orwell his material. The duty of the satirist is to go one worse than reality; and it might be objected that Mr. Orwell is too literal, that he is too oppressed by what he sees, to exceed it. In one or two incidents where he does exceed, notably in the torture scenes, he is merely melodramatic: he introduces those rather grotesque machines which used to appear in terror stories for boys. In one place—I mean the moment when Winston's Inquisitor drives him to call out for the death of his girl, by threatening to set a cageful of famished rats on him—we reach a peak of imaginative excess in terror, but it is superfluous because mental terrorism is his real subject.

Until our time, irony and unnatural laughter were thought to be the duty of the satirist: in *Candide* the more atrocious the fact—and a large number of Voltaire's facts were true—the gayer the laugh. More strikingly than in any other genre, it is indispensable for satire to sound "untrue," an effect Voltaire obtained by running a large number of true things together in a natural manner. The laughter of Voltaire, the hatred of Swift were assertions of vitality and the instinct to live in us, which continually struggles not only against evil but against the daily environment.

But disgust, the power to make pain sickening, the taste for punishment, exceed irony and laughter in the modern satirist. Neither Winston Smith nor the author laughs when he discovers that the women of the new State are practised hypocrites and make fools of the Party members. For Mr. Orwell, the most honest writer alive, hypocrisy is too dreadful for laughter: it feeds his despair.

As a pamphleteer Orwell may be right in his choice of means. The life-instinct rebels against the grey tyrannies that, like the Jehovah of the Old Testament, can rule only as long as they create guilt. The heart sinks, but the spirit rebels as one reads Mr. Orwell's ruthless opening page, even though we have met that boiled cabbage in all his books before:

> It was a bright, cold day in April, and the clocks were striking thirteen. Winston Smith, his chin nuzzled into his breast in an effort to escape the vile wind, slipped quickly through the glass doors of Victory Mansions, though not quickly enough to prevent a swirl of gritty dust from entering along with him.
>
> The hallway smelt of boiled cabbage and old rag mats. . . . It was no use trying the lift. Even at the best of times it was seldom working, and at present the electricity current was cut off during daylight hours. It was part of the economy drive in preparation for Hate Week. The flat was seven flights up, and Winston, who was 39 and had a varicose ulcer above his right ankle, went slowly,

resting several times on the way. On each landing, opposite the lift shaft, the poster with the enormous face gazed from the wall. It was one of those pictures which are so contrived that the eyes follow you about when you move. Big Brother IS WATCHING YOU, the caption beneath it ran.

But though the indignation of *Nineteen Eighty-Four* is singeing, the book does suffer from a division of purpose. Is it an account of present hysteria, is it a satire on propaganda, or a world that sees itself entirely in inhuman terms? Is Mr. Orwell saying, not that there is no hope, but that there is no hope for man in the political conception of man? We have come to the end of a movement. He is like some dour Protestant of Jansenist who sees his faith corrupted by the "doublethink" of the Roman Catholic Church, and who fiercely rejects the corrupt civilisations that appear to be able to flourish even under that dispensation.

"Orwell on the Future"

Lionel Trilling:

The New Yorker, **June 18, 1949**

George Orwell's new novel, "Nineteen Eighty-Four"
(Harcourt, Brace), confirms its author in the special,
honorable place he holds in our intellectual life.
Orwell's native gifts are perhaps not of a transcendent kind; they have their roots in a quality of
mind that ought to be as frequent as it is modest.
This quality may be described as a sort of moral
centrality, a directness of relation to moral—and
political—fact, and it is so far from being frequent
in our time that Orwell's possession of it seems
nearly unique. Orwell is an intellectual to his
fingertips, but he is far removed from both the
Continental and the American type of intellectual.
The turn of his mind is what used to be thought of
as peculiarly "English." He is indifferent to the
allurements of elaborate theory and of extreme
sensibility. The medium of his thought is common
sense, and his commitment to intellect is fortified
by an old-fashioned faith that the truth can be got
at, that we can, if we actually want to, see the
object as it really is. This faith in the power of
mind rests in part on Orwell's willingness, rare
among contemporary intellectuals, to admit his
connection with his own cultural past. He no longer
identifies himself with the British upper middle
class in which he was reared, yet it is interesting
to see how often his sense of fact derives from
some ideal of that class, how he finds his way

through a problem by means of an unabashed certainty of the worth of some old, simple, belittled virtue. Fairness, decency, and responsibility do not make up a shining or comprehensive morality, but in a disordered world they serve Orwell as an invaluable base of intellectual operations.

Radical in his politics and in his artistic tastes, Orwell is wholly free of the cant of radicalism. His criticism of the old order is cogent, but he is chiefly notable for his flexible and modulated examination of the political and aesthetic ideas that oppose those of the old order. Two years of service in the Spanish Loyalist Army convinced him that he must reject the line of the Communist Party and, presumably, gave him a large portion of his knowledge of the nature of human freedom. He did not become—as Leftist opponents of Communism are so often and so comfortably said to become— "embittered" or "cynical"; his passion for freedom simply took account of yet another of freedom's enemies, and his intellectual verve was the more stimulated by what he had learned of the ambiguous nature of the newly identified foe, which so perplexingly uses the language and theory of light for ends that are not enlightened. His distinctive work as a radical intellectual became the criticism of liberal and radical thought wherever it deteriorated to shibboleth and dogma. No one knows better than he how willing is the intellectual Left to enter the prison of its own mass mind, nor does anyone believe more directly than he in the practical consequences of thought, or understand more clearly the enormous power, for good or bad, that ideology exerts in an unstable world.

"Nineteen Eighty-Four" is a profound, terrifying, and wholly fascinating book. It is a fantasy of the political future, and, like any such fantasy, serves its author as a magnifying device for an examination of the present. Despite the impression it may give at first, it is not an attack on the Labour Government. The shabby London of the Super-State of the future, the bad food, the dull clothing, the fusty housing, the infinite ennui—all these certainly reflect the English life of today, but they are not meant to represent the outcome of the utopian pretensions of Labourism or of any socialism. Indeed, it is exactly one of the cruel essential points of the book that utopianism is no longer a living issue. For Orwell, the day has gone by when we could afford the luxury of making our flesh creep with the spiritual horrors of a successful hedonistic society; grim years have intervened since Aldous Huxley, in "Brave New World," rigged out the welfare state of Ivan Karamazov's Grand Inquisitor in the knickknacks of modern science and amusement, and said what Doestoevski and all the other critics of the utopian ideal had said before—that men might actually gain a life of security, adjustment, and fun, but only at the cost of their spiritual freedom, which is to say, of their humanity. Orwell agrees that the State of the future will establish its power by destroying souls. But he believes that men will be coerced, not cosseted, into soullessness. They will be dehumanized not by sex, massage, and private helicopters but by a marginal life of deprivation, dullness, and fear of pain.

This, in fact, is the very center of Orwell's vision of the future. In 1984, nationalism as we know it has at last been overcome, and the world is organized into three great political entities. All profess the same philosophy, yet despite their agreement, or because of it, the three Super-States are always at war with each other, two always allied against one, but all seeing to it that the balance of power is kept, by means of sudden, treacherous shifts of alliance. This arrangement is established as if by the understanding of all, for although it is the ultimate aim of each to dominate the world, the immediate aim is the perpetuation of war without victory and without defeat. It has at last been truly understood that war is the health of the State; as an official slogan has it, "War Is Peace." Perpetual war is the best assurance of perpetual absolute rule. It is also the most efficient method of consuming the production of the factories on which the economy of the State is based. the only alternative method is to distribute the goods among the population. But this has its clear danger. The life of pleasure is inimical to the health of the State. It stimulates the senses and thus encourages the illusion of individuality; it creates personal desires, thus potential personal thought and action.

But the life of pleasure has another, and even more significant, disadvantage in the political future that Orwell projects from his observation of certain developments of political practice in the last two decades. The rulers he envisages are men who, in seizing rule, have grasped the innermost principles of power. All other oligarchs have included some general good in their impulse to rule and have played at being philosopher-kings or priest-kings or scientist-kings, with an announced program of beneficence. The rulers of Orwell's State know that power in its pure form has for its true end nothing but itself, and they know that the nature of power is defined by the pain it can inflict on others. They know, too, that just as wealth exists only in relation to the poverty of others, so power in its pure aspect exists only in relation to the weakness of others, and that any power of the ruled, even the power to experience happiness, is by that much a diminution of the power of the rulers.

The exposition of the *mystique* of power is the heart and essence of Orwell's book. It is implicit throughout the narrative, explicit in excerpts from the remarkable "Theory and Practice of Oligarchical Collectivism," a subversive work by one Emmanuel Goldstein, formerly the most gifted leader of the Party, now the legendary foe of the State. It is brought to a climax in the last section of the novel, in the terrible scenes in which Winston Smith, the sad hero of the story, having lost his hold on the reality decreed by the State, having come to believe that sexuality is a pleasure, that personal loyalty is good, and that two plus two always and not merely under certain circumstances equals four, is brought back to health by torture and discourse in a hideous parody on psychotherapy and the Platonic dialogues.

Orwell's theory of power is developed brilliantly, at considerable length. And the social system that it postulates is described with magnificent circumstantiality: the three orders of the population—Inner Party, Outer Party, and proletarians; the complete surveillance of the citizenry by the Thought Police, the only really efficient arm of the government; the total negation of the personal life; the directed emotions of hatred and patriotism; the deified Leader, omnipresent but invisible, wonderfully named Big Brother; the children who spy on their parents; and the total destruction of culture. Orwell is particularly successful in his exposition of the official mode of thought, Doublethink, which gives one "the power of holding two contradictory beliefs in one's mind simultaneously, and accepting both of them." This intellectual safeguard of the State is reinforced by a language, Newspeak, the goal of which is to purge itself of all words in which a free thought might be formulated. The systematic obliteration of the past further protects

NINETEEN EIGHTY-FOUR TO 1984 / 163

the citizen from Crimethink, and nothing could be more touching, or more suggestive of what history means to the mind, than the efforts of poor Winston Smith to think about the condition of man without knowledge of what others have thought before him.

By now, it must be clear that "Nineteen Eighty-Four" is, in large part, an attack on Soviet Communism. Yet to read it as this and as nothing else would be to misunderstand the book's aim. The settled and reasoned opposition to Communism that Orwell expresses is not to be minimized, but he is not undertaking to give us the delusive comfort of moral superiority to an antagonist. He does not separate Russia from the general tendency of the world today. He is saying, indeed, something no less comprehensive than this: that Russia, with its idealistic social revolution now developed into a police state, is but the image of the impending future and that the ultimate threat to human freedom may well come from a similar and even more massive development of the social idealism of our democratic culture. To many liberals, this idea will be incomprehensible, or, if it is understood at all, it will be condemned by them as both foolish and dangerous. We have dutifully learned to think that tyranny manifests itself chiefly, even solely, in the defense of private property and that the profit motive is the source of all evil. And certainly Orwell does not deny that property is powerful or that it may be ruthless in self-defense. But he sees that, as the tendency of recent history goes, property is no longer in anything like the strong position it once was, and that will and intellect are playing a greater and greater part in human history. To many, this can look only like a clear gain. We naturally identify ourselves with will and intellect; they are the very stuff of humanity, and we prefer not to think of their exercise in any except an ideal way. But Orwell tells us that the final oligarchical revolution of the future, which, once established, could never be escaped or countered, will be made not by men who have property to defend but by men of will and intellect, by "the new aristocracy . . . of bureaucrats, scientists, trade-union organizers, publicity experts, sociologists, teachers, journalists, and professional politicians."

> These people [says the authoritative Goldstein, in his account of the revolution], whose origins lay in the salaried middle class and the upper grades of the working class, had been shaped and brought together by the barren world of monopoly industry and centralized government. As compared with their opposite numbers in past ages, they were less avaricious, less tempted by luxury, hungrier for pure power, and, above all, more conscious of what they were doing and more intent on crushing opposition. This last difference was cardinal.

The whole effort of the culture of the last hundred years has been directed toward teaching us to understand the economic motive as the irrational road to death, and to seek salvation in the rational and the planned. Orwell marks a turn in thought; he asks us to consider whether the triumph of certain forces of the mind, in their naked pride and excess, may not produce a state of things far worse than any we have ever known. He is not the first to raise the question, but he is the first to raise it on truly liberal or radical grounds, with no intention of abating the demand for a just society, and with an overwhelming intensity and passion. This priority makes his book a momentous one.

"To George Orwell"
Aldous Huxley
October 21, 1949

Dear Mr. Orwell,

It was very kind of you to tell your publishers to send me a copy of your book. It arrived as I was in the midst of a piece of work that required much reading and consulting of references; and since poor sight makes it necessary for me to ration my reading, I had to wait a long time before being able to embark on *Nineteen Eight-Four*. Agreeing with all that the critics have written of it, I need not tell you, yet once more, how fine and how profoundly important the book is. May I speak instead of the thing with which the book deals— the ultimate revolution? The first hints of a philosophy of the ultimate revolution—the revolution which lies beyond politics and economics, and which aims at the total subversion of the individual's psychology and physiology—are to be found in the Marquis de Sade, who regarded himself as the continuator, consummator, of Robespierre and Babeuf. The philosophy of the ruling minority in *Nineteen Eighty-Four* is a sadism which has been carried to its logical conclusion by going beyond sex and denying it. Whether in actual fact the policy of the boot-on-the-face can go on indefinitely seems doubtful. My own belief is that the ruling oligarchy will find less arduous and wasteful ways of governing and of satisfying its lust for power, and that these ways will resemble those

166 / "To George Orwell"

which I described in *Brave New World*. I have had occasion recently to look into the history of animal magnetism and hypnotism, and have been greatly struck by the way in which, for a hundred and fifty years, the world has refused to take serious cognizance of the discoveries of Mesmer, Braid, Esdaile and the rest. Partly because of the prevailing materialism and partly because of prevailing respectability, nineteenth-century philosophers and men of science were not willing to investigate the odder facts of psychology. Consequently there was no pure science of psychology for practical men, such as politicians, soldiers and policemen, to apply in the field of government. Thanks to the voluntary ignorance of our fathers, the advent of the ultimate revolution was delayed for five or six generations. Another lucky accident was Freud's inability to hypnotize successfully and his consequent disparagement of hypnotism. This delayed the general application of hypnotism to psychiatry for at least forty years. But now psycho-analysis is being combined with hypnosis; and hypnosis has been made easy and indefinitely extensible through the use of barbiturates, which induce a hypnoid and suggestible state in even the most recalcitrant subjects. Within the next generation I believe that the world's rulers will discover that infant conditioning and narco-hypnosis are more efficient, as instruments of government, than clubs and prisons, and that the lust for power can be just as completely satisfied by suggesting people into loving their servitude as by flogging and kicking them into obedience. In other words, I feel that the nightmare of *Nineteen Eighty-Four* is destined to modulate into the nightmare of a world having more resemblance to that which I imagined in *Brave New World*. The change will be brought about as a result of a felt need for increased efficiency. Meanwhile, of course, there may be a large-scale biological and atomic war—in which case we shall have nightmares of other and scarcely imaginable kinds.

Thank you once again for the book.

Yours sincerely,
Aldous Huxley

THE LEGACY OF
NINETEEN EIGHTY-FOUR

Symptoms of Orwell's 1984
Bertrand Russell

In this short essay, published in 1953, Lord Russell uses *Nineteen Eighty-Four* as a point of departure for his own observations of the decline of individual liberty and the encroaching power of the state—both in England and America.

The essay has value here, however, as it demonstrates Russell's complete sympathies with Orwell's libertarian objectives in writing *Nineteen Eighty-Four*, which specifically were *not* to satirize Stalinist Russia or to criticize the failings of the postwar Labour government in England. Rather, Orwell's eye was on the erosion of freedom and social justice and on the growth of monolithic government apparatuses in all modern political systems. As we examine Russell's note of distress from our vantage point more than thirty years later, it remains difficult to judge whether the forces that he, and Orwell, indicted have been successfully deflected or, in many ways, continue to suggest that the world Orwell sketched for the end of this century may yet be possible.

George Orwell's *1984* is a gruesome book which duly made its readers shudder. It did not, however, have the effect which no doubt its author intended. People remarked that Orwell was very ill when he wrote it, and in fact died soon afterward. They rather enjoyed the *frisson* that its horrors gave them and thought: "Oh well, of course it will never be as bad as that except in Russia! Obviously the author enjoys gloom; and so do we, as long as we don't take it seriously." Having soothed themselves with these comfortable falsehoods, people proceeded on their way to make Orwell's prognostications come true. Bit by bit, and step by step, the world has been marching toward the realization of Orwell's nightmares; but because the march has been gradual, people have not realized how far it has taken them on this fatal road.

Only those who remember the world before 1914 can adequately realize how much has already been lost. In that happy age, one could travel without a passport, everywhere except in Russia. One could freely express any political opinion, except in Russia. Press censorship was unknown, except in Russia. Any white man could emigrate freely to any part of the world. The limitations of freedom in Czarist Russia were regarded with horror throughout the rest of the civilized world, and the power of the Russian Secret Police was regarded as an abomination. Russia is still worse than the Western World, not because the Western World has preserved its liberties, but because, while it has been losing them, Russia has marched farther in the direction of tyranny than any Czar ever thought of going.

For a long time after the Russian Revolution, it was customary to say, "No doubt the new regime has its faults, but at any rate it is better than that which it has superseded." This was a complete delusion. When one rereads accounts of exile in Siberia under the Czar, it is impossible to recapture the revulsion with which one read them long ago. The exiles had a very considerable degree of liberty, both mental and physical, and their lot was in no way comparable to that of people subjected to forced labor under the Soviet Government. Educated Russians could travel freely and enjoy contacts with Western Europeans which are now impossible. Opposition to the Government, although it was apt to be punished, was possible, and the punishment as a rule was nothing like as severe as it has become. Nor did tyranny extend nearly as widely as it does now. I read recently the early life of Trotsky as related by Deutscher, and it reveals a degree of political and intellectual freedom to which there is nothing comparable in present-day Russia. There is still as great a gulf between Russia and the West as there was in Czarist days, but I do not think the gulf is greater than it was then for, while Russia has grown worse, the West also has lost much of the freedom which it formerly enjoyed.

The problem is not new except quantitatively. Ever since civilization began, the authorities of most States have persecuted the best men among their subjects. We are all shocked by the treatment of Socrates and Christ, but most people do not realize that such has been the fate of a large proportion of the men subsequently regarded as unusually admirable. Most of the early Greek philosophers were refugees. Aristotle was protected from the hostility of Athens only by Alexander's armies, and, when Alexander died, Aristotle had to fly. In the seventeenth century scientific innovators were persecuted almost everywhere except in Holland. Spinoza would have had no chance to do his work if he had not been Dutch. Descartes and Locke found it prudent to flee to Holland. When England, in 1688, acquired a Dutch king, it took over Dutch tolerance and has been, ever since, more liberal than most states, except during the period of the wars against revolutionary France and Napoleon. In most countries at most times, whatever subsequently came to be thought best was viewed with horror at the time by those who wielded authority.

What is new in our time is the increased power

of the authorities to enforce their prejudices. The police everywhere are very much more powerful than at any earlier time; and the police, while they serve a purpose in suppressing ordinary crime, are apt to be just as active in suppressing extraordinary merit.

The problem is not confined to this country or that, although the intensity of the evil is not evenly distributed. In my own country things are done more quietly and with less fuss than in the United States, and the public knows very much less about them. There have been purges of the Civil Service carried out without any of the business of Congressional Committees. The Home Office, which controls immigration, is profoundly illiberal except when public opinion can be mobilized against it. A Polish friend of mine, a very brilliant writer who had never been a Communist, applied for naturalization in England after living in that country for a long time, but his request was at first refused on the ground that he was a friend of the Polish Ambassador. His request was only granted in the end as a result of protests by various people of irreproachable reputation. The right of asylum for political refugees that used to be England's boast has now been abandoned by the Home Office, though perhaps it may be restored as the result of agitation.

There is a reason for the general deterioration as regards liberty. This reason is the increased power of organizations and the increasing degree to which men's actions are controlled by this or that large body. In every organization there are two purposes: one, the ostensible purpose for which the organization exists; the other, the increase in the power of its officials. This second purpose is very likely to make a stronger appeal to the officials concerned than the general public purpose that they are expected to serve. If you fall foul of the police by attempting to expose some iniquity of which they have been guilty, you may expect to incur their hostility; and, if so, you are very likely to suffer severely.

I have found among many liberal-minded people a belief that all is well so long as the law courts decide rightly when a case comes before them. This is entirely unrealistic. Suppose, for example, to take a by no means hypothetical case, that a professor is dismissed on a false charge of disloyalty. He may, if he happens to have rich friends, be able to establish in court that the charge was false, but this will probably take years during which he will starve or depend on charity. At the end he is marked man. The university authorities, having learned wisdom, will say that he is a bad lecturer and does insufficient research. He will find himself again dismissed, this time without redress and with little hope of employment elsewhere.

There are, it is true, some educational institutions in America which, so far, have been strong enough to hold out. This, however, is only possible for an institution which has great prestige and has brave men in charge of its policy. Consider, for example, what Senator McCarthy has said about Harvard. He said he "couldn't conceive of anyone sending children to Harvard University where they would be open to indoctrination by Communist professors." At Harvard, he said, there is a "smelly mess which people sending sons and daughters there should know about." Institutions less eminent than Harvard could hardly face such a blast.

The power of the police, however, is a more serious and more universal phenomenon than Senator McCarthy. It is, of course, greatly increased by the atmosphere of fear which exists on both sides of the Iron Curtain. If you live in Russia and cease to be sympathetic with Communism, you will suffer unless you keep silence even in the bosom of your family. In America, if you have been a Communist and you cease to be, you are also liable to penalties, not legal—unless you have been trapped into perjury—but economic and social. There is only one thing that you can do to escape such penalties, and that is to sell yourself to the Department of Justice as an informer, when your success will depend upon what tall stories you can get the FBI to believe.

The increase of organization in the modern world demands new institutions if anything in the way of liberty is to be preserved. The situation is analogous to that which arose through the increased power of monarchs in the sixteenth century. It was against their excessive power that the whole fight of traditional liberalism was fought and won. But after their power had faded, new powers at least as dangerous arose, and the worst of these in our day is the power of the police. There is, so far as I can see, only one possible remedy, and that is the establishment of a second police force designed to prove innocence, not guilt. People often say that it is better that ninety-nine guilty men should escape than that one innocent man should be punished. Our institutions are founded upon the opposite view. If a man is accused, for example, of a murder, all the resources of the State, in the shape of policemen and detectives, are employed to prove his guilt, whereas it is left to his individual efforts to prove his innocence. If he employs detectives, they have to be private detectives paid out of his own pocket or that of his friends. Whatever his employment may have been, he will have neither time nor opportunity to continue earning money by means of it. The lawyers for the prosecution are paid by the State. His lawyers have to be paid by him, unless he pleads poverty, and then they will probably be less eminent than those of the prosecution. All this is quite unjust. It is at least as much in the public interest to prove that an innocent man has not committed a crime, as it is to prove that a guilty man has committed it. A police force designed to prove innocence should never attempt to prove guilt except in one kind of case: namely, where it is the authorities who are suspected of a crime. I think that the creation of such a second police force might enable us to preserve some of our traditional liberties, but I do not think that any lesser measure will do so.

One of the worst things resulting from the modern increase of the powers of the authorities is the suppression of truth and the spread of falsehood by means of public agencies. Russians are kept as far as possible in ignorance about Western countries, to the degree that people in Moscow imagine theirs to be the only subway in the world. Chinese intellectuals, since China became Communist, have been subjected to a horrible process called "brainwashing." Learned men who have acquired all the knowledge to be obtained in their subject from America or Western Europe are compelled to abjure what they have learned and to state that everything worth knowing is to be derived from Communist sources. They are subjected to such psychological pressure that they emerge broken men, able only to repeat, parrot fashion, the jejune formulas handed down by their official superiors. In Russia and China this sort of thing is enforced by direct penalties, not only to recalcitrant individuals, but also to their families. In other countries the process has not yet gone so far. Those who reported truthfully about the evils of Chiang Kai-shek's regime during the last years of his rule in China were not liquidated, but everything possible was done to prevent their truthful reports from being believed, and they became suspects in degrees which varied according to their eminence. A man who reports truly to his government about what he finds in a foreign country, unless his report agrees with official prejudices, not only runs a grave personal risk, but knows that his information will be ignored. There is, of course, nothing new in this except in degree. In 1899, General Butler, who was in command of British forces in South Africa, reported that it would require any army of at least two hundred thousand to subdue the Boers. For this unpopular opinion he was demoted, and was given no credit when the opinion turned out to be correct. But, although the evil is not new, it is very much greater in extent than it used to be. There is no longer, even among those who think themselves more or less liberal, a belief that it is a good thing to study all sides of a question. The purging of United States libraries in Europe and of school libraries in America, is designed to prevent people from knowing more than one side of a question. The *Index Expurgatorius* has become a recognized part of the policy of those who say that they fight for freedom. Apparently the authorities no longer have sufficient belief in the justice of their cause to think that it can survive the ordeal of free discussion. Only so long as the other side is unheard are they confident of obtaining credence. This shows a sad decay in the robustness of our belief in our own institutions. During the war, the Nazis did not permit Germans to listen to British radio, but nobody in England was hindered from listening to the German radio because our faith in our own cause was unshakable. So long as we prevent Communists from being heard, we produce the impression that they must have a very strong case. Free speech used to be advocated on the ground that free discussion would lead to the victory of the better opinion. This belief is being lost under the influence of fear. The result is that truth is one thing and "official truth" is another. This is the first step on the road to Orwell's "double-talk" and "double-think." It will be said that the legal existence of free speech has been preserved, but its effective existence is disastrously curtailed if the more important means of publicity are only open to opinions which have the sanctions of orthodoxy.

This applies more particularly to education. Even mildly liberal opinions expose an educator nowadays in some important countries to the risk of losing his job and being unable to find any other. The consequence is that children grow up in ignorance of many things that it is vitally important they should know, and that bigotry and obscurantism have a perilous measure of popular support.

Fear is the source from which all these evils spring, and fear, as is apt to happen in a panic, inspires the very actions which bring about the disasters that are dreaded. The dangers are real— they are indeed greater than at any previous time in human history—but all yielding to hysteria increases them. It is our clear duty in this difficult time, not only to know the dangers, but to view them calmly and rationally in spite of knowledge of their magnitude. Orwell's world of 1984, if we allow it to exist, will not exist for long. It will be only the prelude to universal death.

Climax and Change
Wyndham Lewis

In this short, trenchant piece, Wyndham Lewis focuses squarely on what he regards as Orwell's principle shortcoming—his romanticization of the working class. Several critics have commented on the implausibility of an effectively managed totalitarian state that disregards 85 percent of its populace as subhuman. Orwell's irony is clear: we normal, average people going about the business of our daily lives are indeed the proles. Lewis goes the critics one better by taking Orwell to task for both making a political generality of this group as well as imbuing it with a naive, fleshy humanity to which Orwell was both attracted and repelled. Lewis contends that *Nineteen Eight-Four* suffers for these indulgences, and Orwell himself comes off as an antediluvian socialist for his inability to overcome what Lewis calls "the *Wigan Pier* business."

At last, in 1945, Orwell's literary ambition was realized. He wrote a good book, *Animal Farm*.

As this is not literary criticism, I need not say very much as to the literary quality either of *Animal Farm* or *1984*. Treating of a society of animals, the theme brings to mind the classical masterpieces, which might, one would say, have inspired him to stylistic emulation. But this is not the case. The language is business-like and adequate but that is all. It is, however, a considerable feat of political lampooning. It is direct and dry, often witty. His "All animals are equal, but some are more equal

than others" is a splendidly witty climax to the
law-giving of the Pigs. And this little book, this
sardonic parable, was a turning-point in the reaction. He showed the same courage in writing this
as he had displayed as a "fighter for Freedom" in
Spain (which subsequently he found was not Freedom after all, but slavery). With *Animal Farm* he
led the wavering lefties out of the pink mists of
Left Land into the clear daylight. Few, it is true,
can or will follow him very far.

But *Animal Farm*, by reason of its success, made
it respectable to think clearly or to write without
humbug, if a young man was so disposed. It was in
a sense an iron curtain that came down on the
period of literary fellow-traveling, the work of an
ex-fellow-traveller.

But for himself, as I have just stressed, he remained with one foot on *The Road to Wigan Pier*:
the other foot in that region which had been finally opened to him by those foreigners of whom
we have read his unqualified praise. To the Europeans of course must be added Burnham, and all
the Trotskyite intelligentsia of the United States.

1984 is Wellsian in form, Wellsian in the style of
its writing, Wellsian in the colourlessness and ano-
nymity of the personae. I have discussed already,
in passing, the reason for the insignificance of the
humans who supply the drama in *1984*. There is,
in fact, very little drama, in consequence of the
extremely unelectrical quality of the human material. O'Brien, one of the two principal figures, is an
uninteresting business man. If all the other humans in Orwell's novels had not been of so uni-
formly devitalized and colourless a type, one would
have assumed that in *1984* the human element
had been keyed down to show off the inhuman
inquisitorial machinery to best advantage.

The manner in which Orwell has utilized the

knowledge he acquired of the Communist attitude to objective truth is admirable. His hideous palaces of Truth and Love are first-rate political creations. His elaborate bureaucratic monstrosities will quite likely one day be historical facts: this is one of those rare books in which we may actually be looking at something existing in the future. Those parts of Goldstein's secret text which we are shown are well written, clear, and plausible. The interminable torturing, culminating on the page with "I Love Big Brother," is impressively chilly and logical. However, O'Brien and his victim are a comic pair sometimes: I think of the part where he bends over the truth-loving Winston and says "How many fingers have I got?", and when the foolish Winston still insists on counting in the way he was taught to do in the good old days of "two and two make four," the button is pressed and he receives a slightly more agonizing dose of torture than the last time. Here and elsewhere mirth is induced instead of terror, partly because an acute sense of the ridiculous is not Orwell's strong point, and then since the human beings involved are prefabricated and bloodless, we experience no sympathetic pang.

The book as a whole is a first-rate political document. There is only one thing I am obliged to point out. The old London lying all around this floodlit bureaucratic centre, this almost balletesque survival, full of the "Proles" which are Orwell's specialty, does not (perhaps oddly) make the scene more real. It is unlikely, in a régime such as Orwell describes, that the millions of ordinary people will be left unmolested, treated indeed as though they were not there. The appetite for power involves the maximum interference with other human beings.

But the hero's Orwellian enthusiasm for the "Proles" ("Proles" meaning "proletariat") imports a silliness into this book which is rather a pity. It is a silliness of the author of *The Road to Wigan Pier*; and that is not the author who was writing *1984*.

This natural life surrounding the artificial lunacy of the votaries of "Big Brother" is the real, unspoilt life of the people: that is the idea. It is the hero's belief that out of these vigorous, sane multitudes will come salvation. O'Brien, the powerful Commissar, is able to read Winston's thoughts. He says to him, "You believe, Winston, that the Proles will revolt and destroy us all. This is an illusion. There is not the slightest possibility of their doing anything of that kind," etc. etc. etc. etc. etc. Winston clings to Orwell's sentimental fancies. It is really Orwell who is on the rack. But he obstinately adheres to his love of the proletariat, whereas he should in fact be loving "Big Brother."

So that my meaning should not be mistaken, I consider a South-side publican, a garage hand, a docker, a city policeman, a window-cleaner, just as good as a Prime Minister, a Lord President of the Council, an Air Marshal, or a Captain of Industry. But I consider Orwell's romancing about the former group an insult to them, for he really thought that they were marked off in some mysterious way from the second group, which they are not. The whole of the *Wigan Pier* business was a very stupid affectation. I explained this at the time I was writing about the *Wigan Pier* book, but it is best perhaps to remind you of the nature of my criticism. One feels in the case of *1984* that it is as though a lot of William Morris bric-à-brac had got mixed up with the hysterical realities of the ghastly time we live in. The gutter-songs of the London children—"Oranges and lemons say the Bells of St. Clements; You owe me five farthings say the Bells of St. Martin's"—echo romantically through

the book. But the London that existed when that
song was written is no longer there—was no longer
there in 1930. The bells of the various churches
rang out clearly once, when London was quite a
small place, and everyone was familiar with their
chimes. But this song is an archaeological relic;
and to use such a song to symbolize the vast and
roaring megalopolis of 1940 or '50 is absurd.

So we have the Old and the New contrasted. The
Wellsian nightmare of a crazed totalitarianism
stands for what socialism becomes when interpreted as Stalin has done: the delightful, old-fashioned
London of the nineteen thirties, 'forties and 'fifties,
with its hurdy-gurdies, its "Oranges and Lemons,"
and anything else you can think of to make it like
the London of Charles Dickens,—that stands for
the socialism of Keir Hardie, or Lansbury, and of
Orwell. For if, having seen what "State" socialism
is apt to turn into, we still remain Socialists, then
this is no doubt the correct symbolical contrast.

No one any longer believes in the *simpliste* notion of workers charged with an easily recognizable identity, causing them to be as distinct as
though all manual workers had black faces, and
all who were not manual workers white faces. No
one believes in the myth any longer of all these
black-faced people rising in revolt, killing all the
white-faced people and there being henceforth a
black-faced world. No one believes this because
they know that it is not an ultimate division,
working-class and nonworking-class; that there are
deeper divisions which ignore these very superfi-
cial ones. They know that proletarian revolt must
be engineered by members of the middle or upper
class, who do this out of ambition. They know that
when a revolution is over most of those who were
manual workers before it are still manual workers;
and few, if any, of the new leaders belong to the

class of manual workers. The Orwell picture is a long-out-dated socialism. His two humanities contrasted in *1984*, of, on the one hand, a virgin virile world of workers, bursting with potential leadership, on the other, a ruling class of the Stalinist party-pattern, is really socialism in one of its XIXth Century forms (probably medieval and guildish confronting the stream-lined, ruthless, efficiency-socialism of today).

I for one would have considered *1984* a better book had the "Prole" business been left out, and a more realistic treatment of the probable condition of the mass of the population been employed.

So, finally, I do not regard Orwell as *un malin* like Sartre, but a parallel with Sartre's case certainly exists. It seemed necessary to Orwell, in the interests of his reputation, not to withdraw from his conventionally leftish position. How conscious he was in following this line I do not know. But it is (and this is my argument) a false position, as with Sartre; and so, too, numbers of other writers obliged to toe a party-line of *some* sort.

In these politics-ridden times writers experience irresistible pressures, this way or that. Yet this pressure in a still free community can be almost as destructive as the writing-to-order in Communist Russia. Every writer should keep himself free from party, clear of any group-pull: at least this is *my* view of truth. My truth is objective truth, in other words. In England the entire intellectual atmosphere is impregnated with liberalism, or rather what liberalism transforms itself into so as to become more-and-still-more liberal. With us the pressure to achieve conformity is very great. Whether in the matter of costume, or hair-cut or intellectual fashion.

Orwell possessed a very vigorous mind, he went much farther on the road to an ultimate political realism than any of his companions or immediate English contemporaries. But you have seen him noting the great advantage the political writer of European origin has over the Englishman. Orwell, I feel, *did* almost wrench himself free. But the whole of his history is one of misdirected energy, and when, at the end, he transcended his earlier self, it was still to retain a bit of the old sentiment, to show his heart was still in the right place, in spite of the cruel and horrible things he had said about "The Great Russian Socialist Experiment."

America's View of George Orwell
John P. Rossi

Orwell achieved a wide following in America only in the final years of his career—and his life. After *Animal Farm* became a bestseller in 1946, the commercial success of *Nineteen Eighty-Four* was fairly secure. Professor Rossi's account, published originally in 1981, traces the factors underlying America's initial indifference to Orwell, which was followed by lavish praise for his last works and the development of a cult that nearly mythologized him.

Orwell's writings—most appearing posthumously in the United States—served, during the fifties, both to inspire an American Left grappling with its disillusionment with Soviet Communism and to fuel the mounting pitch of Cold War anti-Communist sentiment on the Right. Diverse though the political postures of those who embraced it were, for a time George Orwell's message seemed to have universal appeal in America.

It is now almost a third of a century since George Orwell's publication of *Animal Farm* made him famous in the United States. Outside of certain radical and literary circles Orwell was virtually unknown in America before 1946. He had written an occasional piece for journals like the *New Republic*, Dwight Macdonald's idiosyncratic *Politics*, plus a series of "London Letters" for Philip Rahv's radical magazine, *Partisan Review*. In the early 1930's *Harper's* had published some of his earlier works, novels like *A Clergyman's Daughter* and

Burmese Days, and non-fiction pieces like *Down and Out in Paris and London*. They were largely ignored, unread, and unreviewed.

Orwell's initial failure to reach an American audience had many causes. First and foremost, he did not fit into any recognizable political category, right, left or center. Those American intellectuals who knew his work were uneasy with him. He was a self-proclaimed socialist who seemed to take a special pleasure in assaulting his fellow leftists, a foe of nationalism who wrote movingly and beautifully about English patriotism, the English countryside and English customs like tea drinking and pubs. Secondly, in the 1930's he had attacked communism as a form of totalitarianism just as evil as fascism or nazism. Most American leftists, still caught up in the naive belief of "no enemies on the left," felt uncomfortable before this indictment. Finally, most of Orwell's writing before 1946 was of the kind that would have limited appeal in the United States. His fiction and political writings dealt with topics that were of peculiar interest to the English and his essays on such disparate topics as humorous postcards, the public schools or English murder mysteries also fit within a framework that most Americans could not follow. *Animal Farm* changed all that.

Animal Farm was first published in August of 1946. It was an immediate critical and popular success. The initial reviews in the mass circulation magazines like *Time*, *Newsweek*, the *New Yorker*, the *New York Times Magazine*, and so on were all laudatory. Edmund Wilson, doyen of American intellectual reviewers, heaped praise on *Animal Farm*, comparing Orwell as a satirist to Voltaire and Swift. Edward Weeks in the *Atlantic* reviewed *Animal Farm* very favorably but revealed considerable political naïveté by commenting that Orwell's fable showed a "clever hostility if one applies it to Soviet Russia." Whom else the analogy fit is difficult to imagine.

In the politically oriented journals *Animal Farm* got a lukewarm reception. Most of these journals were leftist and just beginning to move away from the sycophantic admiration for "our Soviet Ally." The first drafts of the cold war were beginning to blow through left-wing political circles in America and Orwell's work arrived in this country just as the American Left was struggling to formulate a new attitude toward Russia. The reception given *Animal Farm* in journals like the *New Republic* and the *Nation* reflected the political confusion then rampant in American leftist circles. Isaac Rosenfeld in the *Nation* bitterly attacked *Animal Farm*. He denied that Orwell's interpretation of revolution had any validity when applied to the Soviet Union. According to Rosenfeld, to attempt to apply Orwell's hostile view to Stalin's Russian regime only revealed the reactionary flavor of *Animal Farm*. Rosenfeld also argued that Orwell did not tell his audience anything about the Russian revolution it did not already know. He did not tell them where in America this had been made so clear, certainly not in the pages of the *Nation*, a journal which slavishly followed every contortion of the party line during the 1930's and early 1940's. Rosenfeld's hostile review was matched by George Soulé in the pages of the *New Republic*, then also a consistent apologist for Russian behavior. He found *Animal Farm* "dull" and the analogy to events in the Soviet Union since the revolution "creaking" and "clumsy." Soulé managed to confuse the rather obvious characters of the pigs, Snowball and Napoleon. He thought Napoleon was supposed to be Lenin, failing to discover Stalin in this successful pig who betrayed the revolution. Soulé also was angry at Orwell's portrait of Soviet education with vicious dogs being trained as the secret police. Nor could he see any parallel in Russian history for the slaughter of the horse, Boxer, who had labored so mightily to make the revolution a success. This is an astounding commentary on his blindness to Russian history in the 1930's, especially Stalin's purge of the old Bolsheviks, party faithful, and disillusioned masses who had devoted themselves entirely to making the revolution a success.

The negative views could not offset the growing success and popularity of *Animal Farm*. The Book of the Month Club announced that it had picked Orwell's fable as its selection for August 1946 thus guaranteeing Orwell a large audience. The growing success of *Animal Farm*— eventually it sold over 500,000 copies in the United States—revived interest in Orwell's earlier work. Beginning in 1946 with a collection of his essays, *Dickens, Dali, and Others*, Orwell's early writings began to appear regularly in the United States. Eventually, by 1958 everything of any consequence that he had written was published to growing critical, and often popular, acclaim.

The key to Orwell's success in America, after his relative obscurity, was a matter of timing. Not only was *Animal Farm* a clever story which could be understood and appreciated on two levels, as a children's tale of how success corrupts or as a highly imaginative indictment of the failures and betrayals of the Russian Revolution, but it also appeared at a crucial time in the relationship between the Soviet Union and the West. *Animal Farm* was published just as the cold war began. In fact, it came out less than six months after Winston Churchill's famous "iron curtain" speech at Fulton, Missouri, first brought home the reality of new tensions with Russia to the American public. America was just beginning to discover that the Soviet Union was not the noble, disinterested ally of World War II. In 1946 this realization made its first deep impression on the American mind. This realization made Orwell's brand of "tough" realism very appealing. Possessing impeccable leftist credentials he could not be dismissed as just another reactionary warmonger. After the success of *Animal Farm* Orwell found outlets for his essays which now began to appear regularly in major American journals like the *New Yorker* and the *New York Times Magazine*. His writing won him a larger following in the United States than in England possibly because of America's growing awareness of its international responsibilities and its deepening absorption into the cold war. Orwell's growing American reputation was enhanced in June 1949 by the publication of his grim anti-utopian novel *1984*.

As with *Animal Farm*, *1984* was chosen by the Book of the Month Club as one of its selections. It was also condensed in the *Reader's Digest* for its September 1949 issue, a sure sign that Orwell had established himself as a popular author. This time there were no negative reactions or reviews as had been the case in England where Isaac Deutscher had labeled *1984* nothing more than an ideological "superweapon of the Cold War." The closest thing to a negative review came from Diana Trilling in the pages of *Nation*. Trilling was profoundly impressed by *1984*, but she was put off by the way Orwell played upon the reader's emotions and by the relentless quality of its tone. Still she called Orwell a rarity, a man who places his own brand of realism above the use of political partisanship. After the Berlin blockade, the Communist coup in Czechoslovakia, the growing awareness of Russian espionage and the imminent fall of China. Orwell's political views and predictions no longer seemed extreme or unrealistic. *1984* proved a runaway best-seller, over the next twenty-five years selling eleven million copies, a figure by the way, matching *Animal Farm*. Both novels were made into films in the cold war-haunted 1950's: *Animal Farm* as a clever and powerful cartoon; *1984* as a somber film that failed to capture the terrible atmosphere of Orwell's grim future.

Following his death in January 1950 interests in Orwell's writings remained steady throughout the rest of the decade. In fact, a close examination of the writing about Orwell personally or his publications reveal an interesting example of the way a writer's reputation undergoes ups and downs. Between Orwell's death in 1950 and 1956 over thirty articles or reviews dealing with him appeared in the popular American journals. These varied from brief notes in *Time* or *Newsweek* to longer appreciations of his work in major popular journals such as the *Saturday Review of Literature*, *Harper's*, and *Atlantic*. Only one could be considered negative, a review in the *Nation* of the American publication of *Homage to Catalonia* in 1952. After the mid-1950's interest in Orwell and his work declines sharply. Between 1957 and 1965 the total of the articles and reviews about Orwell drops to six, with four of them jammed in the period 1957–59. They are all favorable. Between 1965 and 1974 interest in his work undergoes a steady, if slow, revival hastened partly by the publication of his four-volume *Collected Letters and Journalism* in 1968. The total of articles and reviews now rises to thirty-two still favorable but no longer exclusively so. An attempt was made in those years to come to grips with Orwell while avoiding mythologizing him. He came to be looked on, not just as a Cold Warrior with a conscience, but as a serious, if flawed novelist, and a journalist of superb qualities.

In his fine essay, "Freedom of the Press," which was to serve as the introduction to *Animal Farm*, but was ultimately dropped, Orwell wrote: "It is the liberals who fear liberty and the intellectuals who want to do dirt on the intellect." This quality of attacking your friends and exposing the weaknesses of your allies was an Orwellian trait. It gave added impact to what he wrote since it lent a note of honesty and disinterestedness to what he had to say. It was also precisely the quality that came to endear Orwell to alienated American leftist intellectuals in the postwar years. American intellectuals, for the most part, had been naive about the menace of communism both before and during the war and had been among the leading apologists for Russian actions during the last stages of World War II. Disillusion set in rapidly. As Conor Cruse O'Brien has noted. Orwell shook the confidence of the Left "perhaps permanently, making them ashamed of their cliches, and made them more scrupulous in their political enthusiasm." Nowhere was this truer than in the United States.

Those who jumped on Orwell's bandwagon read like a "Who's Who" of the American liberal establishment. Edmund Wilson, Lionel Trilling, Philip Rahv, Irving Howe, Arthur Schlesinger, Jr., and Max Lerner are just some of the names. These men were all distinguished by their probity and their determination to find a viable political position for American progressives, something that would serve to distinguish the Left in the United States from the taint of "fellow traveling." What they found appealing in Orwell was his realism, his common sense, his obvious decency, and the clarity of his thinking. Many were disillusioned, or potentially disillusioned, socialists and the man who had discovered the flaws of socialism ten to fifteen years before had a dramatic appeal to them. In truth they also found Orwell's ability to spot a fraud endearing. He was a great hater and saved his special venom for his fellow socialists, men and women, he once wrote, "who take their cookery from Paris and their opinions from Moscow," "all that dreary tribe of high minded women and sandal wearers and bearded fruit juice drinkers who come flocking towards the smell of progress like bluebottles to a dead cat."

The American leftist intellectual, angry with the course of events since the end of World War II and the Russian betrayal of peace during the cold war, found comfort in Orwell's assessment. As they sought a new political direction Orwell became one of their guides. At the same time his attacks on communism and his exposures of Soviet totalitarianism won Orwell a considerable following among American conservatives. There is, at times, a Tory quality to Orwell's thinking, a respect for individualism and a nostalgia for the past, that conservatives found sympathetic. Orwell had written that "all revolutions are failures, but they are not all the same failure," a view shared by American conservatives who were looking for intellectual support for contemporary Western society. Moreover, as Malcolm Muggeridge noted, the bourgeoisie in the West "is always looking for someone who combines impeccable intelligentsia credentials with a passion, secret or avowed . . . for maintaining the status quo." Orwell provided that.

In the late 1940's, early 1950's, Orwell became virtually a saint for the American Right. The Luce press in particular canonized Orwell. *1984* not only was reviewed favorably by *Time* but also a special editorial in *Life* called the American public's attention to it. *1984*, they argued, pointed up the dangers confronting the free world with special impact because "it comes from a leftwinger who is cautioning his fellow intellectuals of the left to beware lest their desire to help the common man wind up in trapping him in hopeless misery." The publication of each new Orwell work in the United States during the 1950's elicited greater praise from the Luce organization. For example, the collection of his essays, *Such, Such Were the Joys* in 1953 was heralded in *Time* for the way it showed that much of Orwell's energy in the 1940's "was devoted to carrying on a guerilla campaign against woolheaded fellow travellers who were poisoning English intellectual life." Before his death Orwell had tried without much success to counter this enshrinement as a conservative hero. He published a letter in *Life* and the *New York Times Magazine* in which he reiterated his loyalty to the Labour party and to the concept of socialism. To those who saw *1984* as an attack on socialism he countered that it was really designed to show up the perversions of communism and fascism. Orwell's letter had little impact on American conservative views of his work. He remained a hero to them.

Following his death in January 1950 Orwell's reputation went through a period where he was as overpraised in the United States as he had been neglected in the past. Each new publication of his works, a process that lasted through the decade, was greeted with enthusiasm in both the popular and the political journals. Just a month after he died. James Stern, an Irish-born novelist, wrote an assessment of Orwell's published work in the *New Republic* that was typical of critical evaluations of the 1950's. Future critics, said Stern, may very well describe Orwell "as the most important English writer to have lived his whole life during the first half of the twentieth century." He then concluded in a vein that was to be repeated over and over again in American journals: "England never produced a novelist more honest, more courageous, more concerned with the common man—and with common sense." This constitutes a virtual anointing.

Orwell's books sold well, especially *Animal Farm* and *1984*, and his popularity grew. The prevalent view of him was consistently positive. Orwell was portrayed at the last honest man, and the words "common sense" and "decency" were constantly associated with him. This is easily understandable if overdone. In a decade that prided itself on its rejection of ideology Orwell's nondoctrinaire brand of socialism, which stressed honesty and fairness, was very appealing. Also, to a generation of intellectuals searching for their roots Orwell was a powerful antidote to their anxiety. It is interesting to note that the mythologizing of Orwell never went as far in England as it did in America. There was a large left-wing audience in England that did not appreciate Orwell's strictures on their beliefs. Moreover, the cold war mentality that came to prevail in the United States in the early 1950's did not mature in as extreme a form as in England. Orwell had his English admirers. Muggeridge, V. S. Pritchett, etc., but their view of him was more balanced and more realistic than many of their American compatriots.

Occasionally, there was a dissent from this lionizing of Orwell in America. Probably the most significant was a bilious review of the American edition of *Homage to Catalonia* by Herbert Matthews in the *Nation*. While calling *Homage to Catalonia* an honest, vivid, personal account of Orwell's experiences in the Spanish civil war, Matthews felt that it only deserved two cheers. Orwell, he argued, was politically ignorant before the civil war and he remained politically ignorant afterward.

He was right about the counterrevolutionary nature of communism but he reached this correct assessment for the wrong reasons. He never really understood the issues at stake in Spain because of the nature of his own political alignment. Spain disillusioned Orwell and in the process poisoned his mind for the rest of his life about the frailties of the Left. It made him overly suspicious of the Left and simplistic in his understanding of its problems. Matthews's review did little to harm Orwell's American reputation. In fact, some of his arguments were so silly as to strengthen Orwell's hold over the thinking of the American Left. To accuse Orwell of political ignorance in 1936 is ludicrous. Before he went to Spain in December 1936 Orwell had already completed the *Road to Wigan Pier* with its long section outlining his views about socialism and politics in general. He had written *Burmese Days* with its indictment of imperialism a couple of years before. Both works showed mature insight into the political realities of the issues of the 1930's. There is also evidence that Orwell had read and studied Marx and the various Marxian commentators before this time. While not yet a committed socialist (Spain completed that process) Orwell had already formulated most of his major political views by 1936.

Matthews's review was just about the last negative comment on Orwell to appear in the United States for quite a while. There was a minor flap in 1955 when the cartoon version of *Animal Farm* appeared. Spencer Brown in the February 1955 issue of *Commentary* published a short essay. "Strange Doings at 'Animal Farm'" in which he noted how critics in the major papers and journals had managed to review *Animal Farm* without referring to its analogy to the Russian Revolution. Brown was angered by the way the pigs were portrayed in the advertising for the film as McCarthy types or Southern senators but not as Stalinist figures. This was corrected, however, in later reviews and advertising and the film did fairly well both critically and at the box office.

Probably the most balanced assessment of Orwell's work in the 1950's came from the pen of Dwight Macdonald, a fellow disillusioned leftist, who like Orwell did not fit into any easily recognizable category. Writing in the *New Yorker* in March 1959, Macdonald analyzed the publication of two books of some importance for contemporary socialism: Leon Trotsky's *Diary* and Orwell's *Road to Wigan Pier*. Both books initially appeared in the mid-1930's and both came from the pens of highly individualistic thinkers. Enormously impressed by Orwell's account, Macdonald called it "the best sociological reporting I know." What particularly impressed him was the nonideological nature of *Road to Wigan Pier* as compared to the doctrinaire quality that ran through every page of Trotsky's *Diary*. A first-class controversialist himself, Macdonald was impressed by Orwell's standards: he was harder on himself and his own side than he was on his enemies, a trait by the way which Macdonald shares with Orwell. Macdonald also contrasted Orwell's feeling for people with Trotsky's perception of everything through the distorting mirror of class. Orwell never romanticized the poor and Macdonald enjoyed Orwell's openly stated determination to judge poverty by his own clearly spelled out standards.

Macdonald was not blind to Orwell's limitations. For one thing, Orwell was too quick with predictions about the collapse of the British middle class or assertions that the British standard of living depended on the possession of an empire. These, of course, were not borne out by the events of the next generation. Much of the abuse of his fellow socialists which runs through the last half of *Road to Wigan Pier* Macdonald found distasteful, a point which has bothered other admirers of Orwell. He was a great hater, and though he found it difficult to hate someone he knew, Orwell seemed to enjoy overwhelming his enemies with rhetorical abuse.

Following the appearance of Macdonald's essay there was relatively little written about Orwell in the United States until the mid-1960's. Now his reputation was firmly established, his books sold well, and he was constantly quoted. For many American intellectuals, especially the cold war-haunted ones, Orwell became a virtual totem against whom the political-literary figures of the 1930's, 1940's and 1950's were constantly measured. American intellectuals enthusiastically reviewed studies of Orwell by Anthony Powell and George Woodcock. On the other hand, Raymond Williams's tendentious, and highly critical, examination of Orwell's career was passed over quietly in the United States unlike in England where it started a reevaluation of Orwell's work. As John Wain had noted in England in the early 1970's it suddenly became fashionable to snipe at Orwell, "Now as then, (cf. 1930s) his truth-telling is dismissed as 'perverse' and his warnings are shrugged off by what he himself called 'the huge tribe known as the right left people'. Now as then, the most vicious digs at Orwell came from men whose basic intellectual position is totalitarian." This was never the case in the United States. There were Americans critical of Orwell, but he remained essentially a highly popular figure here. Finally, the appearance of Orwell's *Collected Letters and Correspondence* in 1968 saw his reputation enhanced in the United States. These four volumes showed Orwell at his best and American reviewers were confirmed in their high opinion of his intellectual honesty, personal decency, as well as the breadth of his interest. Only Mary McCarthy, in a highly critical review of his *Collected Letters*, dissented in any serious way from these glowing estimates. While admiring Orwell, she argued that he was in danger of being treated as a mythic figure in America. She zeroed in on two themes that ran through much of his career: his hatred of arbitrary power and his refusal to join in whatever was fashionable intellectually. These were attractive qualities, according to McCarthy, but they also hid certain flaws in Orwell's thinking. How, for example, to bring about the desired socialist state while detesting power? She also suggested that Orwell's hatred of the intellectually fashionable was the source of his fierce denunciations of his fellow leftists, an observation other writers had missed.

By the 1970's Orwell had entered deeply into the consciousness of the American scene. No longer an eccentric English intellectual anymore Orwell had become institutionalized as an American cult figure. In the words of Irving Howe, an uncritical admirer, Orwell was a hero to an entire generation. "More than any English intellectual of our age, he embodied the values of personal independence and a fiercely democratic radicalism." This is a perception of Orwell that has predominated to the present. To an age tired of intellectual heroes who fade almost with the change of seasons, it is an enormously appealing evaluation.

All or Nothing
Richard Rees

Sir Richard Rees was a close friend of Orwell, one
of the few outsiders who spent time with him at his
remote outpost on the island of Jura in the Hebrides,
where Orwell finished writing *Nineteen Eighty-Four*
while suffering with the tuberculosis that would finish
him little more than a year later.

In this excerpt from Rees's study, *George Orwell:
Fugitive from the Camp of Victory*, he provides an
intimate perspective on Orwell's mood, given his
health, as it affected *Nineteen Eighty-Four*. Particularly, he believes that Orwell wrote the "inquisition"
scene while in a state of extreme physical suffering,
which accounts for its much-criticized sadomasochistic sensationalism.

But there are deeper questions concerning Winston's
ultimate torture and capitulation in Room 101, where
he cries out, "Do it to Julia!" What possessed Orwell
to leave his character with less than even human-
ness in the end? And how important is Winston's
ordeal to what Orwell was really addressing about
modern societies in *Nineteen Eighty-Four*? Rees offers a number of novel conclusions that bear comparison with those in James Connors' essay, "Do It to
Julia," which follows.

1984 is not so obviously a masterpiece as *Animal
Farm*; but it is wider and more ambitious in scope
and has probably been even more influential. It,
too, contains images and phrases—Big Brother,
for example, and *doublethink*—which have become

familiar throughout Western civilization; and it is perhaps mainly thanks to this book that the adjective "Orwellian" can be used wherever English is spoken with almost the same probability of being understood as "Shavian" or "Wellsian." Yet it is not easy to decide how good a book it really is. Writing of *Uncle Tom's Cabin* Orwell called it the supreme example of what he thought of as "good bad" books. "It is an unintentionally ludicrous book, full of preposterous melodramatic incidents; it is also deeply moving and essentially true." ("Good Bad Books" in *Shooting an Elephant*.) He further prophesied that it would outlast the entire works of George Moore and Virginia Woolf, although he could think of no strictly literary test by which its superiority could be proved.

Without conceding that it need be called in any way a bad book, I would make the same prophecy about *1984*, and I would add the entire works of Joyce, with the doubtful exception of *Ulysses*, to the list of shorter-lived books. *1984* is full of melodramatic incidents, but they are not preposterous in the sense of being artistically inappropriate or even—fantastic though one hopes this will some day appear—particularly hard to believe. They are, however, in one or two places rather flatly written and one of them might be called unintentionally ludicrous. But although Orwell must often have been feeling tired and ill when he was writing the book, it has very few weak passages and is, in the main, a sustained and powerful imaginative effort which very few contemporary novelists could approach.

Among Orwell's earlier heroes Gordon Comstock was in rebellion against the money god who commanded him to become a conventional business man; and George Bowling, more modestly, wanted merely to avoid being streamlined, and to be able to call his soul his own, though he lived in fear of a coming regime of thugs with rubber truncheons. But in *1984* Winston Smith is already living under a regime far worse than any that Gordon could have imagined and in which George's worst fears have been realized.

> It was a bright cold day in April, and the clocks were striking thirteen. Winston Smith, his chin nuzzled onto his breast in an effort to escape the vile wind, slipped quickly through the glass doors of Victory Mansions, though not quickly enough to prevent a swirl of gritty dust from entering along with him.

That is the first paragraph of *1984*. Except for the twenty-four-hour clock it recalls the first paragraph of *Coming up for Air:*

> The idea really came to me the day I got my new false teeth. I remember the morning well. At about a quarter to eight I'd nipped out of bed and got into the bathroom just in time to shut the kids out. It was a beastly January morning, with a dirty yellowish-grey sky. . . .

And of *The Clergyman's Daughter:*

> As the alarm clock on the chest of drawers exploded like a horrid little bomb of bell metal, Dorothy, wrenched from the depths of some complex, troubling dream, awoke with a start and lay on her back looking into the darkness with extreme exhaustion.

Poor Winston is going to share Dorothy's extreme exhaustion and not George Bowling's cheerfulness and vigor.

He was born in 1945 and has lived through an

atomic war and the subsequent period of social disturbances out of which the world of the 1980's has crystallized. There are three great world powers— Oceania, Eurasia and Eastasia—which correspond, though only roughly, to the actual power blocs of the present day. There is a continuous desultory war between them which none of them seriously desires to bring to a end, because a state of war creates a favorable atmosphere for their home policies. The three world empires, in fact, prop one another up "like three sheaves of corn." Oceania consists of the Americas, the British Commonwealth, and the British Isles, the latter being known as Airstrip One, with London for its capital. The social and economic system is as follows: a ruling Pary (with a, possibly fictitious and merely symbolic, Leader known as Big Brother) divided into two branches, the Inner Party and the Outer Party. The Inner Party members are the rulers and the Outer Party, to which Winston belongs, consists of secretarial and technical employees. The remaining 85 per cent of the population are known as "the proles"; they have no rights and no responsibilities and are regarded as of no more political significance than animals. The economic system is nominally socialist in that all private ownership, except of petty personal possessions, has been abolished. All property belongs to the State, represented by the Inner Party.

In all this, Orwell is merely exaggerating the tendencies he observed in the world of his day; and he succeeds in packing into *1984* nearly all the ideas of all his previous books. *1984* is often compared to Aldous Huxley's *Brave New World* as though one of them will prove to be a more correct prophecy than the other. But it is their resemblances rather than their differences that are significant. Orwell and Huxley are disturbed by much the same features of twentieth-century life, and the only important difference between them is that Huxley predicts that the hypertrophy of these features will be due to a combination of sloth, or apathy, with brutish hedonism, while according to Orwell it will be due to the same sloth or apathy combined with brutish will-to-power. Why should there not be a large measure of truth in both diagnoses? The ruling Party in *1984* is an oligarchy which appears to have discovered the secret of retaining power indefinitely. It has understood that "the secret of rulership is to combine a belief in one's own infallibility with the power to learn from past mistakes." It does this by correcting its mistakes, but falsifying the past so as to prove that the mistakes were never made; and its members prove this not only to their subjects but to themselves, by the technique of *doublethink*.

> The new aristocracy was made up for the most part of bureaucrats, scientists, technicians, trade-union organisers, publicity experts, sociologists, teachers, journalists and professional politicians . . . As compared with their opposite numbers [i.e. ruling castes] in past ages, they were less avaricious, less tempted by luxury, *hungrier for pure power* [my italics] and, above all, more conscious of what they were doing and more intent on crushing opposition . . .

For the student of Orwell the composition of the new aristocracy is very significant. Triumphant progressivism has shaken off the nudists and sandal-wearers; the "little fat men" of *The Road to Wigan Pier* have become robot bureaucrats with fruity voices and spectacles which in certain lights produce the effect of "two blank discs instead of eyes"; and the folly of the intellectuals in the nineteen-thirties has sown seeds which have blossomed into a full-blown sadism:

... in the general hardening of outlook that set in round about 1930, practices which had long since been abandoned, in some cases for hundreds of years—imprisonment without trial, the use of war prisoners as slaves, public executions, torture to extract confessions, the use of hostages and the deportation of whole populations—not only became common again, but were tolerated and even defended by people who considered themselves enlightened and progressive.

That is from a heretical (but true) history of the twentieth century issued by the Party as a trap for Party members who are suspected of being recalcitrant to the official "truth." It represents, of course, a logical development of Orwell's own views as expressed in his earlier books. Of twentieth-century socialism it speaks as follows:

... in each variant of Socialism that appeared from about 1900 onwards the aim of establishing liberty and equality was more and more openly abandoned. The new movements which appeared in the middle years of the century, Ingsoc in Oceania, Neo-Bolshevism in Eurasia, Death-Worship, as it is commonly called, in Eastasia, had the conscious aim of perpetuating *un*freedom and *in*equality.

The oligarchy is adoptive and not hereditary; it recruits, by examination, intelligent children from the Outer Party. But it deals with the proles in the manner of the Spartans with their helots. The Thought Police take no interest in their opinions but simply liquidate any of them who show signs of initiative or originality. Party members, on the other hand, are spied upon continuously by microphone and "telescreen" (two-way television) and are tortured and brain-washed if they show the faintest sign of lapsing from orthodoxy. All this, too, is a consistent development of Orwell's former predictions. But there are two new features in *1984* which require examination. One is his apparent belief that the oligarchy would be able to treat the proles (85 per cent of the population) as a negligible factor, and the other is the theory that the oligarchy could survive indefinitely with a philosophy, or religion, limited to pure sadistic love of power.

To take the second and simpler point first. O'Brien, the Party philsopher who is concerned with the purging of Winston's heresy, explains the Party's philosophy as follows:

> Power is in inflicting pain and humiliation. Power is in tearing human minds to pieces and putting them together again in new shapes of your own choosing. Do you begin to see, then, what kind of world we are creating? It is the exact opposite of the stupid hedonistic Utopias that the old reformers imagined. A world of fear and treachery and torment, a world of trampling and being trampled upon, a world which will grow not less but *more* merciless as it refines itself. Progress in our world will be towards more pain ... Always we shall have the heretic here at our mercy, screaming with pain, broken up, contemptible—and in the end utterly penitent, saved from himself, crawling to our feet of his own accord. .... A world of victory after victory, triumph after triumph after triumph: an endless pressing, pressing, pressing upon the nerve of power.

I do not suggest that sentiments like this are incredible. Other writers—D. H. Lawrence, for example—have shown good reason for believing that the world of atheistic science and machinery is uprooting the human psyche and thwarting its natural growth and will end by distorting it into monstrous shapes. But in Orwell's case it does appear that his actual *writing* changes for the worse when the dialogue between O'Brien and Winston begins: and in order to judge the above passage we need to retrace Winston's story up to this point.

He is an editor in the Ministry of Truth, where his job is to rewrite the past, as recorded in back numbers of newspapers, so as to make it correspond with the Party's present policy. He is a social misfit, a harborer of unorthodox thoughts, and a predestined victim of the Thought Police. He gets involved in an excruciatingly dangerous love affair with Julia, another secret rebel. He shares some of Orwell's own characertistics. For example, he is attracted by the fine, creamy quality of the paper in an old, or pre-1940, notebook which he buys in a junk shop and uses for a secret diary (his first overt step toward perdition); he is troubled by a cough in the mornings; and he has dreams of a holiday in a Golden Country in the Thames valley, where there are beech woods and slow streams with dace swimming in the pools under the willow trees. As an intellectual he resembles Gordon Comstock and in his nostalgia for the past and for a country life he resembles George Bowling; and the points in which he resembles them are the points in which they resemble their common author. He rents a room over the junk shop, where he and Julia can be together on the rare occasions when they dare snatch a few hours from their "voluntary" after-hours work for the Party. Needless to say, they have walked into a trap. The proprietor of the shop is a member of the Thought Police.

One day they are looking out of the window at a prole woman hanging out diapers on a washing line. It occurs to Winston that the proles are at least keeping the body and the instincts alive through the years of tyranny, and that if he and his kind can keep the mind alive then surely some

day the proles will awaken to mental life; and
although he will be dead he will at least have
contributed to the life of the future.

> "We are the dead," he said.
> "We are the dead," echoed Julia dutifully.
> "You are the dead," said an iron voice behind
> them.

They are about to be arrested, and the voice comes
from a telescreen hidden behind a picture.

> "It was behind the picture," said Julia.
> "It was behind the picture," said the voice.

The picture suddenly falls.

> "Now they can see us," said Julia.
> "Now we can see you," said the voice.

A little later:

> "The house is surrounded," said Winston.
> "The house is surrounded," said the voice.
> He heard Julia snap her teeth together. "I suppose
> we may as well say good-bye," she said.
> "You may as well say good-bye," said the voice.

From then on the story becomes a catalogue of
horrors, and this rather flat introduction to them,
with the overworked repetitions, does suggest to
me that Orwell was tired when he reached this
point in the book. After weeks, or months, in the
cells of the Ministry of Love, Winston is allowed to
see himself in a mirror and he breaks down in tears
on seeing his ravaged face and wasted frame. It is
tragically likely that the whole account of his interrogation and torture, including the exposition of
the Party's sadistic philosophy—"pressing, pressing,

pressing upon the nerve of power"—is a reflection of Orwell's sense of the ruthless ravages of consumption upon his own body. He survived the publication of the book by only seven months.

The first three-quarters of the book are a brilliant, macabre and convincing picture of what life might be like under a totalitarian oligarchy, but it does rather weaken the force of the warning when the dynamic of the system is described in such lurid and oversimple terms. I am convinced that Orwell would have conceived the last part of the book more subtly if his health had not been breaking down.

The other feature of *1984*, besides the Party philosophy, which calls for comment is the description of the proles. Although they constitute 85 per cent of the population, nobody pays any attention to them—except for the Thought Police's periodical liquidation of any outstanding personalities who might cause trouble. They are left to run wild in their slums. "Proles and animals are free." Even the older among them have only hazy memories of the first half of the century, and the constant rewriting of history and news items makes any general knowledge of the past impossible. So they have no means of knowing whether their conditions have improved or deteriorated. Winston Smith's attitude toward them varies. "If there is hope," he wrote in his diary, "it lies in the proles." If they ever became conscious of their own strength, they would only need to rise up and shake themselves "like a horse shaking off flies." But he is very seldom able to feel any hope. "When you put it into words it sounded reasonable: it was when you looked at the human beings passing you in the street that it became an act of faith."

The real trouble seems to be that when Winston

looks at the proles he sees them, as Orwell himself
was once inclined to do, as comic post-card figures:
"Two bloated women, one of them with her hair
coming down, had got hold of the same saucepan
. . ." Or an old man reminiscing in a pub: "Quite
the gent, 'e was—dress shirt, top 'at, black overcoat.
'E was kind of zig-zagging across the pavement,
and I bumps into 'im accidental-like. 'E says, 'Why
can't you look where you're going?' 'e says. I says,
'Ju think you've bought the bleeding pavement?' ";
or a street scene: "Girls in full bloom, with crudely
lipsticked mouths, and youths who chased the girls,
and swollen waddling women who showed you
what the girls would look like in ten years' time."
No wonder his idea of salvation through the proles
appears to him "a mystical truth and a palpable
absurdity." And in any case, as we learned from
Animal Farm, even when the proles do arise and
shake themselves like a horse shaking off flies the
only result is that they fall under the domination
of pigs.

Every one is familiar with the mood in which
any belief in human beings in the mass is an act of
faith and a palpable absurdity. Think of the rush
hour in the tubes, of a bargain sale, of people
reading newspapers or queuing up for the movies.
It is absurd to dream of these people rising up like
a giant and creating a glorious future. But the
mood in which they appear capable of degenerat-
ing permanently into the demoralized mob described in *1984* is also only a mood. Yet the
plausibility of the book does partly depend upon
an uncritical acceptance of this mood.

An important symbol in the book is the "monstrous woman" who spends most of her day between the washtub and the clothesline outside the
window of the room where Winston and Julia meet.
And she is the occasion of one of the only two

passages in which Winston succeeds in contemplating the proles with a little imagination. This woman of fifty is always singing, some trashy popular song, but her voice is still sweet and it suddenly strikes Winston that in her own way she is beautiful. "The solid, contourless body, like a block of granite, and the rasping red skin bore the same relation to the body of a girl as the rose-hip to the rose." And after thirty years of laundering, scrubbing, darning, cooking, sweeping, polishing, mending for children and grandchildren, there she was, still singing.

> The proles were immortal, you could not doubt it when you looked at that valiant figure in the yard. In the end their awakening would come. And until that happened, though it might be a thousand years, they would stay alive against all the odds, like birds, passing on from body to body the vitality which the Party did not share and could not kill.

This is very well; but all the same he still sees the woman as barely human. Touching and pathetic, perhaps, but "monstrous"—this adjective recurs almost every time a prole woman is mentioned. One is reminded of the "twenty scarlet faces" of the "prosperous plumbers" in *Keep the Aspidistra Flying*.

Intellectuals seem to have the greatest difficulty in seeing the unintellectual masses as human beings. Most novelists avoid the problem by not writing about them, though here again D. H. Lawrence is the outstanding exception. It is true to say that no single character in any book by Lawrence is seen as a comic post-card caricature. For him, members of all classes are human and all are equally interestingly human. Another exception, sometimes, is Orwell himself; and on one other occasion in *1984* he allows Winston Smith to mediate with some perceptiveness about the proles.

> They were not loyal to a party or a country or an idea, they were loyal to one another. *For the first time in his life* [my italics] he did not despise the proles or think of them merely as an inert force which would one day spring to life and regenerate the world. The proles had stayed human. They had not become hardened inside. They had held on to the primitive emotions which he himself had to re-learn by conscious effort.

There is an echo here, but a rather forlorn echo, of the poem which Orwell wrote, on his return from Spain, about the Italian soldier.

> . . . he was born knowing what I had learned
> Out of books and slowly.

The poem does not show the Italian soldier as a beefly garlic-stinking desperado—which from the Winston Smith point of view he probably was—but as a vehicle of the crystal spirit. Yet his mother may very well have been just such a broad-buttocked, brawny, contourless "monster" as the prole woman in *1984*.

As opposed to the depressing emphasis upon the monstrousness of the prole woman, the figure of Julia is the one point of relief and contrast against the nightmarish horror of the book. Not that she would be remarkable in the work of a more subtle and sensitive novelist; but in Orwell's work she stands out as his liveliest and most perceptive study of a woman. The shallow and frigid Elizabeth of *Burmese Days* and the warm, generous Rosemary of *Keep the Aspidistra Flying* (based upon the character of his wife Eileen) are well described;

but they are no more than sketches of features in the human landscape surrounding the hero. Julia is something more. If, as is probable, she can be taken as representing Orwell's idea of essential femininity, it is a somewhat "reactionary" portrait, although not really very different from the "progressive" Bernard Shaw's typical woman. Julia is intelligent but completely unintellectual, determined, practical, unscrupulous, capable of generosity but rather narrowly single-minded. Above all, she is realistic and a vigorous puncturer of hypocrisy and cant. She is brilliantly successful in deceit—"I am rather good at staying alive" is how she puts it—but prepared to take extraordinary risks to gain her ends.

The middle-aged Winston is astonished at the coarseness of her language, but is rather pleased by it. "It was merely one symptom of her revolt against the Party and all its ways, and somehow it seemed natural and healthy, like the sneeze of a horse that smells bad hay." With her tough vitality and ability to survive and even enjoy life against overwhelming odds, her self-absorption and total indifference to the wider issues of truth and justice, and her lack of interest in the past and the future, she strikes a poignant note in the book and makes a dramatic contrast to the tormented, far-seeing Winston. The essential difference between them, and Orwell probably meant it to illustrate the difference between men and women, is hinted, at when they visit the enigmatic and formidable O'Brien to offer their services to the underground organization against the Party, which they believe exists; and of which they believe, or at least hope, rashly and mistakenly, that he is a leader. O'Brien asks them to what lengths they are prepared to go. Will they commit murder, treason, blackmail, forgery, disseminate venereal diseases, give their lives, and so on? They answer "Yes." Then are they prepared to separate and never see one another again?

> "No!" broke in Julia.
> It appeared to Winston that a long time passed before he answered. For a moment he seemed even to have been deprived of the power of speech. His tongue worked soundlessly, forming the opening syllables first of one word, then of the other, over and over again. Until he had said it, he did not know which word he was going to say. "No," he said finally.

There is one more feature of *1984*, and perhaps the most significant of all, that remains to be considered. It is the purpose and the effect of the supreme and final torture to which Winston is subjected. The actual description of it is not one of the best things in the book. A cage of hungry rats is attached to his head in such a manner that when the door is opened their only way out will be by eating through his face. What snakes, spiders or weasels are to some people, rats seem to have been to Orwell. In both *Homage to Catalonia* and *Coming up for Air* he compares a man flattening himself on the ground to escape gunfire to a rat squeezing under a door, which suggests that he had looked at rats more attentively than most people; and in *1984* he builds up the horror of the final torture by means of an incident earlier in the book in which Winston nearly faints with disgust at the sight of a rat. But the description of the torture is not very successful. When we read:

> The rats knew what was coming now. One of them was leaping up and down, the other, an old scaly grandfather of the sewers, stood up, with his pink hands against the bars, and fiercely snuffed the air—

we can hardly help being reminded of a schoolboy's thriller.

But, successful or not as a description, the passage is crucial, not only for *1984* but for the whole of Orwell's work. It is the passage, referred to earlier in this book, where Winston screams out: "Do it to Julia! Not me!"—which is what the torturer O'Brien has wanted to make him say. Long before he is threatened with the rat torture he has been to all appearance broken, mentally as well as physically. He has signed every confession presented to him and incriminated everybody, including Julia; he has learned to believe, by means of *doublethink*, that two and two can make five, that the past is whatever the Party says it was and may at any moment change, without changing, of course, because it must always have been whatever the Party at any moment says it was; and so on. But he has not betrayed Julia. He has incriminated her, of course; but he still loves her, and is therefore still a rebel against the Party, which tolerates no personal or private feelings. He will not be cured until all his love is for Big Brother.

It is only when, in his terror of the rats, he has the idea of interposing another human body, Julia's, for them to devour while he shelters behind it, that he is finally cured of his heresy. The cure consists in the loss of his self-respect. He can no longer feel anything for himself, for Julia, or for anyone. He feels he is nothing, and in his nothingness he turns to Big Brother as his only salvation.

This, as I read it, is Orwell's hard saying and his last word. If you would not give your body to be devoured for the sake of your loved one; if, on the contrary, you would shelter behind him or her, you are worth nothing. And so long as men are worth nothing, they will deserve and will get nothing better than conscious or unconscious slavery. It is such a hard saying that one instinctively feels there must be something wrong with it—morbidity, the feverishness of a sick man, spiritual pride? It is really the same idea as Kirilov's in *The Possessed:* that man can only cease to be a slave and become a god by killing himself, because "full freedom will come only when it makes no difference whether to live or not to live." But just as the power philosophy of the Party is presented in fantastic and almost hysterical terms, so one is tempted to say that there is something lurid and oversimplified about the final torture scene and its aftermath of total humiliation. Julia has been through similar tortures, with the same result, and when she and Winston meet again by chance they find they have no feeling at all for one another. Each of them has learned in the torture chamber that "all you care about is yourself."

The only way to criticize this conclusion, it seems to me, is to shake off the spell of Orwell's obsession and say that their real trouble was that they could not forgive themselves for not being superhumanly brave. There *is* in fact a touch of spiritual pride in the moral of the book. But in making this comment we put ourselves in the position of Sancho Panza criticizing Don Quixote. In his personal life Orwell was capable of Quixotic heroism; he made exorbitant demands upon himself, and no doubt he considered that he failed to live up to them. But like the rest of us he had to try to live with his failures, for I do not suppose that even he would have claimed that it is our duty to commit suicide as soon as we have discovered that we fall short of perfection. Indeed—leaving aside the apparent moral of *1984*—I can think of hardly anyone who would have been less likely to say anything so silly. He had plenty of common sense and was often a very acute critic of overweeningly ambitious virtue.

During the last three years of his life he wrote two essays on this very theme: "Lear, Tolstoy and the Fool" and "Reflections on Gandhi" (both included in *Shooting an Elephant*). In the first he criticizes Tolstoy's attempt to renounce his worldly goods and in the second he discusses Gandhi's asceticism. Rather unexpectedly, he is more critical of Tolstoy than of Gandhi, but this is perhaps because he is discussing Tolstoy mainly in connection with his attack on Shakespeare. He points out, shrewdly enough, that the reason why Tolstoy was particularly irritated by *King Lear* may well have been because he saw it as a kind of parody of his own personal story, even including—though he could not have foreseen this—the final exodus from home and wandering to death. According to Orwell, what Shakespeare is, in effect, saying is: "Give away your lands if you want to, but don't expect to gain happiness by doing so. Probably you won't gain happiness. If you live for others, you must live *for others*, and not as a roundabout way of getting an advantage for yourself." A conclusion which Orwell thinks must have been displeasing to Tolstoy.

But did Tolstoy hope to "gain happiness" by renouncing the world? Was he, as Orwell suggests, practicing self-denial for selfish reasons? In order to be fair to Tolstoy we should need to analyze the word "happiness" in the way that Orwell analyzed "I want" in *The Road to Wigan Pier*: I don't want to cut down my drinking, pay my debts, etc.; but in another and more permanent sense I *do* want to do these things. There is also more than one sense of the word happiness. But the main burden of Orwell's criticism of both Tolstoy and Gandhi is that they were otherworldly; that is to say, they were antihumanist. The purpose of their asceticism, he says, was to escape from suffering, and if carried to its logical conclusion it would bring the world to an end.

> If one could follow it to its psychological roots, one would, I believe, find that the main motive for "nonattachment" is a desire to escape from the pain of living, and above all from love, which, sexual or non-sexual, is hard work.—"Reflections on Gandhi"

In the last resort, he insists, one is either for God or for Man. One cannot be for both. And it is only those who choose Man who are really concerned about men's happiness in the world. But this is clearly untrue of some of the greatest saints, who became what they were precisely because they possessed—and exercised—an abnormally great capacity for love. "He that loveth not his brother whom he hath seen how can he love God whom he hath not seen?" This is a complete answer to Orwell's claim that we are compelled to choose between God and Man. And although it is true that in Gandhi's philosophy existence is an evil and escape from the wheel of existence is a good, it is obvious that in practice his life was almost entirely devoted to improving his countrymen's conditions of existence. Not very many humanistic reformers would go, as the otherworldly Gandhi did, to the length of personally cleaning out the latrines in pariah villages.*

It seems to me that Orwell was a good deal

---

* See also A. J. Toynbee's criticism of Gibbon and Sir James Frazer in *A Study of History* and his quotation from Dawes and Baynes *Three Byzantine Saints*: "One of the outstanding features of early Byzantine asceticism is its passion for social justice and its championship of the poor and oppressed."

nearer to the otherworldly Tolstoy and Gandhi and a good deal further from the average humanistic progressive than he himself was prepared to recognize.

> The essence of being human [he wrote in the "Reflections on Gandhi"] is that one does not seek perfection, that one *is* sometimes willing to commit sins for the sake of loyalty, that one does not push asceticism to the point where it makes friendly intercourse impossible, and that one is prepared in the end to be defeated and broken up by life, which is the inevitable price of fastening one's love upon other human individuals.

That is very well said, but he does not seem to have reflected that to be *prepared* to be defeated and broken up by life is already a step in the direction of nonattachment.

Winston and Julia in *1984* were in fact perfectly prepared, intellectually. They knew very well that their secret life together would certainly be discovered and that the end would be torture and submission. In Winston's own words: "On the battlefield, in the torture chamber, on a sinking ship, the issues that you are fighting for are always forgotten because the body swells up until it fills the universe." There may be some rare people of superhuman fortitude to whom this does not happen. But why should Winston have expected to be one of them? And if he did not expect this, why was his spirit broken for ever when he failed to resist under the torture, when he found himself wishing that Julia should be eaten by the rats? Speculation is difficult in such a matter, and perhaps everyone would be shattered as he was by such a revelation of our basic and absolute egocentricity; but it does seem at least possible that a less purely intellectual, a more *profound* nonattachment—which is perhaps only a way of saying a little more humility—might have helped him. Nearly all of us are failures, and we have to learn to live with our failure.

But the only thing that would certainly have enabled Winston to survive the shame of his collapse would have been the perfect humility defined by Simone Weil in her reflections on prayer:

> It means knowing that in the ego there is nothing whatever, no psychological element, which external circumstances could not make disappear. It means accepting that. It means being happy that it should be so.

Winston's love for Julia was the "psychological element" in his ego that he wished to cling to at all costs. The "external circumstance" of torture caused it to disappear. And he could not be happy that it was so. To achieve such perfectly humble resignation he would, of course, have needed to be a saint. But the achievement is at least psychologically conceivable. Orwell, however, requires him to possess such superhuman fortitude that no external circumstance whatever could obliterate his love. And this is probably impossible, and therefore not effectively conceivable at all.

The fact that Orwell chose to set the personal tragedy of Winston Smith at the center of his story is important as a clue to his own psychology. Winston's failure to rise to superhuman heroism, and the consequences of this failure, confirm the impression we derived from *A Clergyman's Daughter* that Orwell's motto should have been "all or nothing." But his prophecy is independent of the particular form in which he embodied it. He could have described the world of *1984* in exactly the same way without introducing any such character as Winston Smith. Nor, for that matter, is it essential that the ruling oligarchy should be a cruel and sadistic one. As we have already observed, Aldous Huxley's theory is equally plausible: that people can be reduced to a servile condition by means of mass suggestion, hypnopaedia and drugs, without any overt brutality or cruelty and without any conscious suffering. The core of Orwell's message in *1984*, stripped of Winston's tragedy and all the sadism, is simply that our industrial machine civilization is tending to deracinate and debilitate us, and will finally destroy us; and the consensus of opinion on this point among thinkers as diverse as Orwell, Huxley, Gandhi, Simone Weil and D. H. Lawrence, to say nothing of the many others, such as Eliot and Koestler, who would go at least part of the way with them, is striking and depressing. All the more so because no one seriously believes that the rhythm of industrialization and mechanization could be relaxed, or indeed that it can possibly fail to go on accelerating (unless interrupted by war) until the whole population of the world has been incorporated into the mass civilization. Nor is it possible even to wish to reverse the process. Industrialization does seem to be the only way by which the conditions of the Asiatic coolie and the African tribesman can be raised to the level which is the prerequisite of anything that we in the West would consider a civilized or even a properly human life. "The belly comes before the soul, not in the scale of values but in point of time," as Orwell himself put it. And while there are still empty bellies to be filled one might as well whistle to the wind as make any reference to the complementary truth that it is possible to lose your soul in the process of gaining the world. Perhaps the only legitimate conclusion of Orwell's in *The Road to Wigan Pier*—"the machine has got to be accepted, but it is probably better to accept it rather as one accepts a drug—that is, grudgingly and suspiciously."

"Do It to Julia"
James Connors

Many critics have asserted that *Nineteen Eighty-Four* marks Orwell's complete sense of despair with the destiny of the modern world. They link Orwell directly with his character Winston Smith, and thus, in the annihilation of Winston's humanity in Room 101, they see Orwell's own values and morality in defeat as well. That Orwell was writing in extremis—battling the tuberculosis that would kill him seven months after the book's publication—also enters into this interpretation of the terminal bleakness of *Nineteen Eighty-Four*.

In this provocative essay, James Connors offers a novel interpretation of the character of Winston Smith, one that calls for a closer reading of the first two-thirds of the book, in which he sees Orwell planting numerous clues that Winston is but a "shadow man" on whom we should not place much hope for heroism or, more simply, a man without the human capacity to act upon what he feels or understands about himself or the world. In so unmasking Winston, Connors identifies the fundamental terror that Orwell sought to dramatize in Room 101—the terror that is not Winston's alone, but that belongs to each and every one of us.

In any assessment of George Orwell's attitudes towards the future, his last novel, *1984*, is of central importance. Does it reflect, as many have believed, a final and complete abandonment of hope in man's ability to create a just and decent society? For those inclined to view the work as something less than a statement of despair, the recent publication of Orwell's collected letters and essays offers some support. Correspondence indicates that he conceived the idea for the novel as early as 1943 and that he began writing in early 1946.[1] The significance of this time factor ties in with evidence available from these years which convincingly documents Orwell's active commitment to political reform. Perhaps the item which is most damaging to those who have argued that with *1984* Orwell turned his back on the future is the letter which he dispatched to F. A. Henson shortly after the work appeared in America. "My recent novel," he wrote, "is NOT intended as an attack on Socialism or on the British Labour Party (of which I am a supporter) but as a show-up of the perversions to which a centralized economy is liable and which have already been partly realized in Communism and Fascism. I do not believe that the kind of society I describe necessarily *will* arrive, but I believe (allowing of course for the fact that the book is a satire) that something resembling it *could* arrive."[2]

One may argue of course that no matter how much evidence is compiled from outside the work to prove that Orwell retained to the end some form of faith in the future, the inescapable fact remains that *1984* appears to be a profoundly pes-

[1]"Letter to Geoffrey Gorer" 1/22/46; "Letter to F. J. Warburg 10/22/48." In *The Collected Essays, Journalism and Letters of George Orwell*, eds. Sonia Orwell and Ian Angus (New York: Harcourt, Brace and World, 1968). IV, 87; 448. All citations are from Orwell's writings unless otherwise indicated.

[2]"Letter to Francis A. Henson" 6/16/49. Italics in original. Parts of this letter were published in *Life* and in the *New York Times Book Review* shortly after the novel appeared. *Collected Essays*, IV, p. 502.

simistic novel. The pervasive and terrifying power possessed by the Party, the deliberate perversion of language, and the final capitulation of the "hero," Winston Smith, in Room 101 all seem to add up to a mockery of modern man's desire for a better world. Unless one can establish the case for Orwell's enduring faith in man and the future by appealing to evidence from *1984* itself, it is doubted whether those who have discerned a defeated Orwell in the work can be persuaded to re-examine the question.

To wish to rescue Orwell from the ranks of the defeated does not entail inflicting upon him some mindlessly optimistic orthodoxy. That would be foolish. But it would be equally foolish to dismiss the commitment which inspired him throughout his career, especially at distressing moments. Though outraged by the performance of the Communists during the Spanish Civil War, he declared upon returning from Spain that his brief exposure to a premature version of the classless society in Barcelona left him committed to its future realization.[3] From a vantage point mid-way in World War II, he reaffirmed his faith: "I myself believe that the common man will win his fight sooner or later, but I want it to be sooner and not later— some time within the next hundred years, say, and not within the next ten thousand."[4] At the outset of World War II, Orwell voiced his fear over the potential attractiveness of Hitler to the English middle class and wondered whether the English would be capable of mustering the determination to cope with the threat of Nazi tyranny. He did not, however, sink into despair, but instead turned

[3]*Homage to Catalonia* (London: Secker and Warburg, 1938), p. 110.

[4]"Looking Back on the Spanish Civil War" in *England Your England* (London: Secker and Warburg, 1953). p. 175. Essay first appeared in 1943.

out a lengthy polemic urging revolutionary social and political reforms so as to enlist the full support of the lower classes in the struggle against Germany.[5] Several years later, about the time he was writing *Animal Farm*, he chided the disillusioned Arthur Koestler for being a "short-term pessimist." All revolutions, Orwell observed, "are failures, but they are not all the same failure."[6] In his essay "Why I Write," published in 1947, he summed up the focus of his career: "Every line of serious work that I have written since 1936 has been written directly or indirectly *against* totalitarianism and *for* democratic socialism, as I understand it."[7] Since Orwell at this time was probably well along in the composition of *1984*, an attempt to scrutinize the latter for signs of hope would appear to be both in order and worthwhile.

Yet, as a glance at the secondary literature dealing with Orwell clearly indicates, *1984* has proven very difficult to reconcile with the prior portion of his career. To my mind the major stumbling block has been the chief character. Winston Smith—to be precise, his betrayal of his lover in Room 101, when confronted with what for him is the one unendurable form of torture, he screams, "Do it to Julia!" I say stumbling block because of the tendency among those who have studied the work to treat Winston as either Orwell's representative or as a symbol for Everyman. To a certain extent, the identification is understandable: Winston as a man in a revolt against an odious regime and as the pathetic object of O'Brien's sinister tortures can be regarded with some sympathy. Unfortunately,

[5]*The Lion and the Unicorn: Socialism and the English Genius* (London: Secker and Warburg, 1941). pp. 88, *passim*.

[6]"Arthur Koestler" in *Dickens, Dali and Others* (New York: Reynal and Hitchcock, 1945), p. 199.

[7]"Why I Write" in *England Your England*, p. 11.

in the light of Winston's capitulation, an approach
which links him with either Orwell or Everyman
can lead to only one conclusion—despair. Edward
Thomas, for example, after wedding Winston and
Orwell on the strength of the former's attempt to
maintain that 2 plus 2 equals four, writes that
"Winston, in trying to see the world as it is on the
evidence of his senses, is the last representative of
the intellectual tradition in which Orwell placed
himself."[8] Having established this connection,
Thomas then sorrowfully concludes that the healthy
tension between fear and hope, which had marked
Orwell's earlier writings, collapsed in *1984*. Virtually the same conclusion has been reached by Richard Rees *via* the Everyman approach. Attributing
to Orwell the belief that "if you would not give
your body to be devoured for the sake of your
loved one . . . you are worth nothing." Rees ac-
cuses the novelist of demanding "superhuman
bravery" from his characters and then laments
1984 as the grim culmination of his "All or Nothing"
philosophy.[9]

For the most part, the identification of Winston
with Orwell and Everyman reflects an almost obsessive preoccupation with events which occur once
Winston is arrested and confined to the Ministry
of Peace. Such a focus is understandable, since
what happens to Winston following his arrest represents the dramatic culmination of the novel. At
the same time, this emphasis has encouraged a
careless reading of what Orwell had been saying
about Winston prior to his arrest—that is, in the
first two-thirds of the novel. The result of this

[8]Edward Thomas, *Orwell* (London: Oliver and Boyd, 1965),
pp. 93, 94.
[9]Richard Rees, *George Orwell: Fugitive from the Camp of Victory* (Carbondale: Southern Illinois Press, 1961), pp. 103–104.

neglect is seen in the failure to examine closely Winston's attitudes and acts prior to his arrest. It is this failure, I believe, which is responsible for the excessively pessimistic interpretations of the novel which have appeared.[10] It is my contention that the Winston who moves through the first two-thirds of *1984* is neither Orwell's representative nor Everyman's, but rather a frightening example of a writer so corrupted by his work in behalf of the Party that he is doomed to failure in his half-understood and belated attempt to revolt against a group of men whose views and values he shares far more than he realizes. It is only by proceeding in this fashion, I believe, that one can grasp the significance of the capitulation scene, that is, identify what is truly terrifying about it and determine what Orwell may have had in mind in handling it as he did.

Throughout Orwell's life and works, perhaps the most persistent theme is lying. He himself decided to quit the British Imperial Service not only because of a growing conviction that imperialism was reprehensible, but also because of an awareness that it steadily sucked the vitality and integrity from those who served it, especially those who served it reluctantly.[11] His first novel, *Burmese*

[10] *Cf. Marcus Smith, "The Wall of Blackness: A Psychological Approach to 1984," Modern Fiction Studies*, 14 (Winter 1968–1969), 423–433. Mr. Smith quite rightly objects to the failure of critics o confront the problem of Winston's characterization. Though I find parts of his argument persuasive, I do not think Winston "is closely and carefully developed along familiar Oedipal lines." To my mind an investigation of Winston's moral character is far more fruitful and also more in line with Orwell's habitual didactic approach to politics and life.

[11] "Shooting an Elephant" in *Shooting an Elephant* (London: Secker and Warburg, 1950), p. 6.

Days, explores this problem several times. Flory, an English merchant in Burma, knows that the pukka sahib code is sheer nonsense: yet he chooses to live in secret rebellion rather than provoke the wrath of the local European club members with "Bolshi ideas." Throughout the novel, both Flory and Orwell (functioning as the omniscient author) insist on the moral degeneration which accompanies such hypocrisy. "In the end the secrecy of your revolt poisons you like a secret disease. . . . It is a corrupting thing to live one's real life in secret."[12] (Significantly Flory, like Winston, attempts a belated rebellion against a system he despises and, like the latter, fails.) Beginning in 1936, the form of lying which most troubled Orwell was political propaganda. His experience in Spain, especially his affiliation with the Trotskyite P.O.U.M., exposed him to acts of falsification that appalled him. Battles and great victories were reported which never took place, and anti-Fascist groups, for example the P.O.U.M., were systematically maligned as a prelude to being actively persecuted as pro-Fascist.[13] Reflecting on this feature of the Spanish Civil War in 1943, he wrote:[14]

> This kind of thing is frightening to me because it often gives me the feeling that the very concept of objective truth is fading out of the world. . . . The implied objective in the line of thought is a nightmare world in which the leader, or some ruling clique, controls not only the future but the past. If the leader says of such and such an event, 'It never happened'—well, it never happened. If he says that two and two are five—well, two and two are five.

[12]*Burmese Days* (New York: Harcourt, Brace and World, 1955), pp. 69–70.
[13]*Homage to Catalonia*, pp. 220ff.
[14]"Looking Back on the Spanish Civil War", pp. 163–165.

The passage, in the light of Orwell's remark that the ideas for *1984* took shape around 1943, neatly identifies a major source of inspiration for the work. More importantly, perhaps, the passage defines a problem which was to agitate Orwell for the remainder of his life: the obligations of the writer as the defender of the ideal of objective truth in a world where powerful political groups frequently sought to manipulate and distort truth. "From the totalitarian point of view," he wrote in 1946, "history is something to be created rather than learned. . . . Totalitarianism demands, in fact, the continuous alteration of the past, and in the long run, probably demands a disbelief in the very existence of objective truth."[15] Two years later he addressed the problem in greater detail. Without denying an intellectual's need to deal with political questions, and without excusing him from the performance of the most menial political tasks (distributing pamphlets), Orwell nevertheless insisted that no writer could remain true to himself if he used his talents as propagandist at a party's request. The inevitable consequence, he warned, "is not only falsification, but often the actual drying up of the inventive faculties."[16]

The relevance of the material above to *1984* and to Winston Smith becomes clear once one begins to assemble and to organize the clues which Orwell sprinkles throughout the bulk of the book. What sort of man is Winston Smith? He is a thirty-nine year old minor functionary in the Outer Party, specifically, a propaganda expert whose chief talent is destroying and re-creating history. In itself

---

[15]"The Prevention of Literature" in *Shooting an Elephant*, pp. 120–121.
[16]"Writers and Leviathan" in *England Your England*, p. 23. Essay first appeared in 1948.

this is a damning occupation, but Orwell goes on to underscore the fact that Winston not only does his job well but actually derives pleasure from doing it.[17]

> Winston's greatest pleasure in life was his work. Most of it was a tedious routine, but included in it there were also jobs so difficult and intricate that you could lose yourself in them as in the depths of a mathematical problem—delicate pieces of forgery in which you had nothing to guide you except your knowledge of the principles of Ingsoc and your estimate of what the Party wanted to say. Winston was good at this kind of thing. On occasion he had even been entrusted with the rectification of the *Times* leading articles, which were written entirely in Newspeak.

Winston succeeds precisely because he has internalized both the jargon and the assumptions of the Party: he has mastered Big Brother's style. Even after Winston has joined the bogus Goldstein conspiracy against Big Brother, he still contrives to work at his job and to do it well. The very day he finally acquires Goldstein's book coincides with one of the periodic turnabouts in Oceania's politics. A rearrangement of the recent past is imperative. Oceania, having just declared war on Eastasia, must be shown in the records as always having been at war with Eastasia; conversely, Eurasia, the recent enemy, must be transformed into a longstanding ally. The switch entails nothing less than a crash program in destroying the past. Yet Winston, despite his involvement in the conspiracy against Big Brother, remains unperturbed by his assignment. "Insofar as he had time to remember it, he was not troubled by the fact that every word

[17] *1984* (New York: Harcourt, Brace, 1949), p 44

he murmured into the speakwrite, every stroke of his ink pencil, was a deliberate lie. He was as anxious as anyone else in the Department that the forgery should be perfect" (p. 151).

A disparity between Winston's intellectual hostility to the Party and his actual performance recurs in several other significant episodes and contexts. On each occasion Orwell identifies a fatal flaw in Winston—the failure to feel, and hence act on, the difference which he comes to grasp sporadically (and only intellectually) between a cluster of private loyalties and traditional values, on the one hand, and Party loyalty on the other. In scenes such as the flashbacks on his mother's death and in his reflections of the proles, Orwell alerts the reader to Winston's inability to relate insight to action. A dream flashback early in the novel discloses that Winston senses in a vague way that he owes his life to his mother's willingness to sacrifice herself. "His mother's memory tore at his heart because she had died loving him, when he was too young and selfish to love her in return, and because · somehow, he did not remember how, she had sacrificed herself to a conception of loyalty that was private and unalterable" (p. 31). Later on, Winston again ponders his mother's death along with that of a Jewish mother whom he has seen on a newscreen pathetically attempting to shield her child from the bullets being fired from an attacking fighter plane. Having made one link, Winston then proceeds to forge still another, this one with the proles. Doubts and misgivings vanish as Winston perceives that the proles, like his mother, are admirable because they had remained loyal to one another and had not become "hardened inside." The passage is a lengthy one but deserves to be quoted in full, both because it furnishes an excellent summary of Orwell's long-standing esteem for the common workingman and because it offers, in the two final sentences, a clear statement of Winston's dilemma.

> . . . she [his mother] had possessed a kind of nobility, a kind of purity, simply because the standards that she obeyed were private ones. Her feelings were her own, and could not be altered from outside. It would not have occurred to her that an action which is ineffectual thereby becomes meaningless. If you loved someone, you loved him, and when you had nothing else to give, you still gave him love. . . . The refugee woman in the boat had also covered the little boy with her arm, which was no more use against bullets than a sheet of paper. The terrible thing that the Party had done was to persuade you that mere impulses, mere feelings, were of no account, while at the same time robbing you of all power over the material world. When once you were in the grip of the Party, what you felt or did not feel, what you did or refrained from doing, made literally no difference. Whatever happened, you vanished, and neither you nor your actions were ever heard of again. You were lifted clean out of the stream of history. And yet to the people of two generations ago, this would not have seemed all important, because they were not attempting to alter history. They were governed by private loyalties which they did not question. What mattered were individual relationships, and a completely helpless gesture, an embrace, a tear, a word spoken to a dying man, could have value in itself. The proles, it suddenly occurred to him, had remained in this condition. They were not loyal to a party or a country or an idea, they were loyal to one another. For the first time in his life he did not despise the proles or think of them merely as an inert force which would one day spring to life and regenerate the world. The proles had stayed human. They had not become hardened inside. They had held onto primi-

tive conditions which he himself had to relearn by *conscious effort.* And thinking this, he remembered *without apparent reference,* how a few weeks ago he had seen a severed hand lying in the pavement and had kicked it into the gutter as though it had been a cabbage stalk. (pp. 136–137)

The last two lines pointedly dramatize the distance separating Winston and the proles. He cannot establish the absolutely vital connection between his perceptions of what makes the proles human and his own actions. No truly human being would have kicked the severed hand into the street as though it were a vegetable. The situation cried out for some sort of compassionate gesture. Had Winston internalized his newly discovered conception of what constitutes "human" behavior, he would have seen the relevance of his reflections to the thoroughly callous action which he had committed. A feeling of remorse or self-loathing—though these would have been "pointless" in the perverted value system of the Party—would have signified the likelihood of more harmony between ideal and action in the future. This possibility, however, the concluding lines of the passage explicitly reject, for by denying such feelings to Winston, Orwell emphatically censures the partial nature of his humanity.

The importance of this passage, especially its connection with the capitulation scene in Room 101, is further heightened when one notes its strategic location in the novel: it immediately precedes the pact which Winston and Julia make never to betray one another. At Winston's insistence, they are going to try to model their behavior on the humanity of the proles. Orwell, however, provides the reader plenty of evidence pointing towards ultimate failure. Earlier passages suggest the relationship was compromised from the start. Julia found Winston attractive because she suspected that he was against the Party. Their initial love-making was infused with political hatred. "It was," writes Orwell, "a blow struck against the Party. It was a political act" (p. 128). Their decision not to betray one another, since it immediately follows the passage in which Orwell stresses Winston's inability to relate thought and action, amounts to nothing more than a tragic piece of self-deception. Subsequent passages, it should be noted, abundantly confirm that Winston lacks genuine feeling for Julia. Shortly after his arrest, he examines his peculiar relationship with Julia. Orwell writes: "He hardly ever thought of Julia. He could not fix his mind on her. He loved her and would not betray her; but that was only a fact, known as he knew the rules of arithmetic. He felt no love for her, and he hardly ever wondered what was happening to her" (p. 282). A few pages later—and prior to his initial confrontation with O'Brien—Winston explores the question again. "He thought: 'If I could save Julia by doubling my own pain, would I do it? Yes I would.' But that was merely an intellectual decision, taken because he knew that he ought to take it. He did not feel it" (p. 242). Moments after this bit of soul searching, both Winston and the reader receive conclusive proof of how feeble and vulnerable a mere intellectual conviction is. A beating, especially a painful blow on the elbow, provides Winston with an answer to the question which he has posed for himself. "One question," writes Orwell, "at any rate was answered. Never for any reason on earth could you wish for an increase of pain. Of pain, you could wish only one thing: that it should stop. Nothing in the world was so bad as physical pain. In the face of pain, there are no heroes, no heroes, he thought over

and over as he writhed on the floor clutching use-
lessly at his disabled left arm." (p. 243)

The material presented up to this point enables
one to identify Winston largely in terms of what
he is not. The capacity for genuine feeling and
self-sacrifice, which he comes to recognize and admire in his mother and in the proles, he himself
does not possess. Orwell, however, also inserts clues
of a more positive kind, clues which show the
extent to which Winston shares the outlook of the
men he imagines he despises. In this category I
would place those passages already cited where
Orwell describes Winston's attitudes towards his
work. But the most revealing episode is the grim
interview which precedes his entry into the Goldstein conspiracy. O'Brien, playing the role of
friendly conspirator, quizzes Julia and Winston
in order to discover what they are willing to do
to terminate the tyranny of Big Brother and the
Party:

> 'You are prepared to commit murder?'
> 'Yes.'
> 'To commit acts of sabotage which may cause the
> death of hundreds of innocent people?'
> 'Yes'
> 'To betray your country to foreign powers?'
> 'Yes.'
> 'You are prepared to cheat, to forge, to blackmail,
> to corrupt the minds of children, to distribute habit-
> forming drugs, to encourage prosstitution, to dis-
> seminate venereal diseases—to do anything which
> is likely to cause demoralization and weaken the
> power of the Party?'
> 'Yes.'
> 'If for example, it would somehow serve our inter-
> ests to throw sulphuric acid in a child's face—are
> you prepared to do that?'
> 'Yes.' (p. 142)

The significance of the passage hardly needs comment. No human being would consent to do the dreadful things which Winston agrees to do. Only a shadow-man capable of mindless party loyalty would answer yes to questions such as these. And Winston, by virtue of long, obedient service as a party "historian," is just that—a shadow-man. The subsequent skillful exploitation of this conversation by O'Brien strongly suggests that Orwell designed the scene to yield this grotesque dimension to Winston. At the end of the painful interrogation which immediately precedes Winston's arrival in Room 101, the latter tries to portray himself as a better human being than O'Brien, who is now functioning in his true role as representative of the party. O'Brien's response is brief and devastatingly effective: he simply plays a tape recording of the conversation in which Winston agreed to murder and lie and treats it as being so compromising that he does not even bother to comment on it (pp. 222–223).

It would seem that Orwell's "plan" was to scatter clues throughout the first two-thirds of *1984* which would serve not only to identify Winston as a certain kind of man, but also to explain why such a man would be unable to sustain a successful rebellion against the Party. To my mind, the plan succeeds. Once Winston is arrested, one suspects that he will cave in and betray Julia.

Yet Orwell's plan, in a sense, works too well. One expects Winston to capitulate without his tormentor having to resort to the ultimate weapon, which in the case of Winston is his fear of rats. Nevertheless that is exactly the form of torture which Orwell employs to bring about Winston's betrayal. Why?

The most plausible explanation, I think, is that Orwell at some point during the writing of *1984* came to realize that he needed a device to ensure the complete involvement of the *average* reader in the capitulation scene. Until O'Brien delivers his analysis of the "worst thing in the world" it is difficult for an ordinary man, possessing the usual assortment of virtues, and vices, to empathize with Winston. I suspect that when Orwell first conceived *1984* and throughout much of the writing of it, he had in mind a very special audience. The fact that Winston is a writer who employs his skills to distort the truth, and thereby becomes progressively corrupted as a human being, indicates that his ultimate failure to act in terms of his newly discovered ideal—personal loyalty—was designed for the edification of the Left wing intelligentsia. Throughout his career Orwell sniped away at this group for both unintentional and willful distortion of past and current events; and invariably, he pointed to timid party orthodoxy as the chief source of this vice. In one of his last essays, he warned his fellow writers that their own attitudes towards truth would have a crucial impact on shaping the intellectual atmosphere of the future and the moral quality of their own private lives. Should the future turn out to be totalitarian, he sternly concluded, "it will probably be because that is what we have deserved."[18] This habitual didactic posture which Orwell assumed towards the Left intelligentsia goes a long way towards explaining how he conceived of Winston and his betrayal: no writer can hope to demonstrate in action his dignity as a human being, if throughout most of his life his actions have displayed a contempt for truth and humanity. At the same time, it also seems clear that Orwell wished to reach a wider audience than the intelligentsia of the Left.

[18]"Writers and Leviathan," p. 17.

And his solution, though badly inconsistent with his portrayal of Winston's character, worked brilliantly. For with—and only with—O'Brien's discussion of the "worst thing in the world," a dimension is suddenly added to Winston's torture which engages the attention of Everyman. It is not Winston's capitulation which terrorizes the reader but rather O'Brien's almost casual analysis of Everyman's fatal weakness. For one man it may be rats, for another it may be fire, but for each man there is one unendurable terror which renders him powerless to act according to the ideals he cherishes.

Just why Orwell chose this device to involve the general reader can be explained adequately, I think, without having to raise the question of whether or not he believed the thesis which he put into O'Brien's mouth. From at least the latter part of 1943, he remained acutely conscious of the fact that the expectations which most men entertain of the future are marred by a failure to make provision for the occurrence of situations or events which they regard as unpalatable. "Before writing off the totalitarian world as a nightmare that can't come true," he wrote in 1943, "just remember that in 1925 the world of today would have seemed a nightmare that couldn't come true."[19] Two years later, he returned to the same problem: "People can foresee the future only when it coincides with their own wishes and the most grossly obvious facts can be ignored when they are unwelcome."[20] In the light of these observations, my own belief is that the sanest approach to *1984* in its entirety and to O'Brien's "worst thing in the world" thesis is to regard them as shock tactics. Writers in

[19]"Looking Back on the Spanish Civil War," p. 165.
[20]"London Letter to *Partisan Review*" in *Letters*, III, 297.

particular, and men in general, must be made aware of the awful possibility that the future *could* become a nightmarish world if they neglect to keep alive the liberal tradition and the values associated with it.

It would be, of course, a gross mistake to argue that Orwell was a comfortable optimist. He was a brooder, and in *1984* he clearly displays a great deal of anxiety about the future. But anxiety is not the same thing as despair. To argue that with *1984* Orwell abandoned hope entails not only a shallow reading of the work, but also a wholly misleading conception of it as his *last* work. Too often one finds the novel presented as the culmination, or the end, of some negative tendency in his thought. But Orwell was not seventy years old when he died, he was forty-seven, and though he had been ill for several years, he was, on the eve of his death, fairly hopeful about his chances for recuperation.[21] If one must regard *1984* as some sort of culmination, I suggest that it be regarded as the most effective of the numerous efforts which this fine man made to prevent the future from becoming a nightmare. And had he lived longer, it doubtless would have been followed by many more.

[21]"Letter to Leonard Moore" 10/11/49. "Letter to T.R. Fyvel" 10/25/49 in *Letters*, IV, 508–509.

Power and the Perfect State
Martin Kessler

The idea of progress finds its endpoint in utopian—
and dystopian—societies. Change is no longer a social
objective; the status quo must be "frozen" forever.
Within such a static framework, machines pose a
special problem, for technology as we have always
defined it implies open-ended improvement, refine-
ment, increased production, and the like.

Science and technology figure significantly in both
Brave New World and *Nineteen Eighty-Four.* Huxley
and Orwell find very different uses for the output of
their respective "perfect" industries—the former, in a
politics based on conditioned consumption and happiness; the latter, in a politics based on perpetual war
and misery.

In approaching the two novels from this perspective,
Martin Kessler reveals the operational mechanisms
that motivate Huxley's and Orwell's fictional worlds,
some of which have uncomfortably telling implications for our own times.

The late Lord Keynes once described his fellow
economists as "the trustees, not of civilization, but
of the possibility of civilization."[1] In this, as both
Aldous Huxley and George Orwell tell us in effect,
Keynes showed himself a true son of the Victorian
Age. For, it is the unique feature of the twentieth

[1]Quoted by R. F. Harrod, *The Life of John Maynard Keynes*
(London 1951), pp. 193–94 from an address before the Council
of the Royal Economic Society.

century that the material requisites for the "possibility of civilization" are at hand. "From the moment when the machine first made its appearance," Orwell's Goldstein (Trotsky) writes, "it was clear to all thinking people that the need for human drudgery and therefore to a great extent for human inequality had disappeared."[2] And in Huxley's *Brave New World* the Controller informs the Savage that, "there isn't any need for a civilized man to bear anything that is seriously unpleasant."[3] While Orwell bases the oligarchical collectivism of 1984 on conspicuous production, and Huxley his Brave New World on conspicuous consumption, they both start from the same premise, that science has solved the problem of production. Indeed, the means whereby these rulers of the not-so-distant future choose to dispose of the surpluses created by a phenomenally efficient productive machine offer the key to their power.

The production problem is thus incidental to the economy of abundance that Huxley and Orwell are describing and in this more than anything else lies their pessimism. Ever since man first started to seek the kingdom of heaven here on earth, the cartographers of the perfect state have been obliged to devote a good deal of time to the question of *how* to provide Utopia's subjects with the means for the enjoyment of perfection. Through the application of science to the production of goods, through the redistribution of existing income and property relationships, through the abolition of "costly" and wasteful desires, the Utopians of the last five centuries had hoped to construct a perfect society in which men and women could enjoy that ultimate

[2]George Orwell, *Nineteen Eighty-Four* (New York, 1949), p. 190.
[3]Aldous Huxley, *Brave New World* (New York, 1946), p. 284.

degree of happiness which, it was implied, they were denied through the folly and wickedness of their present rulers.

True, Utopians have generally been moralists and their morality more often than not has been a little austere for human flesh and blood. But they have rarely been ascetics advocating the willful mortification of the flesh. Thus it was not until after the secularization of the Church in the thirteenth and fourteenth centuries that Utopian works began once more to be written. By the late nineteenth century, indeed, the rapidly accelerating tempo of scientific discovery encouraged the more vulgar of the Utopians to envisage the perfect society solely in terms of the strange and wonderful gadgets which it would have at its disposal. The prophetic novels of Jules Verne, H. G. Wells, and others, all, to a greater or lesser extent, glamorized their Brave New Worlds in terms of the material conveniences and comforts science would put at the disposal of man. The quality of life in such an environment of abundance was either ignored (as in Jules Verne), or, as in the early Wells, described in altogether glowing terms.

As science has transformed fiction into fact (often ahead of schedule), it has become apparent that the remaining material obstacles to Utopia have been—or in the underdeveloped areas of the world are in the process of being—surmounted. It is of course true that there is no certainty that the "subsistence barrier" has been conquered for all time. The Malthusian dilemma will probably continue to be (though perhaps on a "higher plane") a limiting factor to economic expansion. There is every reason to believe, indeed, that the application of limited resources to unlimited desires will continue to challenge man's ingenuity. But—and it is an important but—the emphasis will shift, according to both Huxley and Orwell, from the absolute or relative increase of resources (that is, from problems of production and distribution) to the restriction, control or "guidance" of unlimited desires. From the stomach, the art of politics will move to the psyche.

As a result, the whole quality of existing super- and subordination systems will undergo—and, judging from Huxley's and Orwell's other writings,[4] is already undergoing—something of a sea change. Both men are concerned with those aspects of a modern science (Pavlonian biology, eugenics and narcotics with Huxley; electronic communications media and cybernetics with Orwell) which will enable future élites to "freeze" the *status quo*. Up to now the élite class in political society has never been secure in its power; changes in the mode of production, wars, votes, intrigues (depending on the kind of society in operation) have constantly threatened it. Pareto's "law" of the circulation of élites operated,[5] for the political structure was never hermetically sealed for all time. Even India and China, where the *status quo* had enjoyed apparently unbreakable religious and institutional sanctions, were ultimately forced to submit to a reconstruction of their social fabric.

Indeed, the absolutely "closed society", to borrow Karl Popper's useful phrase,[6] has existed only in the day dreams of rulers and, more usually, of their ideologists. For, to attribute power to an individual or class is one thing; to exercise that power is infinitely more difficult; to exercise it absolutely is (or rather has been up to now)

---

[4]See in particular Orwell, *Such, Such Were the Joys* (New York, 1953), and Huxley, *Science, Liberty and Peace* (London, 1946).

[5]See Vilfredo Pareto, *Mind and Society* (New York, 1935).

impossible. "The King can do no wrong" was a maxim developed by fifteenth- and sixteenth-century lawyers at a time when, practically speaking, there was relatively little the king could do—right or wrong. Compared to the effective powers of a modern democratic state, the most absolute Renaissance tyrant was but a shadow. The twentieth-century democratic state, based on popular consent and with carefully circumscribed powers, is able to: (1) conscript and maintain mass armies, (2) *effectively* regulate the external and internal flow of goods and individuals, (3) impose *and* collect undreamed of per capita tax revenues, (4) obtain almost instantaneous compliance for its directives, and so on. In the case of contemporary totalitarian countries, where the state's power in law is never less than its power in fact (where the potential is always the actual), we have the nearest thing to the absolute exercise of absolute power known in the history of political society. And in the society of the not-so-distant future, Huxley and Orwell somewhat gloatingly tell us, science will have made the power of the state "absolutely absolute," while man—happily shaking off responsibility according to satirist Huxley, unhappily deprived of personal volition according to moralist Orwell—will have created a society where that power will be instantaneously applied.

The important thing to remember about the "dystopias" of both Huxley and Orwell is that they posit a perfectly maleable (and hence perfectly predictable) human nature incapable of experiencing any emotion or exercising any judgment outside of the prevailing (and, in Orwell, continuously changing) frame of reference. The destruction of

[6]Karl Popper, *The Open Society and Its Enemies* (Princeton, 1950), *passiom.*

personal identity in objective reality is thus complete—or nearly complete, for being romantics at heart, both Huxley and Orwell introduce exceptions. Whether or not we can derive any comfort from these essentially impotent rebels we shall leave for more detailed discussion later on. Right now, let us turn to the techniques of *Brave New World* and *Nineteen Eighty-Four* which have succeeded so conspicuously in repealing Pareto's law.

A MATTER OF TECHNIQUE: THE MEANS

In analyzing the "technology" of power available to the rulers of the Brave New World and 1984—and the use ("technique") they make of this power—one becomes uncomfortably aware that neither Huxley nor Orwell assumes a level of technology much more advanced than what is already enjoyed in the more industrialized nations today. Thus Orwell's television screens, which enable a probably nonexistent "Big Brother" to keep tabs on every aspect, private and public, of the lives of his subjects, are already being widely used by industry for quality-control purposes, by military establishments to insure better communications and by state police to track down traffic violators. Similarly, Huxley's "sleep teaching" methods are being widely practiced in our state mental hospitals (albeit for different ends) under such names as hypnotherapy and narcosynthesis. True, we have not yet succeeded—although in Nazi Germany the attempt was made—in applying modern genetic methods to human beings, but our success with animals makes it at least plausible to assume that we could accomplish equally gratifying results with human beings—especially if Huxley's not at all far-fetched prediction of sexless and artificially "hatched" birth were to come true. As yet there is no "soma" on the market which will allow the consumer to escape reality without adverse physical aftereffects, but we do have the next best thing in the form of escapist entertainments which create increasingly effective ersatz experiences. While no cinema or television process has yet succeeded in reproducing the "bear rug thrills" of the "feelies," we have succeeded in simulating the experience of roller-coaster rides and only recently an imaginative movie mogul patented a new system he called "Smellorama."[7]

Examples like these could be adduced for almost every scientific method or technical gadget found in either *Brave New World* or *Nineteen Eighty-Four*. Certainly, the key to the power of the élite, in both instances depends only indirectly on technology. While it is unquestionably true that industrial technology (and, even more important, the social and economic consequences of that technology) has made the exercise of absolute power *possible*, there is no reason to believe—as Huxley apparently does—in a necessary correlation between technological progress and an increase in the actual use of technology for socio-political ends.

Actually, the applications of technology and science forms only a small (though extremely important) part in the techniques of power of these two books. Technology merely makes possible the realization of an operational philosophy designed

[7]See *Challenge*, October 1953, pg. 64.

to "freeze" the existing social structure in perpetuity. As such, it is introduced primarily for literary and pedagogic effect. Instead of a long discussion on conspicuous consumption, for example, we get a description of obstacle golf, escalator squash, and so forth. Instead of an elaborate analysis of the political effects of a directed hedonism we get hilarious accounts of "soma," "feelies," scent and color organs. In Orwell, where reference to technology is even more indirect and where the effect sought is realism rather than satire, technology is rarely hilarious and in one or two instances—as when Julia and Winston are discovered in their hideaway by the television screen—it is positively frightening. The reason why *Nineteen Eighty-Four* seems so much closer to home is that our experience has been almost exclusively with the conspicuous-production and police-state kind of dictatorship Orwell is describing. We have no historical experience with a conspicuous-consumption dictatorship based upon an economy of plenty and absolute psychological conditioning—although this may well come to be the more serious danger in countries like the United States.

An operational political philosophy can have no objective beyond the purely pragmatic one of effectiveness. Asked to justify dystopia, Mustapha Mond in *Brave New World* and O'Brien in *Nineteen Eighty-Four* both answer, in effect, "It works"; when asked, to what end, both must answer in terms of stability and order—or, in less polite language, the maintenance of existing power relationships. True, Mustapha Mond, when justifying himself to the Savage, refers to the happiness of absolutely conditioned people ("they get what they want and they never want what they can get"),[8] but in the con-

---

[8]Huxley, *Brave New World*, p. 264.

text of the novel this is really irrelevant since happiness is regarded as a means for the perpetuation of the Brave New World, not the other way round. As for O'Brien, he does not even bother to justify his exercise of power to Winston. Power for him is its own justification.

Let us leave the implications of such an operational view of power, as Huxley and Orwell apparently see it, for consideration later on when we discuss some of the moral questions raised by the two novels. Right now let us turn to some of the specific subgoals of the political philosophy on which *Brave New World* and *Nineteen Eighty-Four* are based. For the sake of convenience, we shall describe these subgoals, and the means devised for realizing them, separately for the two novels. Wherever there is overlapping (and on the subgoal level this is rare) we shall try to make note of it.

Take Huxley's novel first. Since his aim is clearly satirical (not too successfully realized it seems to me—witness Chapter III where for seven tedious pages he juxtaposes, often sentence by sentence, a lecture by Mustapha Mond on the obscenity of motherhood and a shower-room chat between Levinia and Fanny on the duty of promiscuity), Huxley's techniques must be taken *cum grano salis*. His is only a *caricature* of what could be. In the long run, however, the implications of this caricature—based as it is upon an economy of plenty—are perhaps even more frightening for "liberal" Western society than Orwell's historically better-known scarcity dictatorship based on fear, repression and misery.

The two principal subgoals of *Brave New World*, absolute depth conditioning on the subconscious as well as on the conscious level and a directed consumption economy, are intimately related. Since it is essential that consumption not only be conspicuous but be related toward those goods actually available in society, stability and satisfaction can be obtained only through deliberate standardization of demand rather than through adjustment of supply to a "capricious" (economically and politically speaking) and ever-changing demand. But, in the final analysis, this can be done only by exercising absolute institutional control over human utilities and aspirations. By assuming the possibility of artificial mass production of human beings, Huxley is able to have his Central London Hatchery and Conditioning Centre (Motto: Community, Identity, Stability) begin work before conception, let alone birth. The state is thus in a position to control the very condition of human existence. Life becomes literally a gift of the state.

Not only life, but happiness. It is here, I think, that Huxley makes his most telling criticism of industrial society in the West: our conscious pursuit of happiness as the *summum bonum* of life. The tragedy of *Brave New World* is that everyone (except Bernard and Helmholtz, the product of decanting errors, and the Savage, the offspring of a "vivaporous" mother who, therefore, doesn't count) is happy. The state, as Mustapha explains, *can* provide its subjects with happiness, and while this gift, like all others, has a price tag attached to it, who cares? Only a Savage, as Huxley ironically points out, claims the right to be unhappy.[9]

Nor is this merely a matter of semantics to be resolved with high-sounding platitudes concerning the difference between "real" happiness and "mere" gratification. In *Brave New World* mere gratification *is* real happiness, for the divine discontent, the "longing of the moth for the star," has been snuffed out and it has been snuffed out precisely because

[9]Huxley, *Brave New World*, pg. 288.

the state has benevolently gratified every (conditioned) desire. The danger of the prevailing welfare ideal of the industrialized (originally Western) world—whether it be sought through the state, through other institutions, or even through personal endeavor—is that it is potentially realizable. Perhaps not absolutely realizable as in *Brave New World*, but sufficiently to dull and limit the scope of human aspirations. While it is true that human wants are unlimited (at least, outside of Huxley's novel), it is questionable whether—except in a few rare exceptions—the desire to satisfy those wants is. Given a certain minimal degree of happiness, how many of us will rouse ourselves to risk the pursuit of more?

The happiness of its members is thus the single most important factor in assuring the stability of the Brave New World (unlike Orwell's *Nineteen Eighty-Four* which, much more conventional in this respect, is based on misery). Happiness, in other words, becomes a technique of power. Society *makes* people happy (rather than *allowing* them to be happy) and thus habituates them to the *status quo*.

It does this by: (1) absolutely separating sex from procreation and thus removing one of the biggest variables in human behavior; (2) standardizing aspirations, responses and behavior patterns —in this sense, Huxley's genetic differentiation into separate bio-psychological "classes" of homogeneous types (Alphas, Deltas, Gammas) does not seem to serve any immediate function beyond division of labor; the economy of plenty may require ability differences but the stable and "happy" society is better off without them (habituating Gammas that they are better off than Epsilons and vice versa is just so much extra work); (3) removing all inhibitions to gratification and all sources of pain, the idea being to remove all possible frustration;

and (4) making all gratifications dependent on society and, wherever possible, upon the economy of plenty rather than upon nature or individual ingenuity.

It will be seen that, while technology is essential in realizing each of these subgoals, it is not nearly as important as the value judgments upon which this synthesis between individual happiness and social stability is based. More on this later.

Now let us turn to 1984 which, at first glance, appears to be a much more appropriate nightmare. (The Brave New World, after all, was originally projected for six hundred years, although Huxley, in a 1946 Foreword, spoke in terms of a single century "if we refrain from blowing ourselves to smithereens in the interval.")[10] The horror of *Nineteen Eighty-Four* is much more direct, for we have all had experience (most of it happily indirect) with the kind of society Orwell is describing. It is merely the twentieth-century totalitarian state made absolute by carrying the political principles of twentieth-century totalitarianism to their logical conclusion. A pessimist might observe that *Nineteen Eighty-Four* is the only alternative to *Brave New World*.

What is its animating political principle? Fear, misery and repression, the obverse of *Brave New World* whose animating principle, as we have seen, is happiness through instantaneous gratification of every conditioned desire. The moralist in Orwell is very apparent in all this. For, if the state is forced to deny, repress and distort in order to maintain its power then there must be something to deny, repress and distort. If the state must corrupt man, then he is not corrupt to begin with. Unlike *Brave New World*, the state in *Nineteen*

[10]*Ibid.*, pg. xix.

Eighty-Four cannot control the condition of human existence. It can only condition the future of his existence. Instead of the gift of life, the state can offer only the punishment of death—a serious limitation in its power.

For Orwell was always a great believer in the essential "decency" (a favorite term of his) of man and this belief never left him even when, depressed and sick with tuberculosis, he retired to the Hebrides to write this last and most profoundly pessimistic of his novels. True, Winston Smith (the name is a tribute to the uncommon Englishman, Churchill, and the common Englishman, Smith) is finally destroyed, for not even the strongest man can withstand the new state. But there will be others. They will be crushed, of course, but still the cells and torture chambers of the Ministry of Love will never be empty. Most of the rebels will be unwilling, like Parsons and Ampleforth, and will oppose the state in spite of themselves. No matter, man will still be worth saving even when salvation is no longer possible. To the end, Orwell retained his Western faith in man—not natural man or civilized man, but "man who is born of woman" and "whose days are filled with trouble." He remained a humanist.

That, however, is the extent of Orwell's optimism. For, granted that man will continue to be worth saving, he can't be saved in 1984. The *proles*, who constitute 85 per cent of the population of Oceania and who are left free by telescreens and thought police to enjoy their misery, will not rise. "If there is hope," Winston had written in his diary, "it lies in the proles,"[11] but Orwell, though as a middle-class Western socialist he is obviously unwilling to deny moral superiority to those who work with

---

[11]Orwell, *Nineteen Eighty-Four*, p. 60.

their hands, has Winston crush such hopes. "Until they become conscious," he sadly confides to his diary," they will never rebel and until after they have rebelled they cannot be conscious." Keeping them unconscious, moreover, is not difficult for the state. The state need merely apply the old mildly repressive techniques of nineteenth-century capitalists and the *proles* will revert "to a style of life that appeared to them a sort of ancestral pattern. . . . Heavy physical work, the care of home and children, petty quarrels with neighbors, beer and, above all, gambling filled up the horizon of their minds."[12] The full force of the totalitarian state of 1984 is brought to bear only against the remaining 15 per cent, the party members who staff the offices of the Ministries of Truth (propaganda and the arts), Peace (war), Love (law and order), Plenty (economic affairs). It is these who are the potential candidates for rebellion.

The fundamental problem for the modern repressive dictatorship is how to maintain full employment and at the same time retain the sacrifices on which that dictatorship depends. Restricting the output of goods is obviously no solution, for the idleness and privations resulting from a deliberate policy of economic stagnation are obviously unnecessary and will inevitably lead to rebellion. On the other hand, it is equally clear (to old-fashioned meliorist Orwell at least) that an all-round increase in living standards would—given the capacity of industrial technology—make the continued existence of a hierarchical dictatorship impossible, since the state depends upon institutionalized instrumentalities to do the repressing. (The Brave New World, on the other hand, is self-regulating. Except for the need of industrial technology for

[12]*Ibid.*, pp. 61–62.

division of labor, the Alpha, Beta, Epsilon differentiation is politically unnecessary for the perpetuation of the "happy" dictatorship. Mustapha Mond, for example, is really a superfluous figure.)

In *Nineteen Eighty-Four* this dilemma of the repressive dictatorship is solved in the conventional manner, that is, through war. Other forms of conspicuous production (useless production of statues, wilful destruction, spoilage or hoarding), while they would accomplish the same end, are not satisfactory psychologically. War is not only "a way of shattering to pieces or pouring into the stratosphere, or sinking in the depths of the sea, materials which might otherwise be used to make the masses too comfortable and hence in the long run too intelligent";[13] it also stimulates an emotional atmosphere in which Doublethink can best flourish. As a result, the three superstates of the book—Oceania (the Americas, the British Isles and Atlantic islands, Australasia and South Africa), Eurasia (most of the Eurasian continent) and Eastasia (China, Mongolia, Tibet, Japan and the Pacific islands)—are engaged in continuous warfare with one another. Alliances keep shifting and the wars themselves, while they induce strong emotions, cause few actual casualties and are confined mostly to uninhabited borderlands and floating fortresses. Since none of the three superstates can be conquered by the other two in combination and since, moreover, there is nothing in a material sense left to fight about (each state being economically self-sufficient), wars become artificial techniques whereby the ruling élites in the three states can, in a psychologically acceptable manner, use up the products of the machine without raising living standards.

It would be impossible, however, for the repres-

---

[13]*Ibid.*, p. 157.

sive dictatorship to realize the full benefits of this mode of conspicuous production without "Doublethink"—a discovery that antedates 1984. "Doublethink", as Goldstein, Orwell's orthodox heretic, defines it, "is the power of holding two contradictory beliefs in one's mind simultaneously, and accepting both of them."[14] Without Doublethink the party would not function. For, when the party intellectual lies, it is essential that he both know that he is tampering with reality and at the same time genuinely believe in his life. Only thus is it possible to arrest the course of history. Only thus is it possible for the party to "change" objective reality by tacitly denying its very existence. The constant tampering with history (Winston's job consists in revising historical announcements to fit into the current party line), for example, is part of this massive attempt to destroy the individual's relationship with objective reality altogether. In a sense, as Orwell realizes, the freedom to say that two plus two makes four is the most essential freedom. And while Winston in the end is brainwashed into believing—actually believing—that two plus two equals five, Orwell leaves one with the impression that truth, while it will never prevail, will persist and will have to be continuously brainwashed out of human consciousness. Even Newspeak, the language of 1984 especially designed to encourage Doublethink, will never be totally successful in stopping Thoughtcrime from arising, even though it may be able to suppress the "crime" once it has appeared.

[14]*Ibid.*, p. 176.

CONCLUSION: A MATTER OF MORALS

It has become fashionable among social scientists in general and political theorists in particular to ignore questions of value and to concentrate exclusively on what is. Both the tradition of the natural sciences and the "open-endedness" of industrial society have encouraged this tendency. And, in a sense, this is understandable. A moral judgment of political behavior must, in the very nature of things, be at least partly *ex post facto*. It is no use to evolve theories of "ought" unless they are based on an empirical knowledge of "is."

Indeed, there can be little question but that a valid political theory that is not based on an "objective" study of political phenomena is impossible. By itself, however, such study cannot provide us with political theory, for it will not answer such fundamental questions as: What is the best form of state? Who should rule? How should a state be ruled? When "objective" political scientists try to generalize in terms of historical experience, saying this is how political institutions arose and functioned in the past, they are in fact passing judgment. For, their pragmatic emphasis on the "workability" of political institutions (whatever is, works) implies a value preference for those factors which make it work.

This bring us to the central problem of both *Brave New World* and *Nineteen Eighty-Four*: the system works splendidly. And it works so well precisely because stability (that is, maintenance of the *status quo*) has become the supreme goal to which all other non-operational values, such as truth, happiness, freedom, must be and are subordinated.

In both novels, there is no external value scheme against which either system can be measured.

It is against this sort of operational determinism that Huxley and Orwell rebel. Both are pleading for the right of individuals to be aware of and act upon "apolitical" values. And in *Nineteen Eighty-Four* and *Brave New World* they have shown what is likely to happen when that right is destroyed.

Newspeak, The First Edition
Alfred R. Ferguson

The invention of Newspeak sets *Nineteen Eighty-Four* apart from its dystopian precursors, *We* and *Brave New World*. Orwell was certainly knowledgeable of the totalitarian ploys suggested by Zamyatin and Huxley, and he had witnessed the gross fabrications of fact by the Communists during the Spanish Civil War and in Stalin's purges of the late thirties—in which individuals literally vanished without trace from record and recollection. But none of these tactics of totalitarian control begins to anticipate the sinister implications of Orwell's Newspeak, in which the meaning of language is so reduced that free imagination—individual thought—is systematically eradicated. With the perfection of Newspeak, dissent or deviation from Party orthodoxy becomes impossible. The words with which to express heretical ideas, mentally or verbally, simply no longer exist.

Perhaps Newspeak—and its concomitant, doublethink—are the ultimate horrors of Orwell's novel. On this score, Professor Ferguson presents convincing evidence that we have much to fear in the depletion of meaning that is occurring in language right now.

> "When I use a word," Humpty Dumpty said, in rather a scornful tone, "it means just what I choose it to mean—neither more nor less."
>
> "The question is," said Alice, "whether you *can* make words mean so many different things."

"The question is," said Humpty Dumpty, "which is to be master—that's all."

Lewis Carroll, *Through the Looking Glass*

Orwell's *1984* is both prophetic and historical. The essence of Orwell's meaning, it seems to me, is that totalitarianism for the twentieth century on incorporates something different from all historical despotisms and dictatorships. Something new— a new factor—has been added to the ancient equation of tyranny.

Modern advances in centralized administration and communications, and the modern machinery of terror are new. But these advances are related more to technology than to the induction of a radically new idea.

I believe that what was, what is, what will be "new" in future totalitarian schemes is not the addition of something new, but the negation of a value that up to the present century escaped absolute negation by would-be tyrants, dictators, or despots. The "new" negation is the negation of humanity's common denominator—the free imagination. By the "free imagination" I mean the faculty of perceiving self-initiated, non-conformist alternatives—ways of being, thinking, doing independent of the prescribed way.

In order to perceive alternatives, you must first be able to think creatively. To think creatively, you must possess two essentials: a memory, which is to say a history, and a language. Of these two essentials, language is primary, for without language there can be no coherent, consistent history. But history's secondary status renders it no less essential. It is just that, in point of time, language must precede history. So, perhaps, rather than saying that language is primary to history, it is more correct to say that language is primal. Therefore, for absolute totalitarian control of the present, the past, and the future, language and its fundamental expressive corollary, history, must first be wrenched out of specific referential context and specific relation to external, common-sense reality. This accomplished, both language and history may then become the servants of an absolute master. And this accomplished, life will be defined according to "which is master." And the rest is silence.

How is this to be done? Shortly after the opening scenes of the novel we learn that Winston's department in the Ministry of Truth, the Research Department, is working on a new and final 11th edition of the Newspeak dictionary—the "definitive" edition. Ultimately, by debasing the language through grammatical and syntactical distortion, and by narrowing the vocabulary to relatively few abstractions with non-specific content, this dictionary will make articulate speech issue from the larynx—guttural grunts or shouts—without involving the higher brain centers at all. Thereafter, no one will be capable of any thought external to the reality presented by authority, because the words to express the thought will no longer exist. Big Brother understands, though many of us do not, the interdependent relation between thought and language.

One of the paradoxes of language use is that the more abstract it is—the less concrete, the less specific, the less referential and image-bearing—the more restrictive it is to imagination, the less stimulative to creative thought. Through imagination, through creative thought, we subjectively perceive options and alternatives in relation to the external objective reality of our environment. The intention of abstract language is to restrict or limit the reality represented by a word to one possible meaning. One meaning, one reality—the prescribed meaning, the prescribed reality. Whether or not the prescribed reality has any reference to objective external reality is immaterial—literally. All that matters is, "which is to be master." If the power is not yet absolute, and if the guardians of language and freedom—and it's impossible to care for the one, freedom, without caring for the other, language—if the guardians of language and freedom are sufficiently careless, or befuddled, or cowardly, then it is only a question of time, Orwell tells us in his novel, until the power will be absolute. Whether or not you believe this logical progress is valid depends on whether or not you believe Orwell's apocalyptic vision is valid. For my part, I do not know if his vision is valid in every particular.

But this I do know: I know this to be an unprecedented time, when increasingly we mislead ourselves and each other by masking abstractions as concrete realities; by exploiting the fluidity of language for obfuscation rather than clarification; by making all sorts of noises in the larynx that do not tell us *really* about ourselves, the world we live in, or our relation to it or to each other. And I know that those expressive forms upon which we rely to tell us about ourselves in relation to reality—art, literature, philosophy, history—increasingly these expressive forms condition us to believe there exists no reality external to the individual consciousness. In the novel, the primary objective of Winston's torture is to elicit a conditioned response geared to a totally subjective reality, a prescribed reality valid to the individual consciousness in isolation, and valid to the consciousness of the mass, also in isolation. You recall the scene in Winston's cell, after his conditioning is nearly complete. He reflects on the "reality" that "Big Brother," through O'Brien, the interrogator, has imposed on him:

Anything could be true, Winston thought. O'Brien had said, 'I could float off this floor like a soap bubble.' [Earlier, Winston's conversion is signified by his admitting to O'Brien that 2 and 2 are five.] Winston worked it out. If he thinks he floats off the floor like a soap bubble, and I simultaneously think I see him do it, then the thing happens. Suddenly, like a lump of submerged wreckage breaking the surface of water, the thought burst into his mind: It doesn't really happen. We imagine it. It is hallucination. He pushed the thought under instantly. The fallacy was obvious. It presupposed that somewhere or other, outside oneself, there was a 'real' world where 'real' things happened. But how could there be such a world? What knowledge have we of anything, save through our own minds? All happenings are in the mind. What ever happens in all minds, truly happens.

There can only be a "real world" outside ourselves where "real things" happen, a world upon which the imagination can operate to produce alternative ways of being, thinking, doing, when the language describing that world is concrete, specific, objective, referential, image-bearing. To the extent our language is not concrete, specific, objective, and referential—to the extent it is abstract, meaningless, subjective—to that extent are we shut up in the prison of our minds, trapped into believing that *anything is possible*. And if we believe that *anything* is possible, then, paradoxically, nothing is possible of our own creation. And we become not the determinant of our destiny but those for whom destiny is determined. Here are three examples to support my argument. These examples are from advertising, government, and education. Bear in mind these are only three examples chosen at random from an unlimited choice awaiting the editors of this, our first edition of the Newspeak Dictionary.

Just as the task of the "Ministry of Truth" in *1984* was to "sell" people abstractions that the authority wanted sold, conditioning them to accept the prescribed reality, so too is it the task of the advertiser to "sell" ideas about a given product. And the relation of the product to an objective reality in a real world is as irrelevant as the lies issuing from the Ministry of Truth.

I am looking at an ad selected at random from the November 11, 1974 issue of *Time*, p. 58. The ad is for the "Mustang II Ghia." We won't bother analyzing the name, "Mustang," the Marlboro implications of machismo. Nor will we mention the "II," as if the machine had the personified legitimacy of royal or noble parentage, nor will we mention the "Ghia," which is, I assume, the name of some European designer—but in any case lends an air of the exotic to the otherwise prosaic. Moreover, it's a "Silver Ghia," suggesting something rare and precious. The picture of the car's interior is captioned: "Cranberry interior with crushed velour seating area."

Now, the sentence makes no referential sense. It is totally abstract—unless you are a cranberry freak and want to drive around *inside* one. The "crushed velour" will do, I suppose. "Velour" is really imitation velvet. As for "crushed"—I suppose that goes with cranberry sauce. But what is really interesting about the caption is the last phrase, "seating area." We shall no longer have seats in our cars. We shall now have "seating areas." Remember the rigidly defined terms of the "A" vocabulary in the novel?—the narrowing of meaning? What is a "seating area"? It is anything. And it is nothing. And so the paradox: the more abstract the expression, the less specific and referential, then the less opportunity (i.e., freedom) for individual conceptual understanding, and the greater the opportunity for imposition of understanding by external authority—until "seating area" could mean, I suppose, that you might ultimately be driving while sitting on the floor, unless you select plain ordinary seats as options at extra cost . . . "affordable," of course.

We also note that the "level of style and luxury is uncommonly high." Higher than what? Remember the food production figures in the novel? Remember that the chocolate ration this year was "uncommonly high"? Higher than what, or when? We don't know, for the abstractness of the phrase defies comparison with a "real world" where "real" things happen.

We could go on—"more exciting choices than ever," one sub-head reads. These "choices" turn out to be expensive options. One of these is something called a Dramatic Option, "a moon roof"—not meaning as the grammar of the language dictates, a roof made of a moon, but a plexiglass insertion in the top of the car for, presumably, gazing at the moon, though not, presumably, while driving.

All this is silly stuff, of course. No one takes it seriously. Certainly not the advertiser nor the manufacturer. And, believe me, neither wants you to take it seriously either. The intention of the language in this ad is to make you respond reflexively, automatically—without thinking. A "gut" reaction is all that is desired. All you need do is march in battalions to your Ford dealer, make some sort of guttural sound of assent, originating somewhere in the larynx, and your anxiety will be eased, instantly, as you throw yourself into the arms of Henry Ford II. Perhaps, in time, as did Winston with Big Brother, you will even come to love your benefactor, and the cranberry reality he has created for you.

The next example I want to discuss requires less analysis, because the example and its source are less sophisticated. It is a memorandum from John Dean to Richard Nixon, written at some point during the 1972 election campaign. Here it is: "We must maximize the encumbancy to screw our political opponents."

You will recall that the "B" vocabulary in *1984* consisted of words deliberately constructed for political purposes. In that vocabulary "mini" and "maxi" were outstanding entries: "minitrue," "minipax," "miniluv," and so on. Adjectival forms of these were "minitruthful," "minipeaceful," and so on. We do not yet, in our present non-fictional vocabulary, have "maximizeful." But, I assure you, it is coming. Like this: "Our activity level in the study area was maximizeful, with more impressive increase-wise gradefulness than ever."

In the light shed by recent history, we know exactly what Dean meant. (But suppose there were no history—or only the history Big Brother, or in this instance, Big Richard, had prescribed?) But because history was not obliterated via the "memory hole," as in *1984*, we know that Dean meant this: "In the campaign, the constitutional rights of political opponents must be denied by presidential power." You notice two outstanding features of Dean's language. First, it sounds innocuous, because it is abstract. "Maximize the encumbancy" means anything, everything—and, hence, nothing. Anything is possible. And was. The verbal phrase "to screw" seems specific enough, since everyone thinks he knows what "to screw" means. But as with all jargon and slang, the phrase is neither self-definitive nor referential, relying on context for definition. It is totally abstract, and cannot therefore stand alone, as can the phrase "deny constitutional rights to." So, anything is possible.

And was. It means, or meant, whatever Dick Nixon and Co. wanted it to mean. All that matters is (or, all that mattered was, who has (or had) the power. And, at that time, he did.

The next and last example is from my own field, education. The following statement, published for assimilation by innocent students, attempts to express the educational philosophy of a prominent professor on my campus. I quote it exactly as published, with original errors in grammar and usage left intact.

> I believe that the schooling process has two distinct functions, 1. to serve the individual student, and 2. to enculturate the student into the ongoing culture. Therefore, the only required classes in the schooling process should be those which deal with universals within a particular culture or those which serve the student with skills and knowledge to serve a positively re-forcing life within the culture. Schooling should offer an option rich environment for exploration of self in relation to the world. The role of the teacher is to facilitate the learning process by being a significant other in the life of the learner. In order to be an informed, helpful, friend who is motivated in his or her search for truth so as to serve a model in the learning environment. Schooling should be involved with feeling and action if the intellectualizing is to be meaningful in the life of the learner. To know without feeling and action is to be less than human. The electronic technology available today can provide option rich environments which powerfully expose knowledge to the learner while the teacher is free, 1. to help the student clarify how he feels about what he learns and 2. to structure experiences which will modify the learner's behavior in terms of what he has learned and how he feels about it.

The grammar of this stuff is perfectly hideous, a

kind of Platonic essence of flatulent bafflegab issuing from many quarters of the academy these parlous days—a perfect example of what the author of the Peter Principle terms "Peter Palaver," a pluperfect non-language comprised of abstractions that obscure rather than clarify—a verbal landscape so mucked up with impenetrable jargon that to figure out the meaning, if any, you must slog hip-deep through "word pollution." But, more seriously, and more ominously, you needn't stretch a point too far to imagine this stuff issuing from the "Minied Department" of the Ministry of Truth.

But not quite. Not yet perhaps. The good professor will need considerably more conditioning before he is promoted to Head of the "Minied Department." Unaccountably, he left out such ringing phrases as "optimal interpersonal integration," "extrinsic empathic adjustment," "diffuse cognitive awareness," "optimal peer-group orientation," "undifferentiated synergistic strivings," "vacillating psychosexual responses," "intrinsic interactional identification," and, finally, "maximized intrapersonal integration in the seating area, student-teacher-wise." Such omissions will surely constitute the "thoughtcrime" of the future—and, given the negative reactions of many to any thought expressed in plain, concrete, image-bearing English today, such omissions may constitute the "thoughtcrime" of the present.

We will not examine piecemeal this analysis-defying heap of verbal rubbish. That it is rubbish, abstract rubbish, all can see. That it is dangerous rubbish, fewer may perceive. But consider: Those of us such as George Orwell concerned with preventing the closing-off of alternatives available to the individual, thus making of him a regulated instrument of the State, an automaton totally "enculturate [d] . . . into the ongoing culture," think that the chief means of averting the ultimate disaster is by cultivating the imagination. We cannot cultivate a free imagination unless we possess the ability to express thought concretely. Lacking the ability to express thought concretely, our imagination will not be free to perceive alternatives in relation to the real, elemental, objective truths of the human condition in the real world. Without such truths we shall surely perish.

Through the development of language in our prehistoric past, anthropoid beasts were turned into men. The burden of Orwell's novel is: by the diminution, the abuse, the wrecking and distorting of language, by disconnecting the relation between words and reality—by these means shall men be turned into beasts.

Last spring the Conference on College Composition and Communications representing 3,000 English teachers voted "to uphold the right of students to their own language." Translated into plain English, this means: Because students neither speak nor write with clarity or precision, and cannot therefore think clearly or specifically, or concretely or objectively, these lucky students are to be granted the inestimable "right" to ultimately have some absolute authority subjectively define reality for them. "The question is," as Humpty Dumpty said, "which is to be master—that's all." And the rest is silence.

A Knight of the Woeful Countenance
Malcolm Muggeridge

Muggeridge was a close friend during the later years of Orwell's short life. This affectionate reminiscence reveals intimate details of Orwell's personality, such as his rejection of his middle-class background and Eton education, which manifested itself as humorously in some of Orwell's personal habits and proclivities as it did profoundly in his writings, or his ironically conservative attitudes, to which Muggeridge attributes much of Orwell's appeal to Englishmen.

Muggeridge's account of the exuberant discussions from the hospital bed in which Orwell related plans for future books, as well as the hopes Orwell pinned on his brief marriage to Sonia Brownell—ended by his death only a few days later—should dispel any contention that he intended *Nineteen Eighty-Four* to be his final testament. Rather, Orwell was a man who maintained hope to the end, in his own life and for all humanity.

I first became aware of the existence of George Orwell in the middle thirties when I read some articles of his on the Spanish Civil War which appeared in the *New English Weekly*, a publication founded by A. R. Orage to expound the principles of Social Credit. They provided the basis for *Homage to Catalonia*, one of his best books. These articles made a great impression on me. I liked their clear, simple style, and the obvious honesty of purpose which informed them. They touched a chord of personal sympathy, too. I saw in Orwell's strong reaction to the villainies of the Communist *apparat* in Spain a comparable experience to my own disgust some years previously with the Soviet regime and its fawning admirers among the intelligentsia of the West as a result of a stint as Moscow correspondent of the *Manchester Guardian*. So I sent Orwell an appreciative note, to which I received a polite reply.

Later, when I got to know Orwell, he told me the story of how the articles had been turned down by Kingsley Martin, then editor of the *New Statesman*. I pointed out that, in the same sort of way, my messages to the *Guardian* from the USSR—for instance, about the famine caused by Stalin's collectivization policy in the Ukraine and the Caucasus, and about the arrest of some British engineers on spurious espionage charges—had been either whittled down or unused when they were more than mildly critical of the Soviet regime. Orwell certainly felt very strongly about this matter. Once when we were lunching together at a Greek restaurant in Percy Street he asked me if I would mind changing places. I readily agreed, but asked him why. He said that he just couldn't bear to look at Kingsley Martin's corrupt face, which, as Kingsley was lunching at an adjoining table, was unavoidable from where he had been sitting before.

Orwell was to have a comparable experience with *Animal Farm*, which was offered first to Gollancz. His loathing of progressive publishers and publications, as a result of these incidents, was even greater than mine. He told me once with great relish that his model for the Ministry of Truth in *Nineteen Eighty-Four* had been the BBC, where he worked without much satisfaction during some of the war years. I was not inclined myself to regard Kingsley Martin, C. P. Scott and the other ostensibly 'enlightened' operators in the communications business as being intrinsically more despicable than the Northcliffes, the Beaverbrooks and the Henry Luces, though of course they brought into what is essentially a competitive, profit- or influence-seeking trade an extra dimension of sanctimoniousness. It gave me no anguish to eat my luncheon with Kingsley Martin in vision. Incidentally, neither Kingsley nor Gollancz retracted from their position *vis-à-vis* the Spanish Civil War articles and *Animal Farm*. In his autobiography Kingsley continues to contend that he was right not to publish the articles, and when I asked Gollancz, in the course of a television interview, whether he regretted having turned down *Animal Farm*, one of the few undoubted masterpieces of our time, he replied that, from the professional publishing point of view, it was undoubtedly a mistake, but he still thought that the considerations which led him to make it were valid. One of the great weaknesses of the progressive, as distinct from the religious, mind, is that it has no awareness of truth as such; only of truth in terms of enlightened expediency. The contrast is well exemplified in two exact contemporaries—Simone Weil and Simone de Beauvoir; both highly intelligent and earnestly disposed. In all the fearful moral dilemmas of our time, Simone Weil never once went astray, whereas Simone de Beauvoir, with I am sure the best of intentions, has found herself aligned with apologists for some of the most monstrous barbarities and falsehoods of history.

Orwell himself, of course, would never have accepted this dichotomy; if anything, he would have pronounced himself on the Beauvoir side. He was allergic to institutional and devotional Christianity, and considered himself—in a way, justly—as being temperamentally irreligious. Yet there was in him this passionate dedication to truth, and refusal to countenance enlightened expediency masquerading as it; this unrelenting abhorrence of virtuous attitudes unrelated to personal conduct such as was to be found in the disparity between Kingsley's editorial principles and editorial practice. The point is well put in a hitherto unpublished letter to me from Richard Rees, Orwell's close friend and subsequently mine, dated 8 March 1955, five years after Orwell's death:

> I am at the moment engaged in trying to write a longer and better sketch of Eric (Blair, Orwell's real name) than the one I wrote shortly after his death in which I try to show that his value consists in his having taken more seriously than most people the fundamental problem of religion. *Nineteen Eighty-Four*, for example, is more than a pessimistic political prophesy. The crisis of the book is when the hero, under torture, says: 'Do it to Julia, don't do it to me.' Eric was appalled, like the saints, by the realization that human nature is fundamentally self-centred; and in *Nineteen Eighty-Four* the triumph of the totalitarian state is not complete until it has been demonstrated to the last resister that in the last resort he would sacrifice the person he loves best in order to save his own skin. Personally, I think the book is morbid, because he was so ill when he was writing it. But it *does* reveal his true and permanent preoccupation; and that is why I always think of him as a religious or 'pious atheist.'

The 'longer and better sketch' became Rees's study of Orwell (*George Orwell, Fugitive from the Camp of Victory*, published in 1961), in my opinion easily the best there is. Rees was Orwell's closest friend, whom he chose with his widow, Sonia, to be his joint literary executor, and after whom he named his adopted son. It was in the *Adelphi*, when

Rees was editing it, that Orwell's first published work appeared (as, indeed, did mine), still signed with his own name, Eric Blair, before he had adopted the pseudonym by which he is now universally known. Only someone who was naturally religious—even if unconsciously so—could possibly have made a friend of Rees, whose own view of life was essentially a mystical one. When, to the great grief of his many friends and admirers, Rees died last year (1970), he had just completed his long, arduous, and brilliantly perceptive work on Simone Weil with the publication of her *First and Last Notebooks*—something for which I personally owe him a deep debt of gratitude. I am not saying that Orwell would have shared his admiration for Simone Weil; only that there is support for Rees's view of Orwell as someone concerned with the fundamental problem of religion in the fact that both of them—Orwell and Simone Weil—should have found in Rees their most sensitive interpreter, and Orwell his most intimate friend. Rees came to see me shortly before he died, and we talked about Orwell, as we often did. It struck me then how both of them, in rather different ways, recalled Cervantes's famous Knight of the Woeful Countenance. They were two Don Quixotes who never found a Sancho.

I made Orwell's acquaintance in the flesh through Anthony Powell, with whom for a number of years I was on intimate terms. Now, alas, we are estranged. Powell had spoken to me about Orwell as being an Etonian and a gifted writer, and I mentioned the *New English Weekly* articles. It was arranged that the three of us should lunch together in, I think, a restaurant in Fleet Street, and that was my first sight of Orwell. I had a certain stereotype of an Etonian in my mind, so Orwell's appearance came as a complete surprise. He was dressed in a sort of proletarian fancy dress; an ancient battered sports jacket and corduroy trousers, not actually tied up with string as in old comic drawings, but of the kind that could still be bought in those days in working-class districts and in seaside towns where fishermen live. In this, as in other matters, Orwell was ahead of his time; his costume is now *de rigueur* in public schools and universities, and is more or less the uniform of the middle- and upper-class young. He seemed very tall, the more so because he was so exceedingly thin; his face was decidedly cadaverous, with sad eyes, not particularly bright, and a thin moustache which left a narrow shaved strip between itself and his upper lip. As one can see very clearly in his writings about himself, and in his self-impersonations in his fiction, he was obsessed with the notion that he was physically unattractive. There is, for instance, the ugly birthmark which always shows up with particular vividness on the face of Flory, the hero of *Burmese Days*, in moments of stress and passion. He seems to have seriously believed that the poor smell, as he thought he did himself by comparison with the richer and better favoured boys at his preparatory school and Eton.

This notion of himself as abnormally plain and unalluring was, of course, quite absurd. He was decidedly attractive to both men and women. I personally took to him from the beginning, and grew even fonder of him; not just because of his kindly disposition, true humility and workaday attitude to his writing, and inflexible honesty, but also because there was something charming and winning about him. It was not that he was an amusing talker, or outstandingly original in his ideas. He was original in himself; a card, a dear fellow. If not witty, he was intrinsically funny. For instance, in the extraordinary prejudices he entertained and the naïve confidence with which he propounded them. Thus, he would come out with the proposition: 'All tobacconists are Fascists!', as though this was something so obvious that no one could possibly question his statement. Momentarily, one was swept along. Yes, there was something in it; those little men in their kiosks handing out fags and tobacco all day long—wouldn't they have followed a Hitler or a Mussolini if one had come along? Then the sheer craziness of it took hold of one, and one began to laugh helplessly, until—such was his persuasiveness—one reflected inside one's laughter: after all, they are rather rum birds, those tobacconists. His charming sister, Avril, who kept house for him when he was living in the island of Jura in the Inner Hebrides, gave me another example which greatly pleased me. Talking with a farmer, it seems, he slipped out, as though it was something everyone took for granted, the statement that in the old days ploughmen, following their hand-ploughs, developed an inequality between their shoulder blades, one rising higher than the other, so that special coats had to be made for them taking account of this, some of them even having leather patches for the higher shoulder. The farmer looked incredulous, and subsequent investigation failed to produce any confirmation of Orwell's statement, which he seems to have dreamed up entirely on his own. Even so, I still find myself, if I happen to pass a shop where agricultural clothing is displayed, looking to see whether any of the coats have a single leather shoulder-patch.

I once put the point about Orwell's obsessive sense of being physically unattractive to Cyril Connolly, who was with him at his preparatory school and at Eton. 'He was not a pretty boy', he said laconically, which I took to mean that he was not up to the minimum standard required for participation in the callboy arrangements prevalent at boarding schools. It is likewise obvious that Orwell did not find relations with the opposite sex easy. (Who, by the way, does?) The subject occasionally cropped up during our subsequent meetings; he and Powell and I got into the habit of lunching regularly, quite often with Julian Symons as well. Orwell characteristically held forth upon the logistic difficulties which dogged the penurious amorist. Where was he to go if he could not afford a hotel room and had no private accommodation at his disposal? He himself, he said, had been forced through poverty to avail himself of public parks and recreation grounds. As he dwelt upon his theme, he began to chuckle—a throaty, rusty, deep-down chuckle very characteristic of him. His laughter had the same rusty quality as did his voice, due, I understood, to a throat wound he received in Spain. It would have been a droll experience, I decided, to come upon Orwell stretched out on a summer's evening with the lady of his choice in Kensington Gardens or Regent's Park.

I never met Orwell's first wife, Eileen, but everyone who knew her speaks well of her. As it happened, I saw something of him in Paris in 1945 when she died. I was stationed there for the last year of the war as liaison officer with the French *Services Spéciaux*, and Orwell turned up as correspondent for the *Observer*. He had tried so hard to get into the army, but his poor state of health disqualified him, and he had to content himself with the Home Guard, in which, as a former belligerent, he was considered a gunnery expert. This, says Fred Warburg who served with him in the same platoon, represented a greater danger than anything they had to fear from the enemy. Now, at last, he was in what passed for being a theatre of war, and wearing battle-dress, though naturally trying to look as much like a private, and as little like an officer, as possible. With his quite extraordinary reticence about everything personal, one had no idea how he felt about his wife's death. I stuttered out a few words of sympathy, as one does, and then we talked of other things. My impression is that he was quite stricken.

Somehow, the memory I have of him in those Paris days is particularly clear and loveable. It was not that we did anything much or said anything much, but in the squalid circumstances of a war ending and an empty victory looming, his presence was reassuring. I always think of him as a hero—a hero of our time in the Lermontov style; and never more so than then, sloping about in his battle-dress, and, presumably, seeking out news stories for the *Observer*—though he never spoke about any such activities, and I never saw any of his messages. I had occasion to go to London from time to time, and he would ask me to bring him back some shag he used for making his deplorable cigarettes. It was difficult to track down in wartime London, and I recalled a remark of Mrs Naidu to Gandhi when he was a guest in her house, and she had been desperately searching round for goat's milk and other of his dietetic specialties: 'You've no idea, Mahatma, how expensive it is providing the wherewithal for you to fast.'

We often talked about India, where, as it happened, I had been—actually, teaching at a Christian college in what was then Travancore and is now Kerala—when he was serving in the Burma Police. The generally held opinion is that his time in Burma turned him against the British Raj and made an anti-imperialist and Socialist of him; that to, as it were, purge himself of his involvement in the Raj, he subjected himself to the experiences which resulted in *Down and Out in Paris and London*. From our conversations on the subject, and a careful reading of *Burmese Days*, I consider this to be a great over-simplificaton. In many respects he quite liked his Burma service; Christopher Hollis, a fellow Etonian, dined with him in Rangoon at the time, and found him a perfectly ordinary and relatively contented officer. There was, remember, a strain of violence in him which came out from time to time. Rayner Heppenstall has described one such occasion, when he was sharing a flat with Orwell and came home drunk, and Orwell beat him up mercilessly. It was a source of great pride to him that he was once arrested in Glasgow for drunken disorder, and spent the night in the cells. The parts of *Burmese Days* that most come alive are when he is describing hunting expeditions, and the general attitude of the book is much more Kiplingesque than Marxist. The 'natives' behave despicably; the *Sahibs* may be boors and bullies, but they dominate the scene in a time of crisis. After all, Orwell came from a family with a strong Anglo-Indian background. In a certain sense, he belonged to the Raj; he once told me that he thought *The Road to Mandalay* the most beautiful poem in the English language. I could sense his disapproval when I described to him how in Travancore I used to wear an Indian *dhoti* made of *kadi*, the homespun cloth which was the uniform of the nationalist movement, and live on Indian food which I ate with my fingers, and travel third-class on the railways, and suffer the tortures of the damned by making myself sit cross-legged on the ground. It was all pretty silly, I am sure, but well meant. To him it signified missionaries, whom he regarded with contempt. What he disapproved of, basically, in the Raj was that we in England, as he was fond of putting it, lived off the backs of underpaid, under-nourished and exploited coolies. This is what he felt he must expiate. Indian independence, when it came, gave him no particular satisfaction, but he saw it as an act of retribution.

Orwell's mania to identify himself with the poor and outcast in England had the same sort of basis. They had been wronged by his class, and he must somehow make it up. So he stayed in workhouses, consorted with down-and-outs, and in *The Road to Wigan Pier* gave what he considered to be an authentic picture of working-class life. Actually, as I occasionally ventured to remark to him, I think his data was derived much more from the *News of the World* and seaside picture postcards—two of his ruling passions— and even from Dickens, than from direct observation. In addition to his proletarian fancy dress, he was always trying to conform to what he considered to be proletarian behaviour. Hence the shag and the rolled cigarettes; in a public bar he would whisper that a pint of bitter should be ordered in such a way and drunk in such a way. He was concerned lest his voice and bearing should suggest the Etonian. Here, I really believe he need not have worried; but it is true that, however careful he might be about his clothes, his accent and his behaviour, he was always noticeable; not as an Etonian in a public bar, nor, for that matter, as a down-and-out in a saloon bar, but as Orwell, a dear oddity.

Though I should, I suppose, pass for being much more reactionary (whatever that may mean) in my views than Orwell, in our talk it often seemed the other way round. He was always going on about nancy poets and pacifists and sandal-wearing vegetarians with what seemed to me unnecessary and unfair virulence; he was inclined at times to be vaguely anti-Semitic, and he lambasted contemporary literary mandarins in a way that stirred up even in my breast a tepid desire to come to their defence. The truth is he was by temperament deeply conservative. He loved the past, hated the present and dreaded the future. In this he may well have been right, but it somehow went ill with canvassing on behalf of the Bevanites, and being literary editor of *Tribune*. In his own mind, however, he managed to work it all out, and considered himself the most consistent of beings. Part at least of his great popularity, on both sides of the Atlantic, has derived from this conservative undertow in his leftist course. A bourgeoisie like ours on the run is always looking for someone who combines impeccable intelligentsia credentials with a passion, secret or avowed—but better secret—for maintaining the *status quo*. They found it in a T. S. Eliot, in a W. B. Yeats, in an Aldous Huxley, in an Ezra Pound who has at different times expounded racialist views which would make any Afrikaner go pale with horror. They thought they found it, and perhaps to some extent did, in Orwell; though in his case the confection was characteristically weird.

Immediately after the war I saw Orwell occasionally in London, and, of course, rejoiced over the great success of *Animal Farm*. My older children read it with interest, and one of them wrote to him about it, receiving a charming note in reply. Then I went to Washington as a newspaper correspondent, and by the time I returned Orwell had gone to live in Jura. I had a letter from him there asking me to get him a saddle—God knows why, or what particular kind was required. The furthest I got in carrying out the assignment was to look vaguely at a saddle in the window of a shop in St Martin's Lane. I was living practically next door to Powell, and we quite often went for walks round Regent's Park. The subject of Orwell naturally cropped up from time to time. I think I admired him more than Powell did, but he and Powell had more in common; partly, I dare say, because they were both Etonians, and, in the best sense of the word conservative—something I have never succeeded in being. When word came that Orwell's health had again collapsed, and that he was in a sanatorium near Stroud in Gloucestershire, we decided to go and see him.

We walked the last bit of the way. It was a very beautiful day, and I remember feeling unreasonably cheerful considering the purpose of our journey. Orwell was in a wooden hut by himself. He looked terribly wasted and thin, and I think I knew then that he was likely to die. Visiting tuberculosis patients was, for me, part of the experience of childhood; my father's family was riddled with the disease, and when I was seven I developed symptoms myself and had to go away into the country. So I was familiar with that particular soft, purring cough; that almost mystical transparency of the skin—like a thin sheet of fibre-glass with a furious furnace on the other side. Orwell was in good spirits. He had managed to finish *Nineteen Eighty-Four*, but said little about it. He was as secretive about his work as about everything else. Incidentally, Avril told me that this secretiveness was hereditary; their father had been just the same. Powell and I had been laughing over an incident in a novel by Koestler; the hero, in seducing one of the female characters, through being circumcised, reveals that he is a Jew. Orwell was not as amused as we were. Of course it's not true, he said, that in this country only Jews are circumcised; but it is true that, generally speaking, the upper classes are and the lower classes aren't. He cited his own case at Eton, where in the changing-rooms he was very ashamed at being uncircumcised, and kept himself covered. It was a vintage Orwell point. On the way

back I suggested to Powell that he should tell Eve-
lyn Waugh, who then lived in the neighbourhood
of the sanatorium, that Orwell was there, so that
he might visit him. Whether at Powell's suggestion
or someone else's, I learnt afterwards that Waugh
did go and see Orwell several times, and afterwards corresponded with him in a very delightful
way. Despite all Waugh's efforts to appear to be an
irascible, deaf old curmudgeon, a sort of innate
saintliness kept breaking through. I should have
loved to see them together; complementary figures,
his country gentleman's outfit and Orwell's proletarian one both straight out of back numbers of
Punch.

Shortly afterwards, Orwell was transferred to
University College Hospital, near to where Powell
and I were living. We visited him quite often, but
mostly separately so as to tire him less. He was
full of projects for books he was going to write; on
Conrad, on Gissing—a dismal writer for whom he
had a great admiration—on anti-British feeling in
the United States. He quoted a remark in one of
Hugh Kingsmill's books to the effect that a writer
who has more to write cannot die. I think that
quite often before he would have been glad enough
to die; now he passionately wanted to live. He was
going to remarry, and go to Switzerland; he had
become a famous writer, his financial worries were
at an end. Sonia Brownell who became his second
wife represented everything he had always longed
for; she was beautiful, and in a generous, luxuri-
ant way; gifted socially, the familiar of writers
and painters. Yet I knew it was all a dream; writers still with things to write *can* die. His mind was
turning more than ever on what he had never had
and must not look to have—physical strength and
beauty. He indignantly showed me an advertisement for sock suspenders that he had cut out of a

newspaper; it was based on the notion of Perseus, and showed his gilded winged calves wearing these particular suspenders. How disgusting, he said, to use something so beautiful for so base a purpose! It shocked him more than anything. There seemed rather a lot going on in the world just then to be shocked about, but I let it pass, and agreed that the advertisement was disgraceful.

Sonia and Orwell were married in the hospital. It turned out to be quite an elaborate legal procedure getting permission, the intention being, I suppose, to protect dying millionaires from designing nurses. There was also a long discussion about what Orwell should wear. In the end a mauve velvet smoking-jacket was decided upon, which he wore over his pajamas. Powell bought it for him at Moss Bros. After the wedding (at which I was not present) he continued to wear the smoking-jacket in bed. I see him now in it, sitting up and holding forth about how, when he and Sonia set up house, all the kitchen fitments were to be in black rubber. At the bottom of the bed he had his fishing-rod, all ready for when they went to Switzerland in a few days time by special charter flight. Lucian Freud was going to accompany them. It never happened, of course. He died the day before they were due to leave. Sonia came to see us the same evening. She cried and cried. I shall always love her for her true tears on that occasion.

It turned out that Orwell had left in his will that he wanted a church funeral and to be buried in a country churchyard. Powell and I had the task of arranging the service. First, we went to an undertaker in Warren Street, and he said he would deal with all that side of things. Then we visited the rector of a nearby Regency church. He had, it was clear, never heard of Orwell, but we were able to persuade him that he was a writer of distinction.

When he heard the name of the undertaker he
noticeably cheered up; the two of them were, he
said, in close touch. We imagined them ringing
one another up—'Anything doing today?' The service went off without a hitch, though it was obvious that a good many of those present were
unfamiliar with Anglican liturgy. The thing that
held my attention all the time was the enormous
length of the coffin. It seemed they had difficulty
in procuring one long enough. Arranging for his
burial was more difficult. In the end the problem
was solved by invoking the help of the Astor influence to find a place for him in a country churchyard.
It somehow recalled Bakunin's death in Geneva,
where in the public cemetery, along with other
data, the profession of the deceased has to be
indicated. As being an anarchist is not a profession,
the only thing they could put in Bakunin's case
was: 'Bakunin—Rentier.'

Another provision in Orwell's will was that no
biography of him should be written. This did not
prevent the publication of a number of books about
him, and in the end Sonia decided that it would be
best to announce an authorized biography, with
me as the putative author. I made various vague
moves in the direction of doing it; such as going
through whatever letters and other documents there
are, meeting various people who had been connected with him, and trying to sort out my own
thoughts on the subject. In the end the project
defeated me, partly through my own indolence,
and distaste for collecting and absorbing the masses
of tape-recorded talk, much of it necessarily in-
tensely boring, which would constitute the bulk of
one's material. It seemed to me that Orwell, with
a cunning he sometimes displayed in life, had posthumously laid down a great smoke-screen of boredom between himself and any explorer who tried

to invade the privacy in which he had lived and died. There was the additional difficulty of the validity to be attached to Orwell's own testimony. Is, for instance, the account of his prep-school days in 'Such, Such Were the Joys' to be taken at its face value? Avril considers that, like Orwell's account of their home life, it is grotesquely distorted. She remembers him as a cheerful, eager schoolboy, and their home as a happy and contented one. Even Connolly suggests in the politest possible way that Orwell laid it on a bit thick. Art is a lie and facts are true; but art is the way to truth, whereas facts lead only down the plastic path of fantasy. Orwell is an artist, and as such lived and wrote his own biography. I think, as he wished, his will prove the definitive work.

Countdown to 1984: Big Brother May Be Right on Schedule

David Goodman

While the projections Orwell made about the triumph of totalitarianism in *Nineteen Eighty-Four* can be argued to be prophecy, warning, or merely grim fantasy, the novel makes numerous specific predictions about scientific and techological developments whose reality in today's world cannot be denied.

Futurist researcher David Goodman has made a long-term project of cataloguing Orwell's predictions and identifying and analyzing their real-life counterparts. The degree of accuracy and completeness with which Orwell saw the application of science and technology to political purposes is more than impressive; it lends a discomfiting validity to his more encompassing view of the possibility of totalitarianism in all modern politics.

Indeed, Goodman makes good use of our anxiety to paint an alarmingly possible vignette, based upon recent incidents in Europe and America, that could unleash the totalitarian apparatus that lies in readiness beneath the democratic facades of contemporary governments.

Some Scientific and Technological Predictions from 1984

Predictions in Military Science

1. Think tanks where experts plan future wars.

2. Improved missiles and bombs.
3. Planes independent of earth.
4. Lenses suspended in space.
5. Floating fortresses to guard important sea lanes.
6. Germs immunized against all antibodies.
7. Self-propelled bombs to take the place of bombing planes.
8. Earthquake and tidal wave control.
9. Efficient defoliants that could be spread over wide areas.
10. Soil submarines that could bore through the ground.

Predictions in Police Technology

1. Data banks containing detailed personal information.
2. Rapid access to and retrieval of data.
3. Two-way, flush-mounted televisions.
4. Remote sensor of heartbeat.
5. Tone-of-voice analyzer.
6. Sensitive omnidirectional microphone.
7. Police patrol helicopters.
8. Large telescreens for public viewing.
9. Memory holes for rapid destruction of information.
10. Scanner to detect and analyze human thought.

Predictions in Psychobiology

1. Improved electrotherapy.
2. Better techniques for hypnosis.
3. Improved truth drugs.
4. Control of the sex drive, specifically by abolishing orgasm.
5. The ability to artificially inseminate.
6. Reconditioning by implosive therapy or flooding.

7. New forms of physical and psychological torture.
8. A science of determining thoughts by facial expressions and gestures.
9. Televised group therapy.
10. Subcortical psychosurgery.

George Orwell wrote *1984* to warn the Western world about what he thought the future might hold. But though Orwell succeeded in creating a gripping vision of a thought-controlled, totalitarian world, his novel has failed to halt the forces that he saw leading the way towards totalitarianism. Now, with only a few years to go until 1984, the Western world is potentially much closer to his vision than most people realize. Though *1984* has failed as a warning, it has been succeeding brilliantly as a forecast.

The novel is filled with predictions, from the details of international treaties that would someday avert nuclear war to the future methods used by dictators to guarantee internal security against revolutionaries. Fortunately, some of Orwell's most terrifying forecasts have not yet come true—Big Brother does not stare from every available wall and many personal liberties have remained intact—but a surprising number of Orwell's speculations are now fact, and many others could become so in the near future.

Even as the book was being published, some of Orwell's predictions were beginning to come true. In the novel *1984*, Orwell pictures a world controlled by three great superpowers—Oceania, Eurasia, and Eastasia—which have achieved social and political stability by locking themselves into a nuclear stalemate. In 1949, the year in which the book first appeared and three years after Orwell began *1984*, 12 Western allies formed the North Atlantic Treaty Organization; the Soviet Union exploded its first atomic bomb; and the Chinese communists proclaimed a People's Republic in China. In the novel *1984*, the three superpowers wage continuous "warfare of limited aims" in a quadrilateral of land that includes much of Africa, the Middle East, and Southeast Asia. Today, the U.S., the U.S.S.R., and China struggle to gain influence throughout the Third World.

Even more accurate than Orwell's predictions of international relations are his forecasts of future developments in science and technology. Although the people of *1984* live close to the poverty level, technological progress is not wholly retarded, and throughout the novel Orwell speculates about dozens of future inventions. He talks about lenses in space, for instance, that would focus the heat of the sun on the enemy. These devices closely resemble the solar collectors that engineers are now designing to orbit the earth and beam down microwaves. Orwell mentions the possible use of disease germs immunized against all possible antibodies. Today, work on synthetic RNA and recombinant DNA points toward a major breakthrough in this field within the next five to ten years.

However, some readers object to considering the world of *1984* as even a possible future. Instead of a forecast, they prefer to see *1984* as a grim fantasy—Orwell's extrapolation of only the bleakest of his surroundings into a world where the houses are rotting, the roads are pockmarked by bomb craters, electric power comes on only sporadically, the water is cold, the soap gritty, and the cigarettes crumble to pieces.

But many of the social trends of the last three decades have been towards Orwell's *1984* vision, not away from it, and when the social developments are considered along with the technological similarities between Orwell's vision and the modern day, a future resembling *1984* must certainly be seen as *possible*.

Even more alarming is the realization that certain "triggering incidents" could make Orwell's future a *probable* one. In fact, these triggering incidents might even make the world of *1984* a *preferable* future, because eternal warfare and a loss of liberty would be viewed as the price that must be paid to avoid catastrophic destruction.

FROM POLYGRAPH TO PREDICTIONS

The government of Oceania monitors Party members by means of a remote sensor of human heartbeat. The sensors are located in the two-way telescreens built into every lodging, government office, and public square in Oceania. By tuning in on a certain person, government police can detect when he is lying or engaging in subversive activity.

I am particularly interested in these sensors because I invented such a device, and thus unwittingly helped to make one of Orwell's predictions come true. My work on the invention began when I was a doctoral candidate at the University of California at Irvine and wanted a way to measure simultaneously several of the physiological variables in salamanders. There must be a better way,

I thought, than plunging painful electrodes into a salamander's body.

And I found a better way, thanks to the electric field of extremely minute voltage that surrounds the bodies of all living organisms. A colleague and I developed very delicate voltage sensors that can measure this electric field, and researchers can now detect and record from a distance an animal's heartbeat, respiration, muscle tension, and body movements.

I took great satisfaction in the remote sensor until 1972, when I moderated a program on future studies at the University of California at Irvine. I had just finished recommending that remote sensing be used for painfree research on animals and human burn victims when a student named Marilyn Hart spoke up. She reminded me that in *1984* Big Brother uses such a sensor for a much more sinister purpose—to spy on the thoughts of suspect Party members. After the class was over I looked in my own copy of *1984* and discovered that she was right: Orwell's protagonist, Winston Smith, tries to sit as far away as possible from the remote sensor in the telescreen because "you could not control the beating of your heart, and the telescreen was quite delicate enough to pick it up."

The Orwellian applications of the remote sensor had never occurred to me, and I was shocked to realize that I could be an inadvertent collaborator with Big Brother. I continued reading *1984* and soon resolved to identify the predictions Orwell had made in the book and find out how many had come true.

Several months later, with my colleagues Gary Swift and William Sparks, I counted the predictions that Orwell makes in *1984*. We identified 137 specific predictions, which we divided into two categories—(1) scientific and technological predictions and (2) social and political predictions. We found that about 80 of Orwell's predictions had already (in 1972) been realized.

More than 20 predictions related directly to psychobiology, my own field, but I felt reluctant at first to discuss the psychobiological aspects of *1984* with others in my profession; after all, it is not pleasant to think that we have been preparing a *1984* world. But because of several startling revelations, my reluctance dissolved. First of all, it became known in 1975 that a group of brain researchers, funded by military intelligence, had been working covertly on methods of hypnotic interrogation and behavior control through ultrasonics and electromagnetic radiation. Then, in July 1977, it was revealed that the U.S. Central Intelligence Agency had spent nearly $25 million studying behavior-altering drugs like LSD and pentothal.

In 1978 I returned to the list of 137 Orwellian predictions that we had complied six years earlier. This time I found that *over 100 of the predictions had come true*. There is now no doubt in my mind that *1984* describes a future that is clearly possible.

THE SCIENTIFIC AND TECHNOLOGICAL PREDICTIONS

The governments of *1984* are able to exercise such strict control over their citizens largely because they have adapted the fruits of science and technology to their own ends. Thus, although the scientists and technicians of Oceania are not free to study subjects of their own choosing, the government sponsors huge research projects in certain areas. Specifically, scientists are either psychologist-inquisitors engaged in perfecting psychoscience mind control, or physicists, chemists, or biologists seeking to create ever greater weapons of destruction.

Orwell therefore presupposes a fairly high level of research and development in the world of *1984*, and either explicitly or implicitly he speculates about many future developments in science and technology. I have chosen 30 of these as a sample, and have divided them into three categories—the sciences of the military, the police, and the psycho-scientists—to examine Orwell's foresight in each.

Military science. In the years right after World War II, most of the military devices Orwell envisioned were either nascent ideas held by a handful of scientists or wild speculations still limited to science fiction. But since that time, scientists in the service of the military have doggedly kept pace with Orwell's imagination: today, not one of the ideas listed is beyond contemporary capabilities. For instance, Orwell foresaw "vast laboratories" where "teams of experts are . . . planning the logistics of future wars." Such laboratories have their real-life counterparts today in the RAND Corporation and other think tanks serving the military. The Doomsday researchers of *1984* try to figure out "how to kill several hundred million people in a few seconds without giving warning beforehand." Today the solution is at hand as scientists miniaturize atomic weapons (the smallest in the U.S. arsenal is only six inches in diameter), concoct more deadly chemical and biological weapons (the latter made all the more frightening by the possible use of manufactured virulent microbes), and strengthen enhanced ion beams and laser "death rays" (now proven capable of stopping antitank missiles in flight). Moreover, as Orwell imagined over 30 years ago, planes can refuel in flight as they fly toward enemy targets; ballistic missiles can hit a large city block from a launching pad a continent away; and projectiles such as the cruise missiles operate according to guidance signals from self-contained intelligence.

Orwell's scientists are working to develop "poisons capable of being produced in such quantities as to destroy the vegetation of whole continents." The U.S. military's "Agent Orange," a defoliant widely used in Vietnam, meets that requirement. Orwell's soil submarine would "bore its way under the soil like a submarine under water." U.S. government scientists recently suggested building a machine that would melt its way through the ground with the heat from a nuclear reactor in its prow. Orwell imagined floating fortresses—man-made islands that would prowl the sea lanes and then be able to remain stationary for months or years. Such floating fortresses have not yet appeared, but if a prototype of such an island-weapon could be created before the late 1980s, then all of these "Orwellian" military technologies could be operating within the next five to ten years.

Police science. The technology of police surveillance and citizen control has kept abreast of progress in military science. Orwell accurately foresaw the development of large data banks—today's electronic computers—that would contain detailed information about all Party members. Furthermore, the invention of fiber optics and microwave communications allows modern technologists to store and retrieve this information with the same speed as the inquisitors of Oceania.

Orwell also predicted that television would help solve the police problems of *1984*. He writes of large public television screens in every meeting hall that continuously pour forth news, spurious statistics, and political propaganda. All home televisions are two-way flush-mounted telescreens, equipped with scanning lenses, powerful omnidirectional microphones, and remote sensors of heartbeat. With the telescreen, the government keeps its citizens under almost constant surveillance. Externally and internally, Big Brother Is Watching You.

To improve the telescreens, the scientists of Oceania are hard at work devising tone-of-voice analyzers and brain-wave sensors. Eventually, they hope to enable the secret police to reach their ultimate goal: "To discover, against his will, what another human being is thinking."

All of these devices are within the state of the art of today's technology. Ours could become the most snooped on, computer-analyzed society in history. Television scanners equipped with electronic detectors of heartbeat, brain-waves, and voice stress could collect physiological and behavioral data which could then be conveyed by microwaves or fiber optics to a central data bank for instantaneous cross matching with the electronic profiles of known subversives and dissidents. Suspected persons could be traced, arrested, and imprisoned— just as in *1984*.

Psychoscience. All told, Orwell managed to foresee some of the most important devices of the last three decades. But nowhere was his foresight sharper than in the field of psychoscience. In Oceania, no man's thoughts are inviolate. The Thought Police can tell from a person's "friendship, his relaxations, his behavior toward his wife and children, the expression on his face when he is alone, the words he mutters in sleep, even the characteristic movements of his body" whether he is being faithful to the Party. After identifying a dissident, the Thought Police use drugs, electric shock, and intricate forms of mental and physical torture to force a person to conform to Party norms.

In recent years, the science of psychoscience has gone even beyond that of *1984*. Since 1963, the number of brain scientists has increased tenfold to more than 6,000. In the U.S., the Bureau of Narcotics, the Department of Justice and the CIA have become new sources of research funds. The broadening interface of academic science and government control has already begun spilling into the laboratory from the pages of *1984*.

More than 3,000 therapies to modify behavior are now recognized. Many suggest little more than transmogrified torture: Modern therapists may systematically pound the body or administer electric shocks to improve people's health or cure them of inappropriate habits. Even Orwell's most frightening treatment, a prolonged and intimate contact with a dreaded phobic stimulus (rats in the case of Winston Smith), has been brought into modern therapy under the name of implosion or "flooding."

Truth drugs have recently begun to play a larger role in improving rapport during psychotherapy: nitrous oxide, carbon dioxide, ether, hallucinogens like LSD, sodium pentobarbital, and sodium amytal have all been used to induce an uncensored flow of thoughts: sodium amytal generally is considered the best disinhibitor. For a severe mental case, a psychosurgeon may still be permitted to perform a lobotomy—a severing of some neural tracks of the brain's frontal lobes.

Researchers now routinely insert electrodes into the orgasm center of the brain. Other implant techniques enable scientists to inject chemicals like cocaine directly into the brain, or even to insert supercooled electrodes to freeze certain brain tissues. Some daring psychoscientists have even tried to use the body's own immunological system to destroy certain specified nerve cells, thus altering behavior.

The result of all this scientific progress is a psychocivilized society—a world where people achieve better living through surgery, electric currents, drugs, flooding, structural integration, bioenergetics, hypnosis, and control of body language. Clearly, few, if any, of the possibilities for mind control that Orwell foresaw go beyond the therapy sessions of today's researchers. With respect to the brain and behavior, *1984* science is here now.

THE SOCIAL AND POLITICAL PREDICTIONS

Our studies indicate that *all* of Orwell's scientific and technological predictions have either already come true or could soon come true. But such a judgment cannot be rendered so easily on Orwell's social and political forecasts.

To some futurists, many of these social and political speculations still seem incredible: In Oceania, no part of a Party member's life is personal, not even his thoughts. The government, through the Thought Police, works to convince everyone that external reality does not exist, that the only measure of the past is people's memories and written records, both of which are altered constantly to suit Party dogma. Oceania is a country of constant fear, where public executions, search without warrant, and imprisonment without cause are commonplace.

Some futurists, in fact, hardly acknowledge Orwell as a prophet at all. Both Richard Farmer in *The Real World of 1984* (David McKay Company, New York, 1973) and Jerome Tuccille in *Who's Afraid of 1984* (Arlington House, New Rochelle, New York, 1975) foresee a "satisfied plenty" and "exuberant democracy" ahead for the American people. Although they admit the technological change is altering people's lives, they believe that people will come to accept technological advancement as inevitable and learn to use technology to further, rather than destroy, human privacy.

But the social trends of the last 30 years have brought the West closer to *1984* than ever before, and these trends could rapidly accelerate under certain circumstances. Of course, the correspondence between Orwell's world and our own varies widely depending on the specific feature under consideration, but the overall drift is obvious.

Doublethink. In *1984*, doublethink is a mental facility required of every good Party member. Orwell defines it as "the power of holding two contradictory beliefs in one's mind simultaneously, and accepting both of them." Furthermore, "the process has to be conscious, or it would not be carried out with sufficient precision, but it also has to be unconscious, or it would bring with it a feeling of falsity and hence of guilt."

Essentially, doublethink is Orwell's projection of the tendency he saw in people to subvert reality to ideological abstractions. Orwell especially detested this trait in the liberal Soviet sympathizers who became apologists for Germany after the Hitler-Stalin pact, and this incident formed much of the base for doublethink in *1984*. But doublethink marks all political propaganda to some extent. A recent example was in the late 1960s when the Nixon administration overtly promoted domestic law and order and decried all forms of "civil disobedience" while covertly ordering telephone taps, sponsoring break-ins, opening the mails, keeping its "enemies" under surveillance, and committing other ostensibly lawless acts.

Denial of objective reality. The Party in *1984* teaches its members that "reality is not external. Reality exists in the human mind, and nowhere else." In this way, the good Party member learns how to sift his sense impressions through an ideological filter, acknowledging acceptable information and ignoring everything else.

Such solipsism is now widespread in our age of growing social confusion and eroding traditional values. The increasing use of alcohol and other drugs may be an attempt to avoid a look at life that would be too painful to bear. Politicians also deny objective reality by backing policies that are unrelated to the actual needs of their constituencies.

Newspeak. The linguists of Oceania are busy replacing traditional English with Newspeak, a language so impoverished that "a heretical thought . . . should be literally unthinkable, at least so far as thought is dependent on words."

Today the steady degradation of the English language is a constantly lamented fact. Verbal tests scores have fallen for a decade; bureaucratic gobbledygook grows more dense as the problems of government grow more complex; and politicians continue to mangle the language with their neologisms (as when bombing raids become "protective reaction strikes").

Mutability of the past. In Oceania, history is completely rewritten every day to suit the needs of the Party. Day-to-day falsification of published records helps assure the stability of the regime in power. One of the Party's slogans is "Who controls the past controls the future; who controls the present controls the past."

Revising the records of the past to fit current policies has long been standard procedure in many countries and has recently become increasingly common in the Western world. Histories are rewritten, tape recordings erased, records deliberately "lost," and past statements dismissed as "inoperative."

Big Brother. The gigantic face of Big Brother, the supposed ruler of Oceania, peers down from posters pasted on buildings and billboards. "He is a face on the hoarding, a voice on the telescreen. . . . Big Brother is the guise in which the Party chooses to exhibit itself to the world. His function is to act as a focusing point for love, fear, and reverence, emotions which are more easily felt toward an individual than toward an organization."

With today's paternalistic government and powerful presidency, Big Brother may be somewhat diffused but just as strong. An interesting aspect of Big Brother's presence lies in the composition of his face. He is worshipped solely because of the strength, charisma, and self-assurance that seem to exude from his features. Today, television personalities (and especially newsmen) are often chosen because they have this same kind of face.

Continuous war. The three superpowers of *1984* have adopted continuous war as an expedient to "use up the products of the machine without raising the general standard of living." In this way, "the consequences of being at war, and therefore in danger, makes the handing-over of all power to a small caste seem the natural, unavoidable condition of survival."

Today's arms race is the equivalent of Orwell's

continuous war. In addition, the current struggles in Africa, the Middle East, and Southeast Asia show many of the same qualities as the war in *1984*. With regards to the Orwellian purpose of continuous war, the experiences of the 1960s are enough to remind us that some of the worse violations of personal liberties have occurred during time of war, usually in the name of national security.

Breakup of the family. One of Oceania's greatest methods of personal disorientation is the dissolution of the family. Breaking the emotional ties between man and woman, parents and children, eliminates bonds that would detract from a person's absolute devotion to the State.

In America, the divorce rate more than doubled between 1963 and 1975, with more than one out of every three marriages now ending in divorce. The subsequent withdrawal into self has contributed to a growing aimlessness and a wide search for something to replace personal relationships. Might not the new something be a political adventure?

Unwarranted search and surveillance. In Oceania, as in most totalitarian states, due process of law is merely a toothless legalism. A man's home is the government's castle. Any citizen can have his dwelling ransacked and possessions seized as evidence to be used against him. Telescreens provide almost complete physical surveillance, and even the mind is not exempt from probe.

Personal privacy has steadily eroded in recent years. The surveillance of alleged subversives by U.S. government agencies has been documented by congressional testimony. Both government agencies and private companies employ investigators to make personal credit checks. Some journalists use hidden microphones to collect information for their articles. And satellites orbit the earth maintaining constant surveillance of areas as small as a square yard.

Public hangings. The government of Oceania uses public executions as a warning to critics and malingerers. The criminal displayed after execution by hanging encourages the populace not to break the law or go against Party dogma.

In the U.S., a well-known Texas politician recently recommended public hangings as a deterrent to crime after the Gary Gilmore incident. More generally, the increasing acquiescence of the American public toward violence in the movies and TV bears a close resemblance to the mood of savagery that marks the people of Oceania. The vicarious pleasure taken in violence is one of the strongest parallels between modern society and the world of *1984*.

The social trends of today clearly indicate a general decay of individual liberties, rational thought, personal privacy, and self-determination; a *1984*-type future is getting closer every year. But the critics of *1984* are quick to point out that "it can't happen here" and that *1984* certainly could not come true only five years from now. They maintain that our democratic beliefs run too deep to be destroyed by a predatory Big Brother.

They are partially right. None of the social trends have yet reached the intensity that Orwell envisioned in *1984*, and at the current rate of "progress" an Orwellian future is definitely more than just five years away. Unfortunately, the trends could speed up. Not one of Orwell's predictions is beyond the range of possibility, and almost any of the social and political trends described above could be brought to a head by just *a single triggering incident*.

THE TRIGGERING INCIDENT

Orwell wrote *1984* partially to deprecate the excesses that the Soviet and German states committed before and during World War II, but the novel is not simply a polemic against collectivist societies or a diatribe against dictatorship. During most of his adult life, Orwell was disturbed by the wave of totalitarianism sweeping the world, and he often pointed out how the mentality leading to its spread was growing in England. In his 1939 novel *Coming Up for Air* Orwell's English protagonist muses about "all the things you've got in the back of your mind, the things you're terrified of, the things you tell yourself are just a nightmare or only happen in foreign countries. The bombs, the food queues, the rubber truncheons, the barbed wire, the colored shirts, the slogans, the enormous faces, the machine guns squirting out of bedroom windows. It's all going to happen . . . its just something that's got to happen."

In the course of Orwell's novels, it finally did happen in *1984*. Orwell did not believe that the state he described in the novel would come to the West in just that form, but he did believe that something resembling it could arise. In 1949, right after the book was published, he said: "I believe . . . that totalitarian ideas have taken root in the minds of intellectuals everywhere, and I have tried to draw these ideas out to their logical consequences. The scene of the book is laid in Britain in order to emphasize that the English-speaking races are not innately better than anyone else and that totalitarianism, if not fought against, could triumph everywhere."

Today, the fight against totalitarianism in America has been scaled down from the national obsession of the 1940s and 1950s to become the concern of a limited number of specialists. And yet many of the features of totalitarianism are still growing. If these trends continue, how many years will pass before the tyranny of totalitarianism overtakes the West?

Moreover, what if these trends suddenly quicken? The prospect is so distressing that most people would sooner not think about it. But the facts suggest that a number of different types of events could bring about the abrupt appearance of a *1984*-type government. One such development is the sudden appearance of terrorist groups armed with atomic weapons.

The terrorists would not even have to use atomic weapons to cause a massive reshuffling of social priorities. If they simply issued a clearly credible threat of nuclear attack, governments would have to take drastic steps to stop them or minimize possible damage. Such governmental action would almost inevitably result in some curtailment of individual rights.

Furthermore, most people would willingly agree to give up those rights, as shown by the willingness of airline passengers to waive some of their rights in the face of a real or imagined threat by terrorists. How many more rights would people yield in the face of a threat to thousands of lives or to the structure of their society?

Many people clearly might view a *1984*-type world as a *preferable* future where the alternative is nuclear destruction. If terrorists actually exploded an atomic weapon somewhere in the Western world, the willingness of people to give up their liberties would greatly intensify. A nuclear explosion could easily infuse society with the siege mentality and war hysteria that the Oceania government adapts to its purposes. Some suggestion of what might happen is the state of virtual warfare that prevailed in Italy during the kidnapping of former premier Aldo Moro.

By actually exploding a nuclear weapon, terrorists could destroy almost the entire government of a major country. The result could be a power vacuum that would be filled by either the most powerful insurgent group fighting to gain control or by the group most desiring of power. In neither case would there likely be an overriding concern for individual rights.

Thus a future similar to that of *1984*, where survival is bought only at the price of subservience, could come on schedule if terrorists gain access to atomic weapons in the years before 1984. And, regrettably, the evidence suggests that nuclear technology now is sufficiently diffused that such a contingency is well within the realm of possibility.

For example, a professor at a large American university announced last summer that he had devised a way to immensely simplify the separation of uranium isotopes. By using a carbon dioxide laser, enough weapons-grade U^{235} for a bomb could be produced in about a year; the critical mass for U^{235}, when encased in a beryllium neutron reactor, is only 11 kilograms. The professor pointed out that the cost, approximately $100,000, is within the capabilities of many small organizations.

Several published reports of past years have documented the laxness of the safeguards applied to uranium and plutonium. And if the material is available, the know-how needed to make an atomic bomb is easily acquired. Last year, two college students announced that they had managed to design a working model of an atomic bomb using only unclassified information.

The proliferation of atomic weapons makes a future like *1984* look almost probable. A well-known rule of thumb states that technology of any kind usually takes 30 years to move from the innovators to the consumers. Since atomic bombs were first exploded in 1945, the time may have come for the general distribution of small, portable, and potentially catastrophic nuclear weapons.

Nuclear terrorism is only one type of development that might usher in *1984*. Almost any major disruption of life in the Western world could lead to some loss of personal liberties. Almost any large economic or ecological catastrophe could clear the way for the rise of totalitarianism. For instance, a massive famine in Mexico could lead to a stampede of refugees into the U.S., forcing the American government into much more vigilant security; a conventional border war could escalate into a major nuclear confrontation; and any nuclear war between superpowers would undoubtedly cause a substantial clampdown on individual liberties. The political situation of Orwell's *1984* arises out of a limited nuclear war that Orwell foresaw happening in the 1950s; luckily, that Orwellian prediction did not come true. But the possibility for such a war increases as nuclear weaponry become refined and available.

MUST WE LIVE THIS FUTURE?

The possibility of Orwell's *1984* becoming reality—perhaps even before the date he specified—is clear. Whether or not it really happens will depend on what we do today. We must prepare to act on two fronts—to *prevent* the triggering incidents from taking place, and to *reverse* the social trends that are leading the Western democracies towards *1984*.

In pondering these problems, we should not expect answers from government bureaucracies. As Willis W. Harman of SRI International has noted: "Society tends to hide knowledge from itself that is superficially threatening to the status quo, even though this knowledge may be badly needed to resolve its most fundamental problem." Being organizations that act to define society's status quo, bureaucracies are far too inertia-bound to discover innovative solutions to the potential threat of totalitarianism. Current administrators, trained to react only after a crisis has occurred, cannot confront the challenges of this second phase of the Atomic Age, when weapons-making information is widely disseminated.

An approach that might form a viable starting point for an initiative to prevent *1984* conditions is the suggestion of biophysicist and futurist John Platt that the countries of the world establish Councils of Urgent Studies. These councils would study what Platt calls the "crisis of crises"—the flood of world problems that are occurring simultaneously in the current age of transformation. In doing this, they would have to give immediate attention to the specific crises that could lead to *1984*.

Forming the councils would be a project similar to mobilizing the country's top minds during wartime. "We need full-time interdisciplinary teams," Platt contends in his book *Perception and Change: Projections for Survival*. These teams must include "natural scientists, social scientists, doctors, engineers, lawyers, and many other trained and inventive minds, who will put together our stores of knowledge and powerful new ideas into action-oriented, policy-directed 'social inventions' that will have a chance of being adopted soon enough and widely enough to be effective."

Platt's councils would have two main tasks: first, to identify and appraise potential problems before they become uncontrollable and, second, to solve them. The councils would devise possible solutions to future problems and then seek to implement them by communicating with policy-makers and the general public. With respect to nuclear terrorism, for instance, the councils could study the political and social consequences of terrorist attacks and originate plans to enable society and its institutions to survive.

Platt's Councils of Urgent Studies proposal is only one approach towards finding some way to protect individual liberties in the years ahead. Others need to be developed and implemented lest the remainder of George Orwell's prophecies be realized.

Chronology of Important Dates
Samuel L. Hynes

	Orwell	The Age
1903	George Orwell (Eric Arthur Blair) born June 25 at Motihari, Bengal.	
1917 –21	At Eton.	World War I ends, Nov. 11, 1918.
1922	Joins Indian Imperial Police. Serves in Burma until August 1927.	
1928 –29	In Paris, working as dishwasher; writing. Returns to England end of 1929.	Wall Street crash, October 1929. Beginning of Depression. One million two hundred thousand unemployed in Britain, 1929.
1931	In London, living with poor; hop-picking in Kent; tramping.	Two million seven hundred thousand unemployed in Britain.
1933	*Down and Out in Paris and London* published (January).	Hitler becomes Chancellor of Germany, Jan. 30. Reichstag fire Feb. 27; Hitler suspends civil liberties. Persecution of Jews begins.
1934	In London, working as bookseller's clerk; writing.	Stalin's purge of Russian Communist Party begins.

1935	*A Clergyman's Daughter* (March); *Burmese Days* (June, but written 1931–33).	Germany reoccupies Saar, repudiates Versailles Treaty. Italy invades Abyssinia.
1936	*Keep the Aspidistra Flying* (April). Leaves for Spain, Dec. 15; joins POUM December 30 in Barcelona.	Spanish Civil War begins, July 18.
1937	*The Road to Wigan Pier* (March). Orwell wounded in throat, May 20. Returns to England.	Bombing of Guernica, Apr. 27. POUM suppressed by Spanish Communists.
1938	*Homage to Catalonia* (April). Orwell ill with tuberculosis, goes to Morocco for winter.	Chamberlain, British Prime Minister, meets Hitler at Munich, gives him Czechoslovakia, Sept. 29.
1939	*Coming Up for Air* (June).	Barcelona falls, Jan. 26. Madrid surrenders to fascist troops, March 28, ending Spanish Civil War. Britain and France declare war on Germany, Sept. 3.
1941	Goes to work for BBC as propagandist.	Battle of Britain, summer 1940–spring 1941. Germany invades Russia, June 22.
1943	Leaves BBC, begins *Animal Farm*.	Italy surrenders, Sept. 3.
1944	Completes *Animal Farm*.	Allied invasion of Europe at Normandy, June 6.

1945	*Animal Farm* published (August).	Germany surrenders, May 7. British elect Labour government, July 26. U.S. drops first atomic bomb at Hiroshima, Aug. 6. Japanese capitulate, Aug. 19.
1946	Takes house on Jura, in Hebrides.	First session of United Nations General Assembly, London, Jan. 10.
1947	Enters hospital with tuberculosis, December 20.	Economic crisis in Britain.
1948	Continues writing; returns to Jura in July. *1984* finished (November). Suffers relapse.	British pound devalued. Communist *coup d'état* in Czechoslovakia. Russians close off Berlin to Western powers.
1949	*1984* published (June). Orwell enters sanatorium Jan. 6.	Chinese Communists proclaim establishment of People's Republic of China, Oct. 1.
1950	Orwell dies in London, Jan. 21.	Korean war begins, June 25.

THE CONTRIBUTORS

JAMES CONNORS teaches history at the University of Hawaii, Manoa, Honolulu. He has authored several articles on Orwell.

ALFRED R. FERGUSON is a professor of history at the University of Wisconsin, Osh Kosh.

OTTO FRIEDRICH worked on the editorial staffs of *Stars and Stripes*, the United Press, the *New York Daily News*, and *Newsweek* before joining the *Saturday Evening Post*, where he held several positions between 1962 and 1969. He is the author of *Before the Deluge: A Portrait of Berlin in the 1920's* (1972) and *Going Crazy* (1976), among several other books.

DAVID GOODMAN is a futurist scientist and researcher. He received a doctorate in psychobiology from the University of California, Irvine, and taught there for ten years before establishing his own consulting firm, whose clients include the 3M Corporation. He is the author of numerous articles on futurist topics.

ALDOUS HUXLEY (1894–1963) was an influential British novelist and thinker, best remembered for *Brave New World* (1932), *Eyeless in Gaza* (1936), *Ape and Essence* (1948), and *The Doors of Perception* (1952), among many other works.

SAMUEL L. HYNES has taught English at Swarthmore and Northwestern and is currently professor of English at Princeton. He has published numerous works on twentieth-century British and American literature, among them *Twentieth Century Interpretations of 1984* (1971), a collection of essays.

MARTIN KESSLER was executive editor of *Challenge* magazine, a senior editor of The Free Press, and secretary of *The Encyclopedia for the Social Sciences* before joining Basic Books, Inc., in 1969. He is now president, publisher, and editorial director of that house.

WYNDHAM LEWIS (1882–1957), Canadian-born artist, writer, and satirist, was educated in England. His paintings are collected in the Tate Gallery, Victoria and Albert Museum, and the Museum of Modern Art, New York. He was the author of numerous books, most notably *The Revenge for Love* (1937), *Time and Western Man* (1928), and *The Writer and the Absolute* (1952).

LAWRENCE MALKIN is a member of the Washington Bueau of *Time*. Prior to that assignment he covered economic affairs for the Associated Press in London.

MALCOLM MUGGERIDGE, the British writer, editor, and media personality, served on the editorial staffs of the *Manchester Guardian and London Daily Telegraph*; he was editor of *Punch* from 1953 to 1957. He is the author of numerous books, including the autobiographical *Chronicles of Wasted Time* (1972–1973).

V. S. PRITCHETT, the noted British author and critic, has taught widely in the United States at Berkeley, Smith, Vanderbilt, Brandeis, and Columbia universities. His many works include the autobiographical *A Cab at the Door* (1968) and *Midnight Oil* (1971), and *On the Edge of the Cliff* (1980).

SIR RICHARD REES (1900–1970) is best known for his work as editor of several volumes of essays and papers by Simone Weil, and for his biographies of Weil and George Orwell (*George Orwell: Fugitive from the Camp of Victory*, 1961). Rees was one of Orwell's closest friends—Orwell's adopted son was named for him—and spent considerable time with Orwell on Jura during the writing of *Nineteen Eighty-Four*.

JOHN P. ROSSI teaches in the Department of History, Lasalle College, Philadelphia.

LORD BERTRAND RUSSELL (3RD EARL) (1872–1970) was one of the

towering intellectual figures of the century. A preeminent mathematician, philosopher, logician, and humanist, he was awarded the Nobel Prize for Literature in 1950. He published an enormous body of work on diverse subjects.

MARK SCHORER (1908–1977), the American writer and critic, taught at Dartmouth, Harvard, Berkeley, and Princeton, among other appointments. He published critical biographies of *William Blake* (1946), *Sinclair Lewis* (1963), and *D. H. Lawrence* (1968), plus three novels and three collections of stories.

JULIAN SYMONS is a world authority on crime and detective fiction, author of numerous books of criticism and commentary on the genre, and author himself of twenty-two crime novels. He is a regular reviewer for the *Times Literary Supplement*. Symons was a longtime friend of Orwell.

LIONEL TRILLING (1905–1975), the esteemed American critic, taught at the University of Wisconsin (Madison), Hunter College, and Columbia, and was visiting professor at Harvard and Oxford. His many critical works include *Matthew Arnold* (1939), *E. M. Forster* (1943), *The Liberal Imagination* (1951), *The Opposing Self* (1955), which includes a piece on Orwell, *Beyond Culture* (1965), and *Mind in the Modern World* (1973).

GEORGE WOODCOCK is a prolific writer and editor, playwright, and documentary filmmaker. He taught English at the University of Washington and English and Asian Studies at the University of British Columbia. He is the author of numerous biographies, including the acclaimed *The Crystal Spirit: A Biography of George Orwell* (1966).

Mystery and Suspense Titles
Available from Carroll & Graf

The Third Arm—by **Kenneth Royce**
An intriguing plot places a band of world-notorious terrorists in a confused and vulnerable London in this literate and astonishing thriller that will enthrall fans of John LeCarre and Graham Greene.

$3.50

Channel Assault—by **Kenneth Royce**
A treacherous plot to negotiate a secret "peace" treaty with Hitler and assassinate Winston Churchill brings together a British doctor, his mistress and an American OSS agent in this novel which combines the realism of historical fiction with the gut grip of a thriller.

$3.50

Deadline—by **Thomas B. Dewey**
The Chicago private detective known only as "Mac" in a last minute fight against the corruption of a one-man dominated small town.

$3.50

The House of the Arrow—by **A.E.W. Mason**
An imaginative, well-crafted plot featuring a prominent London law firm, a famous French detective and a very difficult mystery to solve.

$3.50

Murder for Pleasure—by **Howard Haycraft**
A time-honored history of the mystery genre from A.C. Doyle to Raymond Chandler that will delight the general reader and fan alike.

$10.95

The Red Right Hand—by Joel Townsley Rogers
The chilling story of a young couple on their way to be married who pick up an ominous hitchhiker and are involved in a strange accident is a tale of sheer terror.

$3.50

A Sad Song Singing—by Thomas B. Dewey
Masterful suspense and an unusual mystery set "Mac" against Chicago's shadowy world of entertainers and caberets.

$3.50

The Shrewsdale Exit—by John Buell
Brutal highway terrorism destroys a man's family in this poignant and suspenseful tale of innocence confronted by irrational violence.

$3.50

Fog of Doubt—by Christianna Brand
A mystery in the Christie-Carr-Queen manner. A tour de force in which the last words of the novel name the murderer.

$3.50

Fantasy and Science Fiction Titles
Available from Carroll & Graf

Citadel of Fear—by Francis Stevens
A masterpiece of the fantastic, a classic allegory set in Tlapallan, lost city of an ancient race.

$3.50

Om, The Secret of Ahbor Valley—by Talbot Mundy
Set in India in the 1920's this wonderful tale of adventure and mysticism can be fairly called a cross between *Raiders of the Lost Ark* and *Kim*.

$3.95

The House on the Borderland—by William Hope Hodgson
Renowned as one of the greatest cosmic fantasy tales in the English language, this novel is a work of pure imagination which sustains an overpowering level of wonder and mounting horror. It will appeal equally to fans of fantasy, horror and science-fiction.

$3.25